_.y s world

Berkeley's World

An Examination of the Three Dialogues

TOM STONEHAM

OXFORD
UNIVERSITY PRESS

OXFORD

UNIVERSITY PRESS

Great Clarendon Street, Oxford OX2 6DP

Oxford University Press is a department of the University of Oxford.
It furthers the University's objective of excellence in research, scholarship,
and education by publishing worldwide in

Oxford New York

Auckland Cape Town Dar es Salaam Hong Kong Karachi
Kuala Lumpur Madrid Melbourne Mexico City Nairobi
New Delhi Shanghai Taipei Toronto
With offices in
Argentina Austria Brazil Chile Czech Republic France Greece
Guatemala Hungary Italy Japan South Korea Poland Portugal
Singapore Switzerland Thailand Turkey Ukraine Vietnam

Oxford is a registered trade mark of Oxford University Press
in the UK and in certain other countries

Published in the United States
by Oxford University Press Inc., New York

ISBN 978-0-19-875237-0

Printed in the United Kingdom by
Lightning Source UK Ltd., Milton Keynes

Preface

This book began life as a series of undergraduate lectures on Berkeley given in Oxford in 1995. The lectures were developed over the next three years and writing began when I was on sabbatical leave from Merton College in 1998. It seems to many colleagues and students that to spend a whole lecture course on Berkeley is a waste of time. Normally he only appears in undergraduate courses as a foil to Locke and perhaps for a week on his own as undergraduate cannon fodder. But I had become persuaded that Berkeley was a philosophical figure worthy of study in his own right, even by undergraduates. He has some interesting and ingenious arguments, which often appeal to important philosophical instincts. Furthermore, his positive doctrines are only absurd at first glance. When his writing is explored and developed, it reveals a systematic metaphysician of great depth, considerable insight, and undeniable originality. Berkeley deserves more respect than he is normally accorded.

With this in mind, the present book tries to fill the gap between the cursory introduction to Berkeley found in most courses on early modern philosophy and the detailed scholarly study pursued by academics for academics. This makes it vulnerable to criticism from two directions. Those who are looking for a textbook to support their brief discussion of Berkeley as the link between Locke and Hume will find the first part too general, the second too detailed, and the third too advanced. In contrast, Berkeley scholars will find the first part dull, the second unoriginal, and the third controversial but unscholarly. I am prepared to take these criticisms on the chin, for they mistake the intended audience, which is someone who is seriously interested in philosophy, who wants to study and understand Berkeley's thought in the same way one needs to study other great philosophers if one is going to write informed philosophy of one's own. Because philosophical progress, if there is such a thing, is not cumulative, we cannot appreciate the contributions made by philosophers like Berkeley without coming to terms with the full breadth and detail of his thought.

One obstacle I have found in trying to persuade students to take Berkeley seriously is the theistic, almost religious, nature of his metaphysics. It is true that Berkeley was a religious man, and that he did become a bishop, but we should remember that he developed his metaphysical and epistemological views while he was pursuing an academic career at Trinity College, Dublin. Furthermore, a careful examination of his philosophy reveals that he does not in fact have arguments for the existence of the Christian God, and even more dramatically, for the existence of a god at all, if by that we mean the proper focus of a religion. What his metaphysics requires is that there be some other mind, distinct from all the human minds we know. The one place at which Berkeley's religious belief interferes with his philosophical rigour is in his assumption that by putting a mind more powerful than ours at the centre of the world, he has put God there. When thinking and writing about Berkeley, we all use his word 'God' for the metaphysically special mind or minds, but we do not also need to make his mistake of giving this a religious interpretation.

I had intended to write a book which began with a fairly elementary exposition and became increasingly difficult. Instead I have written one which becomes increasingly detailed and many readers will find that the extra detail makes the later stages easier to follow. Either way, I hope that the structure of the book serves to draw the reader deeper into Berkeley's philosophy, encouraging her to ask more and more taxing questions of the text. To this end

Chapter 2 is simply a statement of the interpretation of Berkeley being put forward, with just enough exegetical argument to make it plausible. Chapters 3 and 4, which form the second part of the book, look in great detail at the two principal strands of Berkeley's argumentative strategy, namely the argument that the objects of perception are mind-dependent, and the argument against matter. The detail is necessary to bring out the hidden strengths of Berkeley's arguments, but also provides the pedagogue with some useful exercises in the analysis and criticism of philosophical arguments. The remainder of the book is very different in character, because it involves teasing out the complexities of Berkeley's immaterialism, often working with limited textual evidence, in order to show that it is very close to being a complete and coherent philosophical system. The range of topics discussed is large and the level of argument sometimes quite difficult. Often the issues are ones that do not appear in the secondary literature on Berkeley, or where they do, only in passing. But they are philosophically important issues, and when we raise them in the context of Berkeley's philosophy, we gain a lot of insight into the subtleties of his thinking. Since this has been my primary interest in writing those chapters, I have avoided scholarly disputes as much as possible. Sometimes it has been necessary to criticize alternative interpretations of the text, but in general I hope the philosophical interest of the interpretations I am putting forward will allow the reader to set aside for a while the question of whether this is exactly what Berkeley thought. Let us reserve scholarly arguments for scholarly journals and keep the book interesting for the general philosophical reader. Some will disagree with where I have chosen to draw the line, but a book aimed at non-specialists is a place to exercise judgement, not to defend it.

One thing about this book which will irritate scholars is that at several points I make vague and unsubstantiated historical claims such as 'Philosophers before Berkeley thought *p*'. This would be totally unacceptable were the purpose of these claims to provide evidence for my interpretation of Berkeley. But that is not their purpose: rather I am trying to elucidate Berkeley's views by contrasting them with views he does not hold. To defend my historical claims in that context would make the book unnecessarily weighty. As a graduate student I once wrote an essay on Kant's Schematism which was criticized by my supervisor, who shall remain anonymous, for being 'too scholarly'. Perhaps in this book I have overreacted to the criticism.

There is some need to explain why I concentrate on the *Three Dialogues* rather than the *Principles*. Received opinion is that the *Principles* is the definitive statement of Berkeley's views and the *Three Dialogues* just a populist reworking. As the great Berkeley scholar A. A. Luce puts it in his *Life* (p. 52):

It covers almost all the ground covered by the *Principles*, stressing points of popular appeal, but not repeating all the detail of the argument. For instance, the relativity of the sensible qualities is argued vividly and at great length in the first dialogue, but the refutation of abstract ideas is throughout assumed, rather than re-argued. Nothing of any importance is added, unless the discussions of the Creation and identity in the third dialogue are to be so regarded.

As Luce makes quite clear, his attitude derives in part from regarding the refutation of abstract ideas as central to Berkeley's strategy, and in part from regarding the systematic development of immaterialism, which is begun in the Third Dialogue, as of minor interest. On my interpretation of Berkeley, the argument against abstraction is not of fundamental importance in establishing immaterialism, and the new material added to the *Dialogues* shows how Berkeley had benefited from three years' extra contemplation of his immaterialism. To put it plainly, I think that the *Dialogues* is a more mature work. Admittedly there are some points omitted, and we have to decide whether they were omitted on populist grounds or because Berkeley thought them less important by the time he came to write the *Dialogues*.

The absence of any serious discussion of abstraction in the later works suggests that Berkeley thought there was a different route to immaterialism. In fact, I doubt that abstraction had the role it is usually ascribed in the *Principles*, for the argument is contained in the Introduction, not the main text. Scholars sometimes argue that Berkeley put the refutation of abstraction in the Introduction to give it pride of place, but that seems very unlikely to me: the introduction is the part of a book most likely to be skipped by the reader, and one would think that a book ought to stand on its own two (or more) feet without requiring support from what is explicitly a separate, though related, text. If Berkeley wanted the arguments of the Introduction to be premises for the rest of the book, it is odd that he restarts the section-numbering at the beginning of the main text, for he often refers back to earlier sections of the main text by section number, and if the Introduction was part of the main argument, confusion would ensue. It is true that Berkeley thought many philosophers only managed to maintain the belief in materialism because they endorsed the doctrine of abstraction, but that makes the refutation of abstraction an act of therapy rather than a positive argument for his own position.

The other marked difference between the works, as Luce notes, is the lengthy discussion of the objects of perception in the First Dialogue. This also seems to represent greater maturity on Berkeley's part. In the *Principles* he simply assumed a philosophical doctrine of ideas, in the *Dialogues* he defends it, and defends it against a variety of opponents, of both the direct and indirect realist varieties. It is too easy for a reader of the *Principles* simply to deny that the objects of perception are ideas or sensations. A reader of the *Dialogues* who wants to make the same denial is forced to make a case for his view in the face of powerful arguments. George Pappas has recently written (*Berkeley's Thought*, 18): 'neither Locke nor Berkeley actually held that direct realism is false [though they were committed to its falsity], for neither even so much as considered the theory'. But if we take the First Dialogue seriously, we see that

Berkeley's own view is a form of direct realism, and that he is offering explicit arguments against materialist versions of the theory. Concentration on the *Principles* can obscure this interesting aspect of his thought.

Luce omits to mention two other additions to the *Three Dialogues* that are as important as the discussions of creation and identity. These are the free-will defence against the problem of evil, which rules out several interpretations of Berkeley's theory of action, and the discussion of whether objects such as coaches are mediately or immediately perceived. Three of these four additions are essential to our understanding of Berkeley's account of ordinary, persisting public objects, without which immaterialism looks grotesquely implausible.

What is interesting is that there are some notable omissions from both works. We know there was a second part of the *Principles* planned, and in a famous letter of 1729 Berkeley says that he had made 'considerable progress in it' but it was lost during his travels in Italy. Some indication of the content of that second part may be inferred from a letter he wrote before the publication of the *Principles* (to Sir John Percival, 1 March 1710), in which he mentions

a treatise I have now in press, the design of which is to demonstrate the existence and attributes of God, the immortality of the soul, the reconciliation of God's fore-knowledge with freedom of men, and shewing the emptiness and falseness of several parts of the speculative sciences, to reduce men to the study of religion and things useful.

There is no discussion of divine foreknowledge and freedom in the part of the *Principles* which was published only two months later, suggesting that Berkeley was including in his description of his treatise things intended for Part II. The other clue is the changes and additions he made to the *Principles* and *Three Dialogues* for their 1734 reprint, by which time Part II had been abandoned. These largely concern the nature of spirits and our knowledge of them. In the 1734 reprint more material was added to the *Dialogues* than the

Principles, again suggesting that Berkeley did see it as something other than just a populist restatement.

Most scholars will be concerned by the way I have completely ignored a major part of the Berkeley corpus, namely the *Philosophical Commentaries*. These two notebooks, not discovered until more than a hundred years after Berkeley's death, provide a fascinating insight into Berkeley's mind and his methods of study and writing. Luce aptly describes them as 'the winding paths of a great man's private thoughts on a lofty theme' (Editor's Introduction, p. 5). The word 'private' in that description should already caution us about using these notes to interpret Berkeley's published works. Throughout this book I make the methodological assumption that we can distinguish the question 'What is the philosophical view expressed in the *Three Dialogues*?' from the question 'What is the philosophical view held by Berkeley?' The distinction is important, because in publishing a book a philosopher is making a decision to put forward certain philosophical views as his own and, inevitably, to remain silent on various other topics. He expects his public not to know anything more about his thoughts than he tells them in the book, and to interpret and evaluate his views solely on the basis of what he has published. If, through historical research, we have more information than this, we have the option of ignoring it in favour of trying to reconstruct the philosophy Berkeley intended his readers to attribute to him. And that is exactly what I have chosen to do.

There is, however, a problem with this method, for the published work may be indeterminate on a philosophical point of great interest to us. At this point it is second nature to most historians of ideas to appeal to unpublished work, but that instantly moves us from considering the first question to the second. In order to maintain my interest in the view Berkeley expressed in a particular work, I have followed the maxim *Attribute to Berkeley the weakest view consistent with the published work unless a stronger view would make it considerably more plausible*. This is exactly the same principle we apply every day when reading philosophy written by our contemporaries, and it should make clear that this is a book for those whose interest in Berkeley is more philosophical than historical.

Chapter 7 may strike the reader as a glaring exception to my avowed intention to examine the philosophy of the *Three Dialogues*, for the account of Berkeley's nominalism given there rests heavily on the Introduction to the *Principles*. Here, and at several other points throughout the book, I extend the principle of attributing the weakest view consistent with the *Dialogues* to attributing the weakest view consistent with both the *Principles* and the *Dialogues*. When faced with two works by the same philosopher one is not compelled to interpret him as holding only views consistent with both works, for he may have changed his mind. But here the plausibility condition kicks in, albeit with a rider: *unless there is public evidence that the later work represents a change of mind, attribute a view consistent with both works if and only if that view is more plausible.* Hence I can coherently pursue the policy of appealing to the *Principles*, but not the *Philosophical Commentaries*, when I need to fill in some of the gaps left by the *Three Dialogues*.

Finally, I ought to mention that the *Three Dialogues* is a good read. It becomes a little turgid in the Third Dialogue, but apart from that, students of philosophy should be able to sit down and enjoy the book for itself. Few works of philosophy can lay claim to such literary merit. I am painfully aware how badly my style compares with Berkeley's, but I have tried to write in a friendly and open manner, so that the reader can see through my words to the thoughts they express. That is certainly an objective which Berkeley would have endorsed.

I would like to thank the Warden and Fellows of Merton College for a sabbatical term in 1998 and for assistance in buying books. I would also like to thank audiences at the Universities of Cambridge, Dublin, Edinburgh, Lublin, and York for stimulating responses and, as always, the Oriel Discussion Group, who have listened to and discussed several chapters. Conversations with Richard Glauser,

Plinio Smith, and Rowland Stout have been especially formative. I would especially like to thank the anonymous reviewers for OUP, whose comments I have had to think about very hard. I have tried to accommodate them all, except where that would have meant writing a completely different book. Because I have tried to minimize discussions of the secondary literature, there are many people whose writings on Berkeley have impressed and influenced me but who get no mention in this book: for what I have learnt from them I am most grateful, and for what I have misunderstood I apologize.

T.W.C.S.

Grahamstown, August 2001

Contents

PART 3

Note on Conventions

Terminology

In everyday speech a materialist is someone who believes that there is *only* matter, crucially that the mind is material. Berkeley is also objecting to a weaker view which allows mental substances as well as matter. In order to get a clear contrast with immaterialism, I shall use 'materialism' for the thesis that there is *some* matter. In practice, there is little or no potential for confusion.

There is more potential trouble with 'perceive'. Berkeley uses 'perceive' to mean, roughly, *to have before the mind*. So imagining, dreaming, and remembering are all cases where we perceive something. Our current usage tends to limit perception to the five senses. Since Berkeley's usage incorporates ours, I keep to it except where I want to emphasize that we are talking about sense perception, and then I put in a qualifier, just as I have done in this sentence.

References

Reference to the *Three Dialogues* is given in the form DHP2 212, which should be read as: *Three Dialogues between Hylas and Philonous*, 2nd Dialogue, p. 212. Page references are to the Luce and Jessop *Works of George Berkeley*, volume ii, and these page numbers are reprinted in the margins of most modern editions. Reference to the *Principles of Human Knowledge* is by section number. Thus 'PHK 31' refers to section 31 of the main text, whereas 'PHK Intro 5' refers to section 5 of the Introduction. All other references are given by unsystematic but natural abbreviation, the full details being discoverable in the bibliography.

PART 1

CHAPTER I

Historical Introduction

1.1

George Berkeley (1685–1753) lived during the infancy of the modern world. More than forty years before he was born, Descartes had sown the seeds of the future by providing a conception of the human mind as a tool powerful enough in itself to produce great philosophical and scientific insights. At the beginning of the seventeenth century Galileo (1564–1642) was publicly vilified for using his own intellect and observations, rather than the wisdom of officially endorsed authorities, to address questions about the structure of the solar system. By the end of the century Newton (1642–1727) was praised as one of the greatest thinkers who had ever lived, and the authority of his *Principia Mathematica* (1687) rested not on who he was or who he agreed with, but on the rigour, systematicity, and brilliance of his arguments. A time had been reached when sheer force of logic could persuade people to change their view of the universe and our place in it. It was a victory of reason over tradition.

Berkeley's attitude to this was ambivalent. He had the greatest respect for the power of argument, and saw the intellectual vacuity of appeals to authority. Like many writers of his time, he regularly made disparaging remarks about the 'Schools', which were the medieval universities, and about philosophers who insisted that the writings of particular figures, such as Aristotle, should never be contradicted (*PHK* Intro 20):

> For example, when a Schoolman tells me *Aristotle hath said it*, all I conceive he means by it, is to dispose me to embrace his opinion with the deference and submission which custom has annexed to that name.

While approving the new method of reason, he deplored the results. In all the philosophers he read, Berkeley found only one or other of two views which were both equally unacceptable to him. Either it was argued that the human senses and intellect were incapable of giving us any knowledge of the world, so that 'there is not a single thing in the world, whereof we can know the real nature, or what it is in itself' (*DHP3* 227), or we are granted knowledge of true natures, but this 'modern way of explaining things' reveals the world to be radically unlike the appearance presented to the five senses. We are left with a choice between saying that we know nothing, or saying that what we do know shows the world to be nothing but colourless, odourless, textureless atoms in a void (or Cartesian pure extension). To Berkeley these are both forms of scepticism, for both have the consequence that if we take our everyday experience of the world at face value, we are being led astray. The modern philosophy which Berkeley learnt as a student told him that we should rely upon our own perceptual and intellectual resources to discover what we can about the world. But when others followed this method, the results were absurd to the sensible and quite practically minded George Berkeley.

One solution would be to return to the pre-modern conception of science and philosophy, to insist on the authority of the authorities, and to refuse to follow reasoning where its consequences were unacceptable. But Berkeley could not do this, for he had too much respect for the power of argument. So instead he had to show that the arguments did not after all lead to scepticism, that the ordinary world which we take ourselves to live in was just as it seemed to

us, and that there was no more to reality than that. This philosophical agenda of Berkeley's began early in life. His first known
work, a paper called 'Of Infinites' which he presented to the Dublin
Philosophical Society in November 1707, challenges the coherence
of and explanatory need for infinitesimals, i.e. an infinitely small
fraction of a unit of distance or time. Infinitesimals were essential
to the Newtonian calculus, and in attacking them Berkeley was
both displaying the view that the authority of a great name should
never outweigh the strength of an argument, and also defending
the ordinary conception of distance and time as composed out of
small but finite units.

By 1709, when he published his first book, *An Essay towards a
New Theory of Vision*, Berkeley appears to have worked out the
broad outlines of his solution to the modern predicament. In that
work he was primarily concerned with the visual perception of size
and distance and kept silent about his immaterialism. He argued
that sight alone does not tell us where objects are located in space
or how big they are. For example, if you were to hold your hand up
so that at a single glance you could see both it and a tree, the visual
experience alone would not tell you whether the tree was further
from you than your hand, and thus would not tell you whether it
was bigger than your hand. Nor can we use a priori arguments to
infer size and distance from anything that sight does tell us. Rather,
we learn that seen objects have location in space by correlating
our experiences of sight and of touch. It is because I cannot touch
the tree that I think it is further away from me than my hand.
Officially the work is addressing a problem in the theory of vision,
but there is more to Berkeley's argument than that. To the casual
reader it might appear that Berkeley is accepting that touch gives us
information about the size and distance from us of material objects
(though there is a slip at § 55), but in fact this is nowhere assumed
in the work. Rather he is careful to speak of 'tangible objects' or
'tangible ideas', which he takes to refer to 'the immediate object of
sense or understanding, in which large signification it is commonly

used by the moderns' (§ 45). Furthermore, distance is 'measured by the motion of [the] body, which is perceivable by touch' (§ 45), but he never raises the question of whether proprioception gives us immediate ideas of the motion of our bodies through objective space or only mediately suggests visual ideas of motion. Berkeley knows he can make his points about the apparent visual perception of space without explicitly challenging his reader's assumption that we perceive the material world by at least one of our senses, but as soon as similar questions are asked about touch, such direct realism looks to be on very shaky ground.

At first this argument appears to be another piece of reasoning leaving us in the modern dilemma: either we know nothing about the spatial location of real objects, or what we do know about them shows that our senses are misleading. However, Berkeley's brilliant resolution, stated bluntly at the beginning of his next work, the *Principles of Human Knowledge* (1710), is to reject the assumption that the real object, the real book, is something distinct from the objects of sight and touch. The modern dilemma arises, according to Berkeley, from thinking of the real world as something completely independent of human perceptions. If we make this assumption, then all the arguments lead to scepticism. But if we reject the assumption, it is possible to maintain the ordinary opinion that the very things we see and touch are parts of the real world. Berkeley's great claim is that if there is no mind-independent matter, if all that exists are minds and the ideas they experience, that leaves in place all of the ordinary conception of the world: no philosophy will undermine our instinctive trust in our five senses. And it is as clear to us as it was to Berkeley that any argument for this conclusion needs two stages. First it must be argued that there is no matter, then it must be argued that this immaterialism has no sceptical consequences. Berkeley's two main philosophical works, the *Principles* and the *Three Dialogues between Hylas and Philonous* (1713), both follow this structure. Berkeley wrote the second book to try to make the anti-sceptical nature of his denial of matter more obvious, since most readers of the *Principles* could not accept that the denial of matter was not the denial of the existence of ordinary physical objects such as tables and trees. In that respect the *Three Dialogues* has failed, for Berkeley continues to be unjustly accused of denying the existence of physical objects.

I.2

Berkeley's life was not one exclusively dedicated to philosophy. He went to Trinity College, Dublin in 1700, aged 15, which was a normal age to attend university at the time. He graduated Bachelor in 1704, was elected Fellow in 1707, and was ordained in 1710, as was required of Fellows. However, his ordination did not follow the normal smooth process, for the Bishop of Clogher, St George Ashe, performed the ordination ceremony in his capacity as Vice-Chancellor of Trinity College, without the permission of William King. As Archbishop of Dublin and Visitor to the College, King held jurisdiction over ordinations and in this instance he was not happy with the action Ashe had taken while his back was turned: he ordered Berkeley to be prosecuted at the Archbishop's court. Interestingly, it appears that King's hidden objection to Berkeley's ordination may have been a philosophical one. Clearly Berkeley was intellectually passionate and self-assured enough to risk upsetting those who held great influence over his career. However, he also knew how to protect his own interests, for he wrote a letter of apology to King and the prosecution did not go ahead.

In 1713, after six years of working hard for his college, as a Lecturer, Librarian, and Dean, Berkeley took leave of absence and travelled to London. He was introduced at Court on 12th April by Jonathan Swift, who wrote in his *Journal to Stella*:

I went to court to-day on purpose to present Mr Berkeley, one of your Fellows of Dublin College to Lord Berkeley of Stratton. That Mr Berkeley is a very ingenious man, and a great philosopher, and I have mentioned him to all the ministers, and have given them some of his writings; and I will favour him as much as I can.

Swift was true to his word, subsequently finding Berkeley an appointment with the retinue of the Earl of Peterborough, whom he accompanied to Europe in 1713. He later became tutor to George Ashe, son of the Bishop of Clogher, remaining on tour with him in Italy and Sicily until 1720, when the young man took seriously ill and died. Berkeley returned to London that year and went back to his Fellowship at Trinity College in 1721.

While in Paris in November 1713, Berkeley attempted to arrange a meeting with the philosopher Nicholas Malebranche. There is no record of the meeting, but one of Berkeley's letters suggests that an appointment was made. One can easily imagine how important the meeting would have been for the 28-year-old Berkeley. In the *Three Dialogues* he had taken pains to distinguish his views from those of Malebranche, presumably in response to some misunderstandings he had encountered, but he was undoubtedly very sensitive to the similarities in their philosophies. In fact, Malebranche was as much of an influence on Berkeley as Locke, so there is a sense in which Berkeley would have been paying homage. In Joseph Stock's 1776 biography of Berkeley it is alleged that the meeting was so heated that it led to Malebranche's death. Amusing though this story is, the dates are wrong, for Malebranche died two years later in 1715, and Berkeley is unlikely to have shown disrespect for such an important philosopher.

Back in Dublin Berkeley began to seek a career in the Church, and in 1724 he was appointed Dean of Derry, increasing his stipend from £80 per annum to £1,100. In 1723 he also received an unexpected inheritance of £3,000. Now wealthy and with few duties he could not delegate, he returned to London to raise money for the founding of a college in Bermuda. Berkeley's grand idea was to educate a priesthood for the Americas, who would then Christianize the plantation workers. He was motivated not by a missionary zeal but by a belief that the future lay in the New World, and the foundations of that future would be a class of honest, God-fearing labourers. His fund-raising met with surprising success, and in September 1728 he set sail for Rhode Island, with a royal charter to found the college. His plan was to settle on Rhode Island while a suitable site for the college was found in Bermuda and purchased. Unfortunately the scheme failed owing to two main factors: Bermuda was too far offshore to be a practical location for the college, and the promised Government grant never materialized. While in Rhode Island Berkeley gave support, both moral and material, to the nascent colleges at Harvard and Yale, and on his departure he endowed both libraries, sending Yale eight cases of books. The private subscriptions that had been raised for the Bermuda college were returned where requested, but a number of benefactors wished for them to be used for educational purposes still, so all of the non-returned subscriptions went to support Yale. Berkeley conveyed his Rhode Island estate, known as Whitehall, to Yale in 1732 and endowed three one-year scholarships. This endowment was altered in 1734 to provide for one scholar for three years. So while Berkeley's own educational project in America failed, his three-year sojourn was very influential in the establishment of the American universities.

Berkeley did not go straight back to Ireland, but re-entered London society. In 1734 he was appointed Bishop of Cloyne at the Queen's instigation. Having been absent for nearly his whole tenure as Dean of Derry, he did return to Ireland to oversee his new diocese personally. Berkeley was cultured and very well travelled, but he was also a philanthropist and passionately concerned about the welfare of the Irish peasants. Luce tells a pleasant but revealing story about the very harsh winter of 1739–40, showing how he combined personal generosity with a strong moral sense which would not allow him to waste food needed by others:

On the first Sunday of the great frost the Bishop came down to breakfast without a grain of powder [i.e. flour] in his wig. Mrs Berkeley, the chaplain, and some visitors all called out at once, asking what ailed his Lordship. He replied that a great deal ailed him; there would be a very long frost; the potatoes would perish, and the poor must depend upon flour, or starve. 'So no powder will I, or shall any individual of my family wear until next harvest.' During the frost and until the summer he gave £20 in gold or a banknote every Monday morning to be distributed among the poor of Cloyne, 'besides what they receive daily, hourly, out of his kitchen and housekeeper's room.' (Luce, *Life of George Berkeley*, 199)

It was at this period that he also began to investigate the use of tar-water as a medicine. During his stay on Rhode Island he had heard of it being used to prevent smallpox by the native Americans and, realizing the vast benefits to public health that would accrue could someone discover a cheap, effective, and readily available medicine, he experimented with its ability to prevent and cure a wide range of illnesses. He became convinced on empirical grounds, and began to advocate publicly the use of tar-water for a wide range of ailments. For this he has met with ridicule, both in his own time and ever since, but we should understand his motives. There was a desperate human need for exactly what he thought he had found. He did not propose the use of tar-water because of some obscure or absurd theory of human health, but because he thought there was good evidence that it worked. In such a situation, and for a man of Berkeley's strong principles, there was no real alternative but to do what he did.

In 1752 he resigned his bishopric and moved to Oxford, in order to oversee the education of his son, also called George, at Christ Church. It was there that he died in 1753 while quietly taking tea with his close family. Ever mindful of the folly of unnecessary expense, he willed:

Item, . . . that my body be buried in the church-yard of the parish in which I die;

Item, that the expense of my funeral do not exceed twenty pounds, and that as much more be given to the poor of the parish where I die.

Since he died in a house on Holywell Street, probably number 7, he should have been buried in the churchyard of St Cross, Holywell. However, his remains and epitaph are to be found in Christ Church cathedral, as befitted his social and intellectual status.

1.3

Berkeley's influence on philosophy has been immense. His contributions to mathematics, psychology, economics, and theology are now largely curiosities only of interest to the historian. But his main philosophical works are still studied as part of nearly every undergraduate degree in philosophy. In part this is because he wrote so clearly and his writings are so full of argument that they make excellent 'cannon fodder' for undergraduates to dissect and criticize. But it is also because his arguments are not as easily dismissed as confident materialists would like. He remains a thorn in the flesh of a world-view according to which the natural world consists of mindless and mind-independent items blindly enacting a causal order and occasionally, and rather mysteriously, causing conscious experiences in human minds. With the outstanding success of science in nearly every area of human enquiry, this world-view has become widely accepted. But this is just the 'modern way of explaining things' which Berkeley was concerned to attack. This book will aim not only to make the point that there is a lot of interest and importance in his attacks on this metaphysical picture, but also that his alternative has sufficient merit to be seriously considered by philosophers three hundred years after its inception.

Berkeley's great stroke of genius was to see that the main metaphysical systems of his time, those of Descartes, Malebranche, and Locke, had a common assumption, the existence of matter, *which could be denied*. But Berkeley knew that a proper refutation takes more than merely spotting a deniable premiss: to refute a position by denying a premiss, one must show that the result of denying the premiss is at least as plausible as the result of accepting it, and that is what the *Three Dialogues* aims to do.

CHAPTER 2

Berkeley's World

2.1 Berkeley's World-View

Berkeley held that reality consisted of two types of entity: minds and ideas. These two types of entity are related by perception: minds perceive ideas. Ideas depend for their existence upon standing in this relation to some mind; they are mind-dependent entities. Thus for ideas, i.e. for everything which is not a mind, to be is to be perceived.

It follows from this that the physical, *which I shall use throughout the book to mean simply 'non-mental'*, world is composed of ideas and is thus mind-dependent. This claim, for which Berkeley is most famous, is variously called idealism or immaterialism. It is opposed to the view that the physical world, while it may occasionally stand in some relation to minds, does so only contingently.

Minds, or spirits as Berkeley usually calls them, are active—that is, they can bring about changes in themselves and the world—whereas ideas are entirely passive. It is not the stone which caused the window to break, but the person who threw the stone, for the stone itself has no causal powers. In imagination the ideas we perceive are under our complete control, but in sense perception that control is limited and indirect (I can choose to see the garden by looking out of the window, but I cannot choose what I shall see in the garden, nor even if it is visible). There are two types of spirit: finite created spirits like ourselves and an infinite, uncreated one, namely God. Since God is omnipotent and sense perception essentially involves limited control, God perceives everything that happens in the world without sensing it. Such are the bare bones of Berkeley's metaphysics.

Berkeley's immaterialism is persistently misunderstood. A common mistake is to think that he is somehow denying the existence of the physical world, but the whole dialectic of the *Three Dialogues* is aimed at combating this error. Let me mention at the outset one of the things he points out quite late in the book (*DHP3* 244):

PHILONOUS   You mistake me. I am not for changing things into ideas, but rather ideas into things.

Quite simply, if one is saying that the physical world is made up of the ideas we have, then one is saying that those ideas are parts of the physical world, i.e. that they are physical. The very use of the word 'idea' is misleading (*DHP3* 235–6), for it is normally used *in contrast to* the physical. Berkeley says that he is using it 'because a necessary relation to the mind is understood to be implied by that term' (*DHP3* 236)—that is, it indicates mind-dependence. The confusion is reinforced by Berkeley using 'in the mind' as a synonym for 'perceived', so that mind-dependence becomes 'existing only in the mind'. Though he tries to clarify the point in the Third Dialogue (*DHP3* 250), this is too late to prevent confusion. The suggestion that ideas are physical is original to Berkeley, but his contemporaries would have been familiar with the suggestion that ideas are not necessarily mental objects from the writings of Malebranche, who thought they were neither mental nor material, and from the use of the term 'idea' by Locke to refer to both things in the mind and qualities of objects. However, given that it has so many other connotations, Berkeley might have been wiser to find another word than 'idea'.

For Berkeley the physical world contains the ordinary, everyday objects that we perceive, such as trees, coffee cups, and human bodies. These persisting, public objects are composed of ideas, which are necessarily perceived and neither persisting nor public. A tree is not *an* idea, rather it is a collection or congeries of ideas. Ideas are such things as the green (e.g. of a leaf) which I am now seeing. Clearly Berkeley needs to do a lot of work to show how everyday things ('middle-sized dry goods') might be composed of such fleeting private qualities, otherwise any argument that he has for the most general claim that reality is populated by nothing but minds and ideas will be seen as an attack on the very existence of ordinary persisting, public objects. For obvious reasons, this issue is often described as whether Berkeley's view is consistent with common sense or not.

At the beginning of the *Three Dialogues* Philonous aligns himself with pre-philosophical opinion, describing his 'revolt from metaphysical notions to the plain dictates of nature and common sense' (*DHP1* 172), and throughout the work philosophical opinions are compared unfavourably with the more plausible views of the 'vulgar' (i.e. ordinary people—the term is not pejorative). Philonous goes so far as to say (*DHP3* 229):

I am of a vulgar cast, simple enough to believe my senses, and leave things as I find them.

and (*DHP3* 262):

I do not pretend to be a setter-up of *new notions*.

All of which strongly suggests that Berkeley is intending immaterialism to be compatible with ordinary, non-philosophical intuitions. On the other hand, anyone who can remember first coming across Berkeley's ideas will be aware that they are quite revolutionary: common sense is surely not neutral on the mind-independence of sensible things, and Berkeley's views about the perception of depth (we do not see it but infer it from touch), the causal passivity of the physical world, and the persistence and identity of physical objects are all quite surprising. Surely he has then failed to live up to his commonsensical standards?

This objection misconstrues the role of common-sense intuitions in Berkeley's philosophy. His respect for vulgar opinions does not need to extend to finding them infallible. The point is rather that certain divergences from common sense make philosophical theories quite literally *incredible*. And what is the point of having a philosophical theory one cannot believe? Alternatively, one's grounds for a philosophical opinion might be so strong that it is easier to give up the natural or intuitive view. What concerns Berkeley most are philosophical views which are 'fantastical' or 'paradoxical' (etymologically: beyond belief). That such views are 'repugnant to common sense' provides a reason to disbelieve them, to think them mistaken, but ultimately in the *Dialogues* the appeal to vulgar opinion is comparative. Immaterialism turns out to be more credible than materialism because less in conflict with common sense. Exactly which pre-philosophical opinions one can give up and which one cannot is a delicate matter, but it is clear why Berkeley should think it an attraction of his views that they appear to reconcile what he takes to be a fundamental tenet of common sense, namely that we are in direct perceptual contact with the real world, with what he takes to be an equally incontrovertible philosophical opinion, namely that sensible things are mind-dependent (*DHP3* 262):

My endeavours tend only to unite and place in a clearer light that truth, which was before shared between the vulgar and the philosophers: the former being of the opinion, that *those things they immediately perceive are the real things*; and the latter, that *the things immediately perceived, are ideas which exist only in the mind*.

2.2 Why Did Berkeley Use the Dialogue Form?

It is not normally necessary to pay attention to the literary character of a piece of philosophy in order to understand it correctly, but the *Three Dialogues* is an exception. In choosing to write a dialogue, Berkeley was choosing to present his philosophy in a literary genre which has inescapable elements of fiction. There has to be a context, there have to be characters, and those characters must have some body of knowledge, set of objectives, and argumentative skills of their own. Even if Berkeley had chosen to base his dialogues exclusively on real people, places, and events, their roles within the dialogues would be completely determined by what was written about them. If we are fully to understand this work of fiction written by a philosopher, we need to be explicit in recognizing its fictional elements. Failure to do so can lead us into the mistake of concentrating entirely on what the fictional Philonous is saying and failing to consider what the historical Berkeley is doing in creating the character.

The most important question to ask about the text derives from the fact that a dialogue is a description of a conversation, so any consideration of motive must address both the motives of the participants in the conversation and the motives of the author in describing this conversation to us. These can clearly come apart: for example, in *Mansfield Park* Jane Austen describes many conversations in order to show us Mrs Norris's selfish snobbery, though Mrs Norris is, in those very conversations, trying to display selfless devotion to Sir Thomas and his family. Of course, neither Hylas nor Philonous is self-deceived in this way, but we need to ask what their motives are in pursuing the conversation, and what Berkeley's motives are in describing it to us.

To understand the characters and motivations of Hylas and Philonous we must know a little more about who they are and what their relationship is. The dialogues clearly take place in a college garden, the first and third early in the morning and the second a bit later, on three consecutive days. They begin with an accidental meeting between Philonous, who is taking a regular early morning walk, and Hylas, who is not usually up so early. At the end of the first dialogue, Philonous arranges a second meeting the next day (*DHP1* 207):

PHILONOUS   Hark; is not this the college-bell?
HYLAS   It rings for prayers.
PHILONOUS   We will go in then if you please, and meet here again
to-morrow morning.

Despite Philonous using a polite form of the imperative mood here,
it transpires at the beginning of the Second Dialogue that Hylas did
not make the morning appointment. The third meeting is arranged
by Hylas (*DHP2* 226):

HYLAS   . . . The remaining part of the day I would willingly spend,
in running over in my thoughts the several heads of this morning's
conversation, and to-morrow shall be glad to meet you here again
about the same time.
PHILONOUS   I will not fail to attend you.

In making this arrangement, Hylas does not use the imperative
as Philonous did, but the optative mood, and Philonous' response
is friendly but ironic, given that Hylas had failed to make their
arranged meeting earlier that morning. From such details we can
hazard a guess that they are both members of the same college but
that Philonous is the senior. Philonous' leading role throughout the
Three Dialogues, even when responding to Hylas' questioning in the
Third Dialogue, also suggests seniority. But the gap is not too great
since Hylas describes Philonous as 'a friend' (*DHP1* 171). Perhaps
Philonous is a Fellow of the College, and Hylas is in that interval
between taking a degree and coming up for election (Berkeley, for
instance, took his BA in 1704 and was elected a Fellow in 1707). This
would explain why Hylas, despite knowing Philonous reasonably
well, only knows of his philosophical views at second hand, through
a conversation in which Philonous did not have an opportunity to
take part.

   If this is correct, Hylas' motive in pursuing the conversation with
Philonous is partly genuine intellectual curiosity and partly a de-
sire to impress. It is more difficult to ascertain Philonous' motives.
Given his relative seniority, it seems unlikely that he saw the con-

versations as dialectical combat in which he was aiming to defeat Hylas by argumentative skill. Nor does he show enough respect for Hylas to be using him as a steel on which to hone his arguments. This leaves two alternatives: his intentions could be entirely pedagogic, like those of Socrates in Plato's dialogues—that is, he could be hoping to teach Hylas to think more carefully and critically about materialism and possibly even to persuade him to endorse immaterialism; or his intention could be to defend his reputation in the College against the charge of scepticism and absurdity. If the former is correct, then the discussion of scepticism is just a convenient way to give structure and interest to the conversations, and the refutation of scepticism is not Philonous' main objective. If the latter is correct, then the primary purpose of the conversations is to show how immaterialism avoids the scepticism to which all forms of materialism are committed.

The first few pages of the First Dialogue strongly suggest that Philonous' motives are pedagogic. He expresses an interest in what Hylas is thinking prior to knowing that it has anything to do with philosophy, let alone scepticism. When Hylas does introduce the charge, Philonous makes it clear that he thinks he is no sceptic, but shows little interest or concern about the fact that he is being misrepresented by others. Rather, his main concern is to have Hylas think things through clearly for himself.

Having established the motives of the participants, we need to ask what Berkeley's motives are in describing the dialogues to us. That he does not share the motivation of either participant should be obvious, but nor can we attribute to Berkeley, at least as a primary motive, the desire to rebut the charge of scepticism which had been laid against the *Principles*. Even had rebutting the charge of scepticism been Philonous' main motivation, it cannot be Berkeley's, for the simple reason that Hylas makes it clear at the outset that he knows, at least in outline and at second hand, the content of Philonous' metaphysical views, but nowhere does Berkeley presuppose that the reader is familiar, even just in outline or at second hand, with the content of the *Principles*. In fact, he states that we do not need knowledge of that work (*DHP* Preface 168). Berkeley certainly intends the reader to come away thinking that materialism leads to scepticism and immaterialism does not, but he does not assume that the reader begins with the converse view, or any view at all.

In the Preface Berkeley explains his objective in writing the *Three Dialogues* (*DHP* Preface 168):

it has been my aim to introduce the notions I advance, into the mind, in the most easy and familiar manner;

and refers to 'the principles, which I here endeavour to propagate'. In other words, this book, like the *Principles* before it, attempts to persuade the reader of the truth of immaterialism. If that is Berkeley's intention, why did he choose to write a pedagogic dialogue? It cannot simply be that the character of Hylas allows Berkeley to foresee and forestall the objections of his readers, because he was perfectly capable of doing that in the *Principles*. Rather it must be because a direct philosophical argument proposes a thesis and gives reasons why the reader *should* believe it, but a dialogue, i.e. a description of an imaginary conversation, can be used to show what one of the characters believes and why he believes it, without explicitly proselytizing. Being a work of fiction, a dialogue is more like a psychological description of belief than a simple attempt to persuade. This is precisely how the *Three Dialogues* works: we gradually discover Philonous' metaphysical views and why he holds them, but at no point is there a didactic finger pointing at us insisting we believe so-and-so for such-and-such reasons.

So, by describing the conversation between Hylas and Philonous, Berkeley wants to show the reader why Philonous finds immaterialism so compelling. But he also intends the reader to side with Philonous, to be convinced of the truth of immaterialism. To achieve this, the reader must agree with the grounds which led Philonous to immaterialism, which is to say that the psychological account of Philonous' belief must also be construable as a persuasive argument. Hence, when we read the book critically as a work of philosophy, our task is often to reconstruct the persuasive argument that Berkeley had in mind when he was describing to us the philosophical convictions of an immaterialist.

Finally, we should consider the question of whether to identify Berkeley with Philonous. There is nothing in the text which compels or even suggests this identification, but nor is there anything which rules it out. However, it helps to treat them as different people, for that reminds us that what Philonous is trying to do in a particular speech might be different from what Berkeley is trying to do in describing that speech.

Consider, for example, how to interpret the arguments of the First Dialogue. It would seem that their proper conclusion is that the things I perceive depend upon being perceived by me. Yet in the Second Dialogue, in order to argue for the existence of God, Philonous asserts that they are independent of me. This creates a puzzle about what Berkeley believed, a puzzle which is the subject of Chapter 5 below. One resolution, which I do not agree with, would be to note that Philonous does not need to be committed to the soundness of the arguments he uses in the First Dialogue, for their purpose is merely to persuade Hylas. If Philonous has a pedagogic aim, then he needs to show Hylas the errors of his beliefs, and to do that he must draw out conclusions to which Hylas is committed, even if Philonous is not. Hence the First Dialogue does not give the reasons which Philonous has for believing that the objects of perception are ideas. And if we assume that Philonous is just Berkeley's spokesman, it follows that Berkeley is not committed to the soundness of those arguments either.

However, it is a mistake to identify Berkeley with Philonous to the extent of attributing to Berkeley the pedagogic aims of Philonous. For example, Philonous aims to persuade Hylas that materialism is more sceptical than immaterialism, but he fails to persuade Hylas of the truth of immaterialism. Berkeley, in contrast, certainly wants his readers to be converted to immaterialism, and the scepticism debate is just one aspect of that. Also, Hylas does not embody a consistent or well-thought-out materialist position of the sort it might be worth systematically refuting, rather he is a fecund source of disparate ideas and objections. So even if Philonous were not committed to the soundness of the First Dialogue's arguments (but see *DHP2* 212), it is another matter altogether whether Berkeley is. Since Berkeley lays out the arguments with a great deal of care and detail, and never casts doubt on them, his reader may reasonably assume that he endorses them. Hylas certainly assumes that Philonous endorses them, but given their (fictional) relationship, Philonous might have a motive to allow that mistake to go uncorrected, whereas it is very unlikely indeed that Berkeley was similarly motivated to let his readers erroneously attribute arguments to him.

2.3 The Argument of the *Three Dialogues*

The debate between Hylas (a name which derives from the Greek for 'matter') and Philonous (whose name means 'lover of mind') is over who is the greatest sceptic, agreed on both sides to be someone who 'denies the reality of sensible things, or professes the greatest ignorance of them' (*DHP1* 173). The conversation begins because Hylas has heard reports of Philonous' immaterialism and finds it unbelievable. Hylas rather uncritically accepts materialism, the view that reality contains some things which are neither minds nor mind-dependent, and Philonous tries to persuade him that all versions of this view lead to scepticism. Beyond materialism, Hylas has no fixed philosophical views and is prepared to use any argument that comes to hand. In the First Dialogue Philonous persuades Hylas that the immediate objects of perceptual experience (sensible things) are mind-dependent, that they are not part of material reality, and thus Hylas is forced to 'deny the reality of sensible things'. In the Second Dialogue the argument is that any notion of matter distinct from sensible things is either incoherent or empty ('an obscure surmise of I know not what': *DHP2* 223), forcing Hylas to 'profess the greatest ignorance'. By the Third Dialogue Hylas is a convinced sceptic and tries to show that immaterialism equally leads to scepticism (*DHP3* 229). To this end he fires a barrage of objections at Philonous. These are real objections that would occur to a critical reader and Philonous, on behalf of Berkeley, has to do more than merely repeat what has gone before. Rather he is forced to develop his views in philosophically substantial ways. The three most important developments are his distinction between those ideas which are parts of physical reality and those which are not, his instrumentalist account of science, and his account of the identity of public objects.

While debating with Hylas in this way, Philonous can be seen to be laying out the major steps in a positive argument for immaterialism. At the very highest level of generality, the argument is:

[1] All sensible things (objects of perception) are ideas;
[2] some ideas have real existence;
[3] all the (perceived) features of the physical world can be accounted for in terms of minds and ideas;
[4] so the world consists of nothing but minds and ideas.

The first three steps correspond very roughly with the presentation of the argument in three separate dialogues. As a dialectical strategy, this shows some advance over the *Principles*, where the argument is summarized (*PHK* 4):

For what are the forementioned objects [houses, mountains, rivers] but the things we perceive by sense, and what do we perceive besides our own ideas or sensations; and is it not plainly repugnant that any one of these or any combination of them should exist unperceived?

This argument is often criticized on the grounds that a materialist will only accept both premises if there is an equivocation on 'perceive'. Thus he might accept that in the ordinary sense of 'perceive', which is roughly to discover about something with one of the five senses, we perceive physical objects but not ideas, and in the specialist philosophical sense of 'perceive', which is to have present to consciousness, we perceive ideas but not physical objects, but deny that the conjunction of these entails that physical objects are composed of ideas. Another common criticism is that the argument undermines the premiss that we perceive physical objects, rather than showing that physical objects are composed of ideas. In the *Principles* Berkeley does little to counter these objections, but we can already see that the dialectical strategy of the *Dialogues* is well designed to do that. The first move is not to argue that we only perceive ideas but rather to agree on a neutral characterization of what we perceive in the ordinary sense and then argue that those sensible things are mind-dependent. This addresses the first criticism of the *Principles* argument. The second and third moves address the second criticism.

2.3.1 *The First Dialogue*

The objective of the First Dialogue, then, is to establish that sensible things are 'in the mind'—that is, they depend for their existence upon being perceived (which is Berkeley's objective, not that of Philonous). This is achieved by (1) getting clear what the sensible things actually are, (2) systematically showing, for the full range of sensible things, that they are mind-dependent, (3) addressing two sorts of objection, one which attacks the argument by proposing an alternative model or theory of perception, and one which attacks the conclusion. At (1) Berkeley explicitly argues that all we ever perceive are qualities of objects, and only by perceiving their qualities do we perceive objects themselves. Within the realm of the sensible there is no distinction between the quality and the thing which has the quality, for if you take away the qualities, there is nothing left in the perception. Less explicitly, Berkeley is also limiting the sensible things to the sorts of property for which a momentary perception is sufficient. For example, the colour of something can be conclusively established with a quick look (in the right conditions), but whether something is made of gold or not, though often judged on the basis of a quick look, is sensitive to other evidence. Thus being made of gold, as opposed to looking golden, is not a sensible quality but something we infer from the sensible qualities of an object.

Part (2) takes up most of the First Dialogue. Philonous guides the discussion through the qualities typically associated with each of the five senses and then through those qualities still sensible but not tied to a particular sense, being figure (shape), extension (size), motion, and solidity. Berkeley provides him with three basic arguments which he uses selectively on each of these qualities. The arguments are: an Assimilation Argument, which aims to show that the quality in question should be assimilated to another quality which is undeniably mind-dependent—for example, a great heat is painful; an Argument from Conflicting Appearances, which notes that the perceptual experiences of different people, different species, and even one person over time conflict with each other and thus cannot all be of a material world, concluding that none are; and a Causal Argument, which is *ad hominem* against the materialist, pointing out that even if materialism were true, the direct objects of experiences would not be their material causes.

In part (3) Hylas raises five objections. One is merely an attempt to reject (1), which elicits some important but scathing remarks about the notion of a substance or substratum in which sensible properties are supposed to inhere, and the others split into two groups. Two objections offer alternative theories of perception based on distinctions which are meant to undermine the arguments of part (2). Thus it is suggested that we should distinguish the act of perceiving from the object of perception, and while the former is obviously 'in the mind' the latter need not be. Alternatively, we might distinguish the ideas we perceive from the objects they represent, which we are enabled to sense indirectly by having the ideas. Both theories are found wanting, but even if they were shown to be reasonable, that would not undermine the argument but force it back to a prior question of what is the correct theory of perception. As we shall see, Berkeley does not think of his view as a *theory* of perception so much as the obvious default view from which any deviation must be justified. The remaining two objections present a different problem, for they challenge the conclusion of the arguments at (2) directly. It is suggested that it is possible to conceive of a sensible thing which no one has perceived and that vision in particular shows its objects to be spatially distant from us. Berkeley, through Philonous, simply denies both of these suggestions. Against the first he offers the infamous argument that to conceive of an unconceived tree is as contradictory as to see an unseen tree. Against the second he offers a selection of arguments taken from his earlier book on vision, namely that dreamt objects also appear at a distance, that when we approach an object what we see, as defined in (1), changes, so the qualities seen before the approach are not shown to be at a distance, and that anyway distance is 'a line turned endwise to the eye' (*DHP1* 202) and hence only visible as a point.

2.3.2 *The Second Dialogue*

The Second Dialogue begins with a discussion of the 'modern way' of explaining sensory perception in terms of the impact of particles on the nerves and the transmission of this to the brain. Philonous' main reply, that the brain is just another idea, seems very odd, but the point is not important because the explanation presupposes materialism and thus can only be used in its favour as part of an inference to the best explanation, and the immaterialist has a perfectly good and, as Philonous here suggests, perhaps better explanation, namely that our perceptual experiences are caused by another mind. This issue dismissed, Hylas finds himself in a state of scepticism, but Philonous avoids this by pointing out that the conclusion of the First Dialogue, namely that sensible things are mind-dependent, leads to the denial that we perceive the real world only if one's criteria for reality exclude ideas (mind-dependent qualities). But for ideas, to be is to be perceived, so when they are perceived, they really do exist. In Berkeley's famous slogan: their *esse* is *percipi* (*PHK* 3).

The obvious objection to this move is that this sort of existence is second-rate. Berkeley offers a two-part reply to this. The first part points out that our sense perceptions are not dependent on our will. From this we can deduce that they must depend upon some other mind, namely God. Even if proving the existence of God is very important to the historical Berkeley, the important philosophical point here is simply that some of our ideas are real in the sense of not being our own creations. The second part of Berkeley's response is to argue that there is no coherent alternative conception of real existence (except that of spirits) against which the existence of ideas might be compared unfavourably.

The strongest move Berkeley could make here would be to give a general argument to the effect that the idea of mind-independent existence is incoherent. Some commentators claim to find such an argument in the *Principles*, specifically in the discussion of abstraction and the unconceived-tree argument. Whatever the merits of this as an interpretation of the *Principles*, in the *Dialogues* the tree argument comes much earlier and abstraction is only mentioned in passing. Rather the strategy in the *Dialogues* is the weaker one of showing that every suggested interpretation of matter, i.e. of mind-independent existence, is either involved in some kind of contradiction or meaningless. Thus Hylas offers four conceptions of matter, as cause or occasion of our ideas, as instrument of God's will, and as entity in general, each of which Philonous argues against. Though this is a weak strategy, it has one advantage over the stronger, namely that if one was convinced that one had a coherent conception of matter, then a watertight general argument against the possibility of such a conception would only lead one to doubt the premises, but if it could be shown that one's actual conception of matter was incoherent, then, pending an alternative conception, one would have to cease believing in matter. Given that in the First Dialogue he has dismissed the thought that the objects of perception are mind-independent, Berkeley can reasonably claim that Hylas' four suggestions do exhaust the alternative conceptions of matter.

2.3.3 The Third Dialogue

The Third Dialogue consists of a series of objections and replies. These occur in no particular order, which emphasizes the dramatic effect of Hylas thinking through the principles of immaterialism and offering up objections as and when they occur to him. However, it is possible for us to identify five grounds on which Hylas is offering objections: theological, scientific, metaphysical, epistemological, and credibility. The replies are not merely restatements of what has gone before but often require Berkeley, in the person of Philonous, to make substantial new philosophical claims.

In response to objections based upon science, Berkeley has two things to say. The first is that scientific laws, such as the relation between mass and gravitational attraction, though often phrased in terms of matter, do not actually invoke anything other than such sensible qualities as extension and solidity. The second is that while scientists may (mis)conceive what they are doing in terms of discovering the nature of some material world which lies beyond and explains the phenomena, all that is really happening is that (DHP3 243)

by observing and reasoning upon the connexion of ideas, they discover the laws and methods of Nature, which is part of knowledge both useful and entertaining.

This is a tantalizingly brief statement of an instrumentalist view of science. Instrumentalists hold that scientific theories do not describe an unobservable reality which works like some mechanism lying behind and controlling the phenomena, but rather that theories are tools allowing us to discover patterns in the phenomena which we can then use to explain and predict occurrences in the world we experience.

In response to several objections raised at different points by Hylas, Berkeley develops, through Philonous, a means of distinguishing imagination (and dreams) from perception and, within perception, illusion from veridical experience. The objection is that he cannot make these distinctions without invoking the correspondence of ideas to reality and thus without presupposing a distinction between ideas and reality. For the first distinction he invokes three criteria, namely vividness, coherence, and (partial) independence of the will (*DHP3* 235). He notes that the first is contingent: there is no reason why dreams and imaginings should not be at least as vivid as sense experiences. So the distinction really rests on the second two criteria.

Within the realm of sense experience, the distinction between true perceptions and illusory ones is made in terms of prediction: a perception is illusory when, if taken as veridical, it would mislead in the sense of lead one to make incorrect predictions about what else one might experience. Thus the effects of foreshortening make a statue placed high up look in proportion, but if I were to infer from that visual experience that it would appear in proportion when looked at from a different angle or when touched, then I would be misled. So Berkeley can accept that foreshortening is a visual illusion.

A final objection worth mentioning is over the publicity of physical objects. Ideas, it would seem most natural to say, are private in the sense that only one person can have each idea. This seems to entail that no two people (or the same person at different times) can perceive the same sensible thing. The response is that no two people can perceive the same idea, but they can perceive the same physical object, because objects are collections of ideas, we perceive a collection by perceiving (some of) its parts, and two people can perceive the same collection by perceiving different parts of it. To make this plausible, Philonous tries to undermine the notion of absolute or objective identity, according to which we never perceive *the very same* thing but only similar or otherwise related things. In its place he suggests, and I think Philonous is here speaking for Berkeley as well, that the notion of sameness is relative to a way of conceptualizing the world. To take Berkeley's own example (*DHP3* 248), suppose the interior of a house was demolished, leaving only the roof and the structural walls, and a completely new interior was built (the rooms could be different sizes, shapes, heights, the staircases in different places, etc.), are we left with the very same house or not? It would seem that the answer to this question relies not upon an objective notion of identity but upon a fairly arbitrary convention.

The dialogue ends with a lengthy discussion of a problem raised by Lady Percival, the wife of Berkeley's friend Sir John Percival. In the biblical account of creation, we are told that God first created the world, then animals, then man. The problem is what the created world consisted in before there were any minds to perceive it. The obvious answer, that it consisted in ideas had by God, runs into the problem that since God is immutable, he must have had these ideas for eternity, so the creation of the physical world cannot have consisted in his coming to have certain ideas. Philonous' struggles with this problem, while heroic, are philosophically unnecessary. Having proved the existence of God from the existence of the physical world, Berkeley then suggests that we can determine the nature of that God from the nature of the physical world. It seems unlikely that this method of philosophical theology will produce precisely the God of the philosophers, who is infinite, eternal, immutable, benevolent, omniscient, and omnipotent. So one solution is to deny God's immutability. Another, which Berkeley endorses, is to say that the existence of the inanimate world prior to the animate, which is not only a commitment of the biblical account of creation, but also of evolutionary accounts, consists in

God having formed conditional intentions that if there were someone to perceive, then they would perceive such-and-such. This is a
form of phenomenalism.

2.4 Interpreting Immaterialism

Misinterpretations of Berkeley's immaterialism abound. The satir-
ist Jonathan Swift, who was a friend of Berkeley's, showed typical
incomprehension by instructing his servants not to open the door
to Berkeley when he visited, on the grounds that Berkeley believed he could walk through doors. A similar misunderstanding is
attributed to Samuel Johnson, the lexicographer, by Boswell: apparently Johnson kicked a stone, saying 'I refute him thus'. Both
forget that solidity is a sensible quality and thus not a feature of dis-
credited matter. The poet Yeats wrote of 'God-appointed Berkeley
that proved all things a dream', but Berkeley was keen to distinguish the real, perceived world from the chimeras of dreams. And
there are too many to mention who have attributed to him the
view that when I leave my study, or even when I close my eyes, the
table (rather than just my idea of it) ceases to exist.

These mistakes can easily be rectified by looking at what Berkeley
actually wrote, but they arise from a serious need to grasp the
essence of his philosophy, which is a need we should respect. If
Berkeley is not saying these things, then what *is* he saying?

One answer is that he is simply responding to Locke, that he
accepts Locke's empiricist premisses and is merely drawing out
their consequences. If this was the case, we could understand him
as arguing for a conditional and assuming its antecedent. However,
the *Three Dialogues*, perhaps more than the *Principles*, makes it clear
that this is not the case. The bulk of the argument in the First
Dialogue is directed not against Locke's indirect or representative
theory of perception, which holds that we see, hear, and touch
material objects by having ideas of those things before the mind, but
against the direct realist view that (some of) the immediate objects

of perception are mind-independent. In the Second Dialogue the conception of matter being attacked is as much that of Descartes and Malebranche as it is of Locke, and while Berkeley does appear to accept empiricist restrictions upon what ideas are available to a mind, he never uses this as an argumentative tool.

Another interpretation, made famous by Bertrand Russell, is that, according to Berkeley, perception alone tells us nothing about the 'true intrinsic nature of physical objects' (*The Problems of Philosophy*, ch. 4, p. 19), but only about our ideas. Philosophical argument, however, is meant to reveal that the physical objects to which our ideas correspond are not material, but are ideas in God's mind. While one can see how Russell formed this opinion, it is a travesty of the historical Berkeley. One of the most important objectives for Berkeley, as is clearly brought out by the dramatic structure of the *Three Dialogues*, is to do away with the idea of true intrinsic natures and return epistemic sovereignty to perception (*DHP3* 245):

PHILONOUS ... We both therefore agree in this, that we perceive only sensible forms: but herein we differ, you will have them to be empty appearances, I real beings. In short you do not trust your senses, I do.

Much of Russell's philosophy can be seen as a response to Cartesian scepticism, and he is trying to understand Berkeley in this light. Berkeley, however, is not responding to Descartes's problem of how, on the basis of what is subjectively available, we can know about the objective world, but rather denying that there is a problem here. For Berkeley the objective world is subjectively available in perception, so once perception occurs, there can be no further gap which needs to be bridged.

Berkeley has also been interpreted as taking part in the Logical Positivist project of analytically reducing all talk of the physical world to talk of experiences. Thus Warnock (*Berkeley*, 175) attributes to Berkeley the view that

the sentence 'It seems to me and to God, and it would seem to anyone else, as if there were an orange on the sideboard' *means the same as* 'there is an orange of the sideboard'.

It is doubtful that Berkeley had Warnock's concept of an analytic equivalence of one sentence to another (I am not sure that I do), but what is really wrong with this interpretation is that it misses the ontological nature of what Berkeley is saying. To say that we could replace without loss all our talk of physical objects with talk of experiences falls short of the claim that what there is in the world are minds and ideas. Also, this interpretation would have to take Berkeley's talk of a mind perceiving an idea as a slightly confused way of saying that the person had an experience, i.e. that it seemed to that person as if such-and-such. This makes the double error of doing away with Berkeley's clear understanding of having an idea as standing in a relation to a thing, and committing him to mentalizing the world, to reducing physical facts to facts about minds.

The two main strands of the interpretation I shall develop in this book are (1) that Berkeley believed in the existence of a physical world distinct from the minds that perceive it but dependent for its existence upon being perceived, and (2) that Berkeley sharply distinguished perceptual knowledge, which is of particulars and unmediated by concepts, from knowledge of general truths, which essentially involves concepts and is thus peculiarly human and fallible. The first point has been vigorously asserted by T. E. Jessop and A. A. Luce, who edited the definitive edition of Berkeley's works, but it can seem very hard to see how one might combine the distinctness and the dependence. In a 1959 lecture Jessop wrote:

Berkeley does not mentalize [corporeal things]. They are exactly what they are experienced to be—coloured, sounding, hot, cold, spatial, hard. These adjectives cannot be applied meaningfully to anything mental. It was not he, but the contemporary philosophers and scientists against whom he was arguing, who made the blunder of regarding such qualities as mental . . . Berkeley was just as revolutionary in rejecting their inner world of mental sensations as he was in denying their independent world of unperceivable material entities. (*George Berkeley*, 31–2)

In favour of this interpretation we can note that Berkeley uses the adjective 'mental' only once in the *Three Dialogues* (DHP3 250— 'mental operations') and once in the *Principles* (PHK Intro 9— 'mental separation'), both times to describe acts of mind, not objects of perception. But there are two major obstacles to the interpretation. One is that Berkeley often talks of ideas as sensations, and the other is that the dependence of ideas on the perceiving mind seems to undermine their distinctness from that mind. On the first point we cannot suggest that the usage is a slip of Berkeley's because the Assimilation Argument of the First Dialogue draws explicit parallels between sense perception and sensations such as pain. So it seems that Jessop must attribute to Berkeley the view that the sensations such as pleasures, pains, itches, and tickles are no more mental items than colours and shapes. Is this too ridiculous to be the view of the historical Berkeley? First we should ask why one might believe that pains are mental. Because they cannot exist unperceived? Because they are as they seem and seem as they are? These are also properties of ideas and thus, *on this interpretation*, not marks of the mental. So we should ask the Jessop question: to what do the sensation adjectives apply? Minds? Well, we do talk of someone being in pain, but that is equivalent to their feeling a pain, which looks like a relation between them and something else. And this something else need not be mental, for when one feels pain, what is painful, what hurts, is usually an event, and this may be a mental event (remembering the loss of a loved one) or may be a physical event (stubbing a toe). The underlying reason for thinking that pains and other bodily sensations (note the adjective: bodies are physical) are mental is a reluctance to see them as part of the real world, as being 'out there', but this reluctance is premissed upon a materialist conception of reality according to which what is real is necessarily mind-independent. If we are following Berkeley as far as to say that the physical world is composed of items for which to be is to be perceived, then nothing about the character of pains prevents them from being part of the physical, i.e. non-mental, world. So there is no problem with Berkeley talking of sensations, so long as we remember that it is the materialist who thinks that sensations are mental.

There remains the concern that one cannot establish the mind-dependence of ideas without undermining their alleged distinctness from the mind. Jessop argued for the distinctness of ideas from minds by claiming that what we experience, the ideas we have, are not mental qualities but physical ones such as shape, size, and colour. In other words, if we agree with common sense that we immediately perceive the physical world, then what we immediately perceive, namely ideas, cannot be mental on pain of the absurd consequence that physical objects such as trees are mental (cf. *DHP3* 262, quoted above).

The mind-dependence derives from the claim that sensible qualities are as they seem to be, that there is no possibility of sensible things seeming to be other than they are (though that is not to say that Berkeley cannot distinguish veridical from misleading perceptions). If this is to establish mind-dependence, the transparency has to be explained not by our having a special faculty of knowing, but by the nature of the things known about. This is argued in the First Dialogue, where Philonous tries to show that how things seem is in part dependent upon the mind that perceives. And if things perceived are exactly as they seem to be, then it follows that how they *are* is in part dependent upon the mind that perceives them. This is the mind-dependence of ideas, but it falls short of their being mental entities, unless one were to make the unwarranted materialist assumption that only the mental can be known transparently.

There is the residual worry that the dependence of how things seem upon the mind that perceives them might be causal and thus compatible with the independence of the objects of perception, but this can be dealt with in the Berkeleian system by the assimilation of causation with voluntary action. If my mind in part caused the carpet to look burgundy, then I would be able to control it, but I cannot.

The error of thinking that Berkeley mentalizes the world is encouraged by interpreting his philosophy as a direct response to Locke's representative realism. According to representative realism we perceive material objects by having representative ideas of them. Thus there are two sorts of objects of perception: ideas and material things; the former are immediate, internal, and mental, the latter are mediate, external, and physical. If Berkeley is interpreted as denying the existence of the external object, then it seems that he is only left with internal, mental objects. This is a mistake, for the point of the categorization of the immediate objects of perception as mental (or for Malebranche, as neither mental nor physical) is to *contrast* them with material things. For the immaterialist, no such contrast is necessary or possible, so there is no bar to thinking of ideas as physical.

The second strand of my interpretation of Berkeley stems from what appears to be an inconsistency, or at least dangerous looseness, in how Philonous describes the objects of perception. On the one hand, at the beginning of the First Dialogue he explicitly limits the sensible things to a small class of qualities (*DHP1* 175):

PHILONOUS   This point then is agreed between us, that *sensible things are those only which are immediately perceived by sense*. You will farther inform me, whether we immediately perceive by sight any thing beside light, and colours, and figures: or by hearing, any thing but sounds: by the palate, any thing beside tastes: by the smell, beside odours: or by the touch, more than tangible qualities.

The important thing about this limitation, which rules out such claims as that we (immediately) see dogs or hear lawnmowers, is that the sensible qualities allowed are ones which can be wholly present to the senses. Whether something is a dog or not depends on more than how it looks to me right now, but whether something is brown or loud or smelly does not.

On the other hand, Philonous often talks, as we all do, of perceiving houses, trees, mountains, etc. A common way for commentators to resolve this tension is to suggest that Berkeley has a strict sense and a loose sense of 'perceive', and certainly there are passages where he writes of what is 'strictly' perceived (e.g. *DHP1* 204). However, this resolution looks like attributing to Berkeley a very misleading way of covering up an unpalatable consequence: since actual sense experience is limited to what we strictly perceive (the rest being 'suggested' or inferred), it would follow that on Berkeley's principles we do not really have sense experience of everyday objects. If that is the true doctrine, then Philonous wins the argument with Hylas only by sleight of tongue.

An alternative resolution goes like this: everyday objects are collections of ideas, and those collections include ideas had by several people at several times in several sense modalities, so no one is ever confronted with a 'complete' object (=collection of ideas). That gives us the strict sense in which we do not perceive objects: we only ever perceive part of an object at once. However, there is nothing wrong with saying that I see something when all that is currently in sight is part of that thing. When my neighbour walks past the window, there are parts of him, such as his legs, which I cannot see, but there is no question that I can see him. So Berkeley can allow that, speaking quite literally, we do have sense experience of everyday objects, though strictly speaking (and this is the 'strictly speaking' of everyday speech) we only ever see part of them.

If this interpretation is right, then we need to take very seriously the ontological distinction between sensible things and everyday objects, and the correlative distinction in how we know about them. Sensible things are completely revealed in sense experience, so the relation of perception provides us with perfect knowledge of them. Everyday objects are rather different, for there is more to be known about them than is revealed in any given perceptual encounter. This knowledge depends upon defeasible inferences. Consider the well-worn example of an oar half in water and thus looking crooked. If I judge that the oar is straight, there are many mistakes I might have made, and all will be consistent with my current sense experience. Thus it may turn out, on closer inspection or by reference to what other people know, not to be an oar but a mast or just a very smooth branch, and it may turn out that when I feel it, or take it out of the water, it still appears crooked. Whenever we judge that something falls under a concept, we are liable to this sort of error, hence perfect perceptual knowledge cannot involve concepts. My knowledge of how things are visually here and now, and my knowledge that there is a straight oar in front of me, are of different types and are arrived at by completely different routes.

This point may not appear particularly significant, but we shall see that many of Berkeley's arguments can be properly appreciated only if we are very clear about whether we are talking about ideas or things (=collections of ideas). Also, it will turn out that along with the epistemological distinction, Berkeley has a rather different attitude to the reality of what we know in the two cases.

2.5 Is Berkeley an Anti-Realist?

Berkeley is often called an idealist, and certainly he thinks that the world is ideal in the sense of composed of ideas, but idealism also connotes a denial of realism, and this is a less clear-cut issue. One way of denying realism about something is to say it does not exist: this is the sense in which I am an irrealist about ghosts and Berkeley is an irrealist about forces such as gravity (*DHP3* 257). But as the dispute between Hylas and Philonous makes clear, Berkeley is insistent that he does not deny 'the reality of sensible things' (*DHP1* 173), for that is the very scepticism he is trying to combat.

There are other ways of denying realism about something than saying it does not exist. For example, I do not want to deny that some flavours of ice cream are nicer than others, but I do not think that being nicer than chocolate is a *real* feature of strawberry ice cream. My reason for thinking that the distinction, though it exists, is not a real one is that if I decide that strawberry is nicer than chocolate, then it is: thinking makes it so. Now what is crucial to this being an anti-realist view is not just the truth of the conditional 'if I think it, then it is true', but the idea that it is my thinking it which *makes* it true.

Superficially it appears that Berkeley is committed to this sort of claim about sense perception, because there is no possibility of how things seem and how they are coming apart: if I seem to hear a noise, smell an aroma, or see a colour, then there was a noise, aroma, or colour which I heard, smelt, or saw. The first point to note is that, as the second strand of my interpretation makes clear, we do not perceive *that* the carpet is burgundy, rather we perceive certain sensible qualities and judge that the carpet is burgundy. Merely judging it does not make that so, since I may be wrong. However, we do need to establish whether the doctrine of *esse* is *percipi* is anti-realist. The doctrine entails that if someone at some time perceives a sensible quality, then that quality exists. Does perceiving make it so?

To see why this is not anti-realist in the sense we are considering, we need to look again at the example of chocolate and strawberry ice cream. There we seem to have two distinct facts, a mental one (my judging that strawberry is better than chocolate) and an apparently non-mental one (strawberry being better than chocolate), and the claim is that the one *makes* the other the case, and therefore the latter is not real. Notice that the facts need to be distinct for the conclusion to follow that one *makes* the other: my judging that strawberry is better entails that I made a judgement about strawberry ice cream, but this has no implications for the reality of my judgements. So if Berkeley is to be a thinking-makes-it-so anti-realist, we must find two distinct facts, namely that a sensible quality appears to someone at some time, and that there is such a sensible quality, and show that the first *makes* the second. But given that Berkeley understands an appearance of a sensible quality to someone as that person being related to that actual quality, the two facts are not sufficiently distinct. The former trivially entails the latter.

So Berkeley can argue that he is a realist about sensible qualities despite their being mind-dependent, in exactly the same way that we are all instinctively realist about pains. Though pains only exist when they are perceived, we do not make our pains exist (except by pinching ourselves or whatever). Similarly, sensible qualities only exist when perceived, but the perceiver does not make them exist. In the course of arguing for the existence of God, Berkeley often says such things as 'sensible things . . . depend not on my thought' (*DHP2* 212), which is clearly a claim to some form of realism. The obvious exception to this is imagination, but that is precisely why sense experience is of reality and imagination is not. What mind-dependence does or does not amount to is discussed in Chapter 5. The distinction between making my sensations exist, which I cannot do, and affecting my perceptions by acting on the world, which I can do, is crucial here. Hence Berkeley's theory of action is essential to his metaphysics. That is discussed in Chapter 6.

There is an important general point about realism here. One clear definition of anti-realist idealism is that it makes the facts about the physical world depend upon contingent facts about minds. But we must be careful to distinguish dependence of the physical upon purely mental facts from dependence upon facts about how minds are related to the non-mental. For Berkeley a fact about what we will is purely mental but a fact about what we sense is not, for sense perception is a relation between us and something else (namely sensible qualities). The idea of perception as a relation is discussed in Chapter 3. He would be happy with the thought that, to the extent that the physical depends upon our acts of will, it is not real. However, what we sense, and thus what the sensible qualities are, does not depend upon any human volition (though we can act on the world and thus cause changes in the sensible qualities, our choice is limited to whether we act, not what the effects of those actions will be).

This is Berkeley's case for being a perceptual realist, but there will be a different story to tell about judgements, in so far as those go beyond what is currently being perceived (which is nearly always). Suppose I hear certain sounds and judge that someone is mowing the grass. When I look out of the window I see that the machine in use is a strimmer: is my judgement that someone is mowing the grass true or false? Well, holding the sensible qualities to be fixed as I have specified them, the truth of the judgement depends upon whether using a strimmer counts as mowing, and what determines that but a human decision about the concept *mowing*? Such decisions are not normally ones that face me when I make the judgement, but for all that they have had to be made at some point. This is fairly obvious in such cases as *mowing*, but has general application. It even applies to basic shape and colour concepts: whether two trees or birds are the same shape or not depends upon how close one looks for differences, and that in turn depends upon our interests and the conventions that express them; and what but a human convention determines that orange is not a shade of red? Every judgement involves classifying something, and Berkeley thinks that the categories by which we classify are our own invention. He takes the nominalist slogan 'everything that exists is particular' extremely seriously, denying that any two sensible things have anything in common, from which it follows that there can never be an objective ground for classifying them together. So it would seem that, by holding all the sensible qualities fixed, the truth of our judgements *does* depend upon human actions.

According to Berkeley the real, physical world which God created, and we know about directly through sense perception, consists of isolated sensible qualities. From God's point of view, no two sensible qualities have anything in common. However, finite minds like ours have a tendency to group or categorize them. The ordering of ideas into types, such as being red or square, is discussed in

Chapter 7. The ordering of ideas into particulars, such as this table or that dog, is discussed in Chapter 8. This human tendency to categorize enables God to impose patterns on the sensible qualities, patterns which are in reality arbitrary but seem natural to us, so that we can predict and control the physical world to our benefit. Some of our classifications will be better, some worse, than others, but only in the sense of more or less useful. None corresponds to objective features of reality. To this extent Berkeley is an anti-realist: what we call truth in any of our judgements is really just a long-term utility.

Appendix: A Quick Reference Guide to the Three Dialogues

First Dialogue 171–207

This dialogue has three important stages of argument. After the preamble and the discussion of scepticism, Hylas is very quickly persuaded that the only objects of immediate perception are sensible qualities (174–5). This is the first stage.

The second stage (175–94) aims to show that sensible qualities are mind-dependent. Philonous discusses the five senses in succession and then the so-called primary qualities, and uses three main arguments selectively. See the table opposite.

In the third stage Hylas tries five ways of avoiding the conclusion. The first and last offer alternative theories of perception, the second has been dealt with at 174–5. The third and fourth are straightforward denials that sensible qualities are 'in the mind'.

195: Distinction between act of perceiving and object of perception.
197: There must be a material substratum in which sensible qualities inhere.
199: The unconceived tree: it is possible to conceive of a sensible object which no one has perceived.

	Assimilation argument	Conflicting appearances	Causal argument
Touch (hot/cold)	175–8	178–9	179
Taste (sweet/bitter)	180	180	
Odours	180–1	180–1	
Sounds			181–3
Colours		183–7	187
Figure and extension		188–9	
Motion		190	
Solidity		191	
Absolute extension	[Inseparability] 192–4		

201: The objects of perception are spatially distinct from us.

203: Representative Realism: ideas are signs of material objects.

Second Dialogue 208–226

The dialogue begins with an argument to the effect that empirical evidence to do with the causation of experience cannot favour materialism (208–10), since the evidence deals only with the relations between sensible objects (209), and anyway there is an explanatory gap (210).

Hylas then charges Philonous with scepticism (denying the reality of everyday objects) on the ground that he accepts the arguments of the First Dialogue. Philonous replies (211–12) that they do not entail scepticism on his standards of reality for sensible objects. Philonous then offers several versions of the argument for God's existence (212–15).

Hylas notes (215) that Philonous has not yet *proved* the non-existence of mind-independent matter. Hylas offers four conceptions of matter:

215: It is the causal intermediary between God's will and our ideas.

218: It is the instrument of God's will.

220: It is the occasion of our sensations.

222: It is entity in general (as opposed to specific qualities).

There is progressively less content to these conceptions of matter, until Philonous is able to claim that Hylas 'meant nothing' (226).

Third Dialogue 227–263

In this dialogue Hylas raises a series of objections to immaterialism in no particular order. The dialogue is very dense with argument and counter-argument, but the main points raised by Hylas can be divided into five groups.

1. *Theological*

231: We have no clearer idea of God (nor ourselves, 233) than we do of matter.

236: Surely God is responsible for all evil?

240: If ideas derive from the mind of God, then God must feel pain, which is an imperfection.

243: Since all mankind falsely believes in matter, surely God is a deceiver?

250: Creation: ideas in God's mind are eternal and thus cannot be created, but ideas in our minds cannot be created before us, yet the Bible says that God created the earth and the animals before he created Adam.

2. *Scientific*

241: There are scientific explanations in terms of matter.

244: Are we not left with just the empty forms of things?

245: How do we account for knowledge only available from microscopes?

3. *Metaphysical*

234: The reality of sensible things does not require them to be actually perceived, but only to be perceivable.

235: How does the idealist distinguish between real things, imagined things, and dreamt ones?

247: Two people cannot share an idea, so they cannot see the same thing?

249: If ideas have extension but minds do not, how can ideas exist *in* minds?

4. *Epistemological*

238: The crooked oar: how do we distinguish true from false perceptions, if not in terms of correspondence to something real?

245: How do we account for disagreement about the nature of objects?

5. *Credibility*

237: Repugnant to the universal sense of mankind.

244: Immaterialism is dangerously novel, so it is politically unwelcome.

244: Surely it is at least controversial to say all things are just ideas?

PART 2

CHAPTER 3

The Sensible

3.1 What Do We Perceive with Our Senses?

At the outset, Hylas and Philonous agree on a criterion of unacceptability in metaphysics, namely that someone 'denies the reality of sensible things or professes the greatest ignorance of them' (*DHP1* 173). Since Philonous does want to deny the reality of material things, he must address the important question: What do we perceive with our senses? He must find an answer to this question which is (*a*) sufficiently general to encompass everything we do or might perceive, and (*b*) sufficiently specific for Philonous to be able to prove something about *all* the sensible things, namely that they are none of them material, that they are all mind-dependent. Now we ought to be sceptical whether an answer meeting both these conditions can be given. For example, we might try to address (*a*) by saying that we perceive things, events, processes, and their properties, but this is clearly too vague to rule out matter. But trying to address (*b*) by saying that we perceive images or sense-data rules out too many of the things we ordinarily take ourselves to perceive. In the *Principles* Berkeley takes the answer that we perceive only ideas to be 'evident to anyone who takes a survey of the objects of human knowledge' (*PHK* 1), and many materialists would have concurred. However, in the *Three Dialogues* this conclusion is reached in stages:

first he tries to characterize what we perceive in a metaphysically neutral manner, and then to argue that all those things are in fact mind-dependent. One way of criticizing Berkeley is to argue that his characterization of what we perceive is not neutral and that the materialist need not accept it. Berkeley's account (*DHP1* 174–5) of what we perceive by sense has three elements:

(1) All sense perception is immediate.
(2) Only a restricted set of qualities (sounds, smells, etc.) can be perceived immediately.
(3) Sensible things are nothing but collections of sensible qualities.

The argument for (1) is roughly that there are several types of thing we know about mediately and those are not things we are said to know by sense. No argument is given for (2), but when we try to work out why Berkeley found it so obvious, we shall uncover better grounds for (1). (3) is argued for briefly, and though a substantial premiss is missing, Berkeley is in a reasonably strong position here.

(1) *All sense perception is immediate.* Philonous gives three examples: seeing a diversity of colour, hearing a variety of sounds, and feeling heat and weight, which are compared in each case to our thoughts about the cause of what we see, hear, or feel. There are two notions of mediation in play in this discussion: (*a*) our knowledge is mediated if it is the product of an inference from something else we perceive; (*b*) our knowledge of something is said to be mediated if that thing is the cause of something else we perceive. It is worth our distinguishing these two notions of mediation, though Berkeley does not, because they raise different issues. For example, when I hear certain sounds I am normally also said to hear the lawnmower which is the cause of those sounds, though there is no need for me to make an inference from the sounds to the lawn-

mower. Equally, I make plenty of inferences from my perceptions which are not causal.

Taking mediation as defined by (*a*), Berkeley's point initially seems quite plausible since we often do distinguish between, on the one hand, things we actually saw (heard, felt, etc.), and, on the other, what we inferred from our experience. However, if Berkeley is to persuade us that his immaterialism does not deny the reality of sensible things, he needs a very sharp distinction between what is sensible and what is not, and unfortunately our everyday distinction between perceiving and inferring is vague in too many cases. For example, did I actually see that the postman had delivered, or did I merely see some letters land on the doormat and infer that he had delivered? The problem here is that for ordinary purposes we say that we saw the postman had been, but sometimes, such as when questioned in a court of law, we would claim to have inferred it. Is the former loose talk, the latter more precise? Or is the former perfectly correct and the latter a specially introduced sense of 'infer'? Berkeley gives us no way of resolving these questions and thus no way of making a sharp sensible–insensible distinction out of this notion of mediation. However, as we shall see in 3.1.2, he does have a way of making a sharp distinction here to which he might have appealed if he had not thought the point so obvious.

Interpreting mediation as in (*b*), Berkeley seems at first to be simply mistaken: we do normally say we heard a violin, saw the lightning, smelt the wine, etc., even though our experience of these is causally mediated via sounds, flashes, aromas, etc. In Berkeley's defence we should note that there are times when we do not say we heard something, like a violin, even though we did hear a sound caused by it, when, for example, it was dropped on the floor. Similarly, while we sometimes see the lightning and not just its effects, if the lightning causes the lights to fail, seeing the lights go off is *not* seeing the lightning. In general, we tend to say that we see, hear, etc. the cause of the sounds, flashes, and aromas when the effect is typical, but not when it is not. Berkeley has a good explanation for this since he thinks that objects are bundles of qualities, so experiencing some of the qualities is experiencing (part of) the object, whereas experiencing qualities which are not included in the bundle is not experiencing the object at all but, at best, something related to it (see Chapter 8, especially 8.3.4 on direct perception). If we add the plausible principle that a whole cannot cause its parts, then we can see why Berkeley thought that all cases of mediation by causation were ones in which we do not say that we saw, heard, etc. the cause as well as the effect. Unfortunately, this would not shore up the argument for (1) without circularity, since Berkeley's argument for the bundle conception of objects relies upon his claims about the objects of perception.

It is worth making clear that Berkeley is only claiming that mediate perception is not *sense* perception. It is still a form of perception, and perception is the having of an idea before the mind. So if someone mediately perceives something, that idea is before his mind. The difference consists in how the idea comes to be before the mind. In mediate perception the idea is suggested by or inferred from another perception, whereas in immediate or sense perception it is independent of all other perceptions. So it is possible, and even sometimes quite easy, to mistake mediate perceptions for sense experiences. For example, if I desperately want to see a golden plover, the movement in the heather might suggest to me a bird-like shape, leading me mistakenly to think I saw a bird. What has merely been mediately perceived, and thus may or may not correspond to the way the world is, is taken to be an immediate or sense perception. This possibility is essential for Berkeley, since as we shall see, he does not think sense perceptions can be of what is not there to be sensed. The mediate/immediate distinction does not mark a difference between two types of perception, between two relations we might stand in to objects, but a difference between the causes of perceptions. If an idea is mediately perceived it is perceived, in exactly the same sense as if it were immediately perceived.

(2) *Only a restricted set of qualities can be perceived immediately.* Berkeley's point here is that all we see is light, colour and shape, all we hear are sounds, all we smell are odours, all we taste are tastes, and all we touch are 'feels' (as in 'the feel of this pen is cold, hard, smooth, etc.'). Hylas simply accepts this point as a consequence of the claim that all sense perception is immediate, but on neither interpretation of mediation does it follow. To see this suppose we claim, *contra* Berkeley, that in good viewing conditions we can see whether something is a sparrow or not. On the one hand, this does not even look like a borderline case of inference, for we just see it, and on the other, it is the property of being a sparrow itself which I claim to be able to detect visually in good conditions, not an effect of it. And yet being a sparrow is not just a matter of colour and shape, so it is presumably ruled out as not immediately perceivable by Berkeley's claim (2).

Many recent commentators think Berkeley has smuggled in an assumption here, namely that immediate perception is infallible, that I cannot make a mistake about what I immediately perceive. Though we might be pretty reliable at detecting sparrows visually, we can still make mistakes precisely because there is more to being a sparrow than having a certain look. However, even if I make such a mistake, I was still right about how things looked to me then. So if one makes the assumption that immediate perception is infallible, (2) does follow from (1).

There are two problems with (2) on this interpretation. First, if we make the assumption, what plausibility there was in (1) is lost, since it would seem obvious that we can and do suffer visual, auditory, etc. illusions. Secondly, it has been argued that there is not even a restricted part of our sense experience which is infallible. Before showing how Berkeley is able to address both these problems, I want to suggest that his assumption is more fundamental than simply that immediate perception is infallible. What Berkeley assumes is a model of perception which has this as a consequence. I shall call his model the Simplest Model of Perception or SMP for short. Berkeley thinks SMP has a special status, for it is the view any deviations from which need to be justified. It is the default account of perception.

> *The Simplest Model of (Sense) Perception* (SMP)
>
> '*S* perceives *O* (by sense)' describes a two-place relation between a mind and a sensible thing/quality. The relation of *perceiving* or *being aware of* is a pure relation, much like a spatial relation (hence 'before the mind'), in that it is not constituted, either wholly or partly, by any concurrent event in or state of one of the relata. The relation is neither an action nor an event, and does not have qualities or features itself. The only possible differences between two perceivings are in the identities of the subject or the object (the five senses are distinguished by their objects). Since the subject is not perceived, changes in the subject can affect the content of the perception only by changing the object of perception. If *S* perceives *O*, then what *S* perceives, the content of the perception, is completely determined by *O*. Sameness of object entails sameness of perceptual content, and consequently perceptual (as opposed to inferential) error is not possible.

To understand SMP, consider its relation to the debate about whether Berkeley holds an act–object model of perception or an adverbial model (e.g. Pitcher, *Berkeley*, 198). Pappas makes the situation very clear when he describes the adverbialist as saying that the distinction between act and object 'collapses' (*Berkeley's Thought*, 125). It is standardly assumed that if this distinction collapses, we are left with just the act, the perceiving, and consequently the difference between seeing red and seeing green must be the difference between seeing redly and seeing greenly. But a collapse can go either way: the object could collapse into the act or the act into the object. SMP holds that we do not have a duality of act and object, but merely an object (and a subject, of course, but the identity and properties of the subject are irrelevant to the content of the perception, to what is perceived). This alternative is obscured by the universal assumption that if *S* perceives *O*, then there is a (mental) event which is a perceiving of *O* by *S*. SMP simply denies this: when *S* perceives *O*, *S* and *O* exist, and they stand in a relation, namely perceiving, but their standing in this relation is neither constituted nor enabled by any concurrent event or occurrence in *S*. *S* can stand in the relation of being one metre away from *O*, and perhaps only stand in that relation because she walked to that spot, and yet her standing in that relation to *O* is neither constituted nor enabled by any concurrent event in *S* (or *O* for that matter). The act–object model of perception would be better called the 'subject–act–object model' to make clear its commitment to a third element in the perceptual relation, and then SMP would be a subject–object model. (To complete the taxonomy, we should call the representative theory of perception the 'subject–object–object model'.) On SMP, then, the only way to account for the difference between seeing red and seeing green is to advert to a difference in the objects, and similarly, according to Berkeley, for the difference between seeing and hearing.

Now it might seem that SMP is obviously false if it is ever true that we perceive ordinary physical objects, such as the African violet on my desk. But this does not rule out SMP from being the default model of perception for two reasons. One is that at this point in the argument Berkeley is trying to establish what kinds of thing we do perceive, so to assume that we do perceive such things as African violets would be question-begging. Secondly, he has been careful to limit the discussion to immediate perception, and this gives him two options for later accounting for the common-sense claim that we do perceive ordinary physical objects. He could claim that this is mediate perception, or he could claim that while we do sometimes immediately perceive physical objects such as plants and desks, any errors we make about them are not perceptual errors but inferential errors. Since his account of the mediate/

immediate distinction entails that everything mediately perceived is also immediately perceived, he takes the latter option. Just as long as 'how things seem' includes not only how things perceptually appear but also how we are inclined to judge them to be on the basis of our perceptual experience, Berkeley can even allow that there is a potential gap between how things seem and how they are, while maintaining that perceptual error is impossible.

Berkeley nowhere makes an explicit statement of SMP, so the attribution is based on inference. First, assuming SMP makes some apparently poor arguments quite plausible, and secondly, at a couple of points Hylas proposes alternative models of perception which are rejected, and SMP seems to be what we are left with.

There are a variety of reasons why an assumption may not be made explicit, ranging from the philosopher not noticing it to his trying to cover it up. Given his objectives in the dialogues with Hylas, Philonous has no reason to make all his assumptions explicit. In Berkeley's case, it would seem that he thought that SMP is obviously the default position, that unless there could be shown to be some problem with it, SMP is self-evidently the best account of perception. Since all the important arguments for immaterialism depend upon SMP, it is unfortunate that Berkeley did not spell out why he thought it such a good model of perception.

SMP has two important merits. The first is phenomenological: sense perception seems to the perceiver to be simple *openness* to objects and their properties. The way things look, feel, sound, etc. appears to the subject to be fully determined by how they are, and SMP entails that the phenomenology does not mislead. The second merit is more theoretical: SMP has the perfect explanation of why the sensible world appears to our senses the way it does, namely that it necessarily appears as it is. Any deviation from SMP will need to give an account of what determines appearances, and this can only be done by introducing, for theoretical purposes, an extra item, such as a mental event, object, or representation, which has properties which can explain why things appear as they do. Given that (a) there is no reason to believe in these items except for the need to explain something which (b) SMP does not need to explain, then it does seem that SMP has a natural advantage. However, if someone can sustain a challenge to either (a) or (b), then SMP loses its initial credibility.

(a) is typically challenged by saying that there is in common sense a three-way distinction between the perceiver, the perceiving, and what is perceived which allows the middle term to vary without the others varying. This would be to say that the same person can perceive the same thing in different ways because the character of their perceiving of it, i.e. how they perceive it, changes. If this were true, then common sense is committed to an act–object model of perception. Hylas proposes an act–object model at DHP1 195 and it is rejected. If that argument works (it is discussed in 3.3.1), then common sense is either mistaken or not committed to the three-way distinction. Berkeley holds the latter.

(b) is more often challenged, on the grounds that the world does not always appear as it really is, hence in some cases (the illusory ones) SMP must be modified to explain what determines appearances. This argument from illusion attempts to show that there must be a third (mental) element in perception, which might be an event, object, or representation, depending upon which model replaces SMP. Now, as we shall see in 3.2.2, Berkeley himself uses arguments from illusion but draws a rather different conclusion: not that SMP needs modifying by the introduction of a third mental component, but that SMP is correct and all the objects of perception are mind-dependent. This commits him to saying that in the cases we call illusions, the world actually is as it seems to be, but he is happy with that commitment (DHP3 238).

If we allow Berkeley to assume SMP, then he can use the intuitive distinction between perception and inference to give content to (1), the immediacy of all sense percepton, and use SMP to defend it. Given (1) and SMP, (2) follows quite directly.

(3) *Sensible things are nothing but collections of sensible qualities.* This thesis was simply assumed at the beginning of the *Principles* but is argued for here. It is effectively a theory of object identity, namely that sensible objects are nothing but bundles of qualities. Given that Berkeley wants to uphold the commonsensical view that physical objects are sensible, he is also committed to a bundle-of-qualities theory of physical objects. Hylas accepts (3) without expecting this consequence. In the passage we are considering (*DHP1* 175) Philonous offers a subtraction argument based on the facts of perception. Later in the First Dialogue he argues against the intelligibility of the alternative (*DHP1* 197–9) and in the Third Dialogue he gives an argument from the nature of identity (*DHP3* 247–8).

The argument at *DHP1* 175 has two steps. First, (2), the restriction on what can be perceived, entails that 'if you take away all sensible qualities, there remains nothing sensible', and secondly, this entails (3). It looks as though the conclusion of the first step is independently plausible: if we sense no qualities, then we sense nothing. However, one might question whether this really entails (3), by noting that (2) is consistent with the claim that sensible things are distinct from their qualities, but we can only sense them *by* sensing their qualities. That we always sense some qualities, if we have any sense experience at all, does not entail that we *only* have sense experience of sensible qualities. Berkeley would want to secure this move by arguing that if we only sense something (*x*) by sensing something else (*y*), then we *mediately* perceive (*x*), and mediate perception is not sense perception by (1). However, the materialist might object that the relation between an object and its qualities provides an exception to this rule. Though our perceiving the object depends upon our perceiving the quality, and is thus mediate, this is possible because there cannot be a quality without something that has it, and a particular quality, such as the sound of that lawnmower I can hear, can only be identified, as I have just done, by referring to the thing which has the quality. Perception can only allow us to identify the particular quality, which it does, if it involves some awareness of the thing which has the quality.

Effectively this objection to Berkeley's argument charges the bundle-of-qualities theory with being committed to the existence of free-floating qualities, qualities which are qualities of nothing, attributes which have no subject. Since such things are supposed to be unacceptable, it is concluded that there must be sensible things over and above sensible qualities. Berkeley's response is threefold. First, he accepts that every quality must be had by some substance, but in the case of sensible qualities, being perceived by a mind suffices. In one clear sense, the 'subject' of the green I now see is not some physical substance but the mental substance which is me. Secondly, he questions the coherence of the relation between a quality and the alleged non-mental substance which is supposed to have that quality (DHP1 197–9). Furthermore, that relation is clearly impossible when the quality in question is mind-dependent, like a pain (DHP1 176). Thirdly, he can show that the bundle theory has the resources to accommodate all talk of the identity of physical objects without recourse to physical substance (DHP3 247–8). Thus the objector has made two errors: he thinks that the general requirement that qualities exist in substances entails that sensible qualities exist in non-mental substances, when all along they exist in the mind that perceives them; and he thinks that talk of physical objects as possessing qualities requires us to accept physical substances over and above those qualities.

So Hylas was wrong to accept (3) without further argument, but that does not matter for Berkeley's purposes, since the further argument is forthcoming and none of the arguments which are used in the First Dialogue for the mind-dependence of sensible things actually depends upon (3).

At one point Hylas becomes suspicious that the arguments for mind-dependence only work for qualities and not for things (DHP1 199):

HYLAS   ... Now, I grant that each quality cannot singly subsist without the mind. ... But as the several qualities united or blended together form entire sensible things, nothing hinders why such things may not be supposed to exist without the mind.

Philonous of course responds by saying that this is an odd thing for someone to say who has already agreed to (3), but he also introduces a new and independent argument, the famous inconceivability of an unconceived tree. It helps to suppose Hylas had put his point slightly differently:

Of course we cannot allow the existence of some isolated quality, such as greenness, except as it might be perceived by someone. However, if we consider not just greenness alone, but the green of this tree along with all its other qualities, then it is possible for that quality to exist without a mind perceiving it. So the quality cannot exist alone without a mind, but if there is a fully equipped tree which has the quality, then there is no need for a mind to perceive it.

One response to this improved objection, which Philonous makes, is that nothing in the arguments for mind-dependence turns upon separating the qualities in this manner. In fact he argues that some qualities, such as visible shape, cannot exist without others, such as colour (DHP1 193). But the tree argument addresses the problem directly by purporting to show that no sensible object, however construed, can exist without the mind. In brief, the claim is that to conceive something unconceived is as much a contradiction as to see something unseen, and what is conceived is in the mind, so it is impossible to conceive something without the mind.

This is often called Berkeley's Master Argument and is thought to be the central argument for immaterialism, so that its failure is decisive against Berkeley. The demerits of this as an interpretation, and the soundness of the argument, are discussed in 4.1 and the appendix to that chapter. For the moment we can see that even if it does not work, Philonous' first response to the objection still stands, and the progress of the argument for immaterialism is not interrupted.

3.2 What We Perceive is Mind-Dependent

Granting the initial plausibility of SMP—and we shall return to that issue—we get a substantial answer to the question of what we perceive, namely a restricted set of qualities each of which can be completely disclosed to a single sense modality at a single moment, *and nothing else*. We now need to address the question of whether these qualities which are sensed stand in the relation of being perceived necessarily or only contingently. Berkeley's preferred way of expressing his thesis here is in terms of existence: to be is to be perceived. This has led Anthony Grayling (*Berkeley: The Central Arguments*) to argue that Berkeley's central argument is an argument about the concept of existence. Another way of expressing the thesis would be in terms of *de re* necessity: everything perceived, every sensible quality, is such that it has the property of being perceived necessarily. Something has a property with *de re* necessity when it is not possible for that thing to lack that property. Since *de re* necessity is closely tied to the notion of essence, the two formulations are equivalent. For simplicity I shall talk of the properties of being necessarily perceived and contingently perceived, where something necessarily perceived is perceived in all possible worlds in which it exists.

Since Berkeley is trying to show that it is a necessary truth that everything perceived is necessarily perceived (the double modality rules out it being contingently true that only the necessarily perceived perceivables are actually perceived), he must remain neutral at the outset on the question of the contingently unperceived. Once he has argued for the impossibility of contingently unobserved qualities, he can then go on to explain the vulgar belief in such things. This he does by distinguishing what is contingently unobserved *by us* from the contingently unobserved *tout court*.

Berkeley uses two major forms of argument for mind-dependence, the Assimilation Argument and the Argument from Conflicting Appearances. The Assimilation Argument has some plausibility in some cases but does not generalize either to all the qualities perceived by a specific sense (*DHP1* 178) or to all the senses. The Argument from Conflicting Appearances has the fascinating property of having been almost universally accepted throughout its long history while being surprisingly unclear in detail. I shall try to spell out some of the detail.

3.2.1 *Assimilation*

The most detailed version of the Assimilation Argument tries to show that sensations of temperature are to be assimilated to sensations of pleasure and pain. Philonous gives the argument for intense heat and then tries to generalize. The generalization is implausible: the argument rests on showing that the sensation of intense heat *is* a pain, whereas it would seem that gentle warmth *causes* pleasure. Still, if the argument for the case of intense heat works, it should unsettle the materialist, who wants to make a sharp distinction between mind-dependent sensations, such as pain, and sensory experiences.

The target is the view that (intense) heat is both something we can experience (i.e. a sensible quality) and independent of being perceived. A suppressed but uncontroversial premiss is that pain is something we can experience but mind-dependent. It proceeds by dilemma.

[1] The experience of intense heat is painful ('is not the most vehement and intense degree of heat a very great pain?' *DHP1* 176).

[2] First horn: there is one object of experience (sensible quality) here, which is both hot and painful.

[3] Given that the pain is mind-dependent, so is the heat. QED.

[4] Second horn: there are two objects of experience (sensible qualities), heat and pain.

[5] BUT this is phenomenologically implausible,

[6] AND if they are distinct, the heat and the pain should be logically independent, but it is not possible to experience the heat without the pain.

The phenomenological claim at [5] is difficult to establish conclusively, but is supported by the well-known phenomenon that we cannot tell merely from the sensation whether we have come into contact with something very hot or very cold, as in the case where someone is blindfolded and touched with a piece of metal at $-10°$ C. The claim at [6] is more important, for it is most natural for the materialist who thinks that there are two sensations here to insist that the sensation of great heat causes the sensation of pain. This does entail that one could have the former without the latter. It has been alleged that some painkilling drugs can do precisely that—they can cut out the pain without cutting out the sensitivity to, in this case, temperature. Maybe that is the case, but it is difficult to the point of being impossible for us to imagine what an intense heat would feel like without the pain. The unimaginability of that sensation suggests that even if there is a possible experience which we would want to call the experience of intense heat without pain, that experience is not a part of what we actually experience when we burn ourselves.

So the argument on the second horn of the dilemma is plausible but inconclusive. However, the generalization is difficult because one can clearly see that the pleasures caused by mild temperatures, or the pains caused by bright lights or loud noises, are more easily separable from the associated sense perception. All the materialist need accept is that, for the sense of touch and perhaps taste and smell, in certain extreme cases we cease to perceive the qualities of objects and merely experience our own sensations. However, there is a slightly deeper moral than this, for Berkeley has unsettled the sharp distinction between sense perception and sensation. In our encounters with the world we have a wide range of experiences. Berkeley has shown that the materialist must make a sharp divide in those experiences between the mind-dependent and the independent qualities, a sharp divide which has no clear phenomenological basis.

3.2.2 Conflicting Appearances

The form of Berkeley's argument here, at its most general level, is: if one assumes that what we perceive is only contingently perceived, and that there is no perceptual error, then conflicting perceptions reveal the perceiver-independent world to be inconsistent, which is absurd. Given that the existence of conflicting appearances is undeniable, we are invited to conclude that what we perceive is not merely contingently perceived.

In the twentieth century this form of argument was roundly criticized for ignoring the obvious possibility that there is perceptual error. In his book on Berkeley, Geoffrey Warnock expressed a now quite commonplace thought: 'for unless we begin by supposing that things *cannot* appear to be otherwise than they are, why should we be at all put out by the obvious fact that they can and do?' (*Berkeley*, 148). This is a straightforward challenge to SMP, which Berkeley's argument certainly presupposes. Instead of arguing for SMP, Berkeley's method is to assume SMP for the purpose of putting forward his views and then to consider and reject (two or perhaps three) of the alternatives. I propose to grant him the legitimacy of this tactic, on the grounds that SMP has some intrinsic attractions. But we should be aware that the success of the First Dialogue (for Berkeley, though not so much for Philonous) ultimately rests on the rejection of the alternative models of perception.

The Argument from Conflicting Appearances has also been criticized for lack of internal cogency. Berkeley was certainly aware of one version of this criticism and may even have been the first to spot it, for he put it forward in the *Principles* (*PHK* 15). There he says that the most the argument can prove is that *not all* the sensible things exist independently of being perceived. At some points in the First Dialogue he seems to forget this point (e.g. *DHP1* 181), but at others he gestures towards an answer to it, which we shall examine below.

Bertrand Russell offered a different criticism of Berkeley's argument:

[Berkeley] argues that we do not perceive things but only colours, sounds, etc., and that these are 'mental' or 'in the mind'. His reasoning is completely cogent as to the first point, but as to the second . . . [he] relies, in fact, upon the received view that everything must be either material or mental, and that nothing is both. (*History of Western Philosophy*, 626)

Apart from the common mistake of confusing 'in the mind' with 'mental', Russell makes a legitimate point, namely that Berkeley often assumes in his arguments that a sensible quality which existed without the mind, i.e. one which was only contingently perceived, would have to subsist in matter and thus be material. There are two aspects to this assumption of Berkeley's. One is that there cannot be qualities which are not the qualities of some substance. So if sensible qualities could exist without the mind, i.e. without any mental substances, then there must be some non-mental substance. The other is that any non-mental substance is material. Russell wants to question this second assumption, but it is, for Berkeley, definitional of the material. It is not as if he thinks that there is a substantive and independent conception of the material world, the existence of which is in question. Rather, the question is whether the objects of perception are contingently perceived or necessarily perceived, and these options are exhaustive and exclusive. More interesting would be a challenge to the first assumption. It might be suggested that mind-independent qualities do not subsist in any substance and that physical objects are merely bundles or collections of such qualities. Now it would seem that Berkeley ought to take this possibility seriously, since he agrees with the claim about physical objects. However, failure to do so does not affect the Argument from Conflicting Appearances, since the crucial premiss is the consistency of the mind-independent world. If the flower looks one way to me and another to you, then we could generate the problem by saying either that a material substance cannot have inconsistent qualities at a time, or that a single bundle of material qualities cannot, at a given time, contain inconsistent qualities.

The first version of the argument given by Philonous shows the structure quite clearly (*DHP1* 178–9):

PHILONOUS   Those bodies therefore, upon whose application to our own, we perceive a moderate degree of heat, must be concluded to have a moderate degree of heat or warmth in them: and those, upon whose application we feel a like degree of cold, must be thought to have cold in them.

HYLAS   They must.

PHILONOUS   Is it not an absurdity to think that the same thing should be at the same time both cold and warm?

HYLAS   It is.

PHILONOUS   Suppose now one of your hands hot, and the other cold, and that they are both at once put into the same vessel of water, in an intermediate state; will not the water seem cold to one hand, and warm to the other?

HYLAS   It will.

PHILONOUS   Ought we not therefore by your principles to conclude, it is really both cold and warm at the same time, that is, according to your own concession, to believe an absurdity.

The initial principle to which Hylas agrees and which leads to the absurdity is a combination of SMP and materialism weakened by the Assimilation Argument (the weakening Hylas accepts is to reject materialism, but not SMP, for intense heat). Hylas next agrees to a consistency principle: a single object cannot be both hot and cold at the same time (and in the same part, we should add). Then we are given an example where something is perceived to violate the consistency principle, resulting in an inconsistent triad of SMP, materialism about all perceived moderate degrees of warmth, and the consistency principle. But stopping here does not lead to the desired conclusion that 'heat and cold are only sensations existing in our minds' (*DHP1* 179). If we assume that SMP and the consistency principles are non-negotiable, the materialist need only say that at least one of the perceived warmth and chill is not in the water itself, but this does not rule out that the other is in the water itself and thus that we sometimes perceive mind-independent qualities. In other words, generating an inconsistency requires materialism about *all* perceived qualities, but the materialist need only say some sensible qualities are independent of being perceived.

This weakness is even more obvious in the next version of the argument (*DHP1* 181):

PHILONOUS Or can you imagine, that filth and ordure affect those brute animals that feed on them out of choice, with the same smells which we perceive in them?

HYLAS By no means.

PHILONOUS May we not therefore conclude of smells, as of the other forementioned qualities, that they cannot exist in any but a perceiving substance or mind?

Here Philonous is confusing relativization to a mind with mind-dependence. What someone sees (hears, smells, etc.) is shown, by the conflicting appearances, to be relative to circumstance, viewing conditions, and the observer, but it does not follow that there are no observers who, when in the right circumstances and viewing conditions, can see or smell things as they really are independently of being observed. As it stands the argument does not get to its conclusion, even when we grant SMP. This is what Berkeley himself pointed out in the *Principles* (*PHK* 15).

What is usually thought to be necessary to make the argument work is an indistinguishability principle to the effect that anything indistinguishable from what exists only in the mind can itself exist only in the mind. Once made explicit, such a principle is far from obvious, but it at least suffices to complete the argument. Since we cannot tell, on the basis of our perceptual experience alone, whether we are seeing things as they are in themselves or merely their appearances and we cannot always be seeing them as they are in themselves, it is only ever their appearances which we see.

Berkeley may be appealing to something more subtle altogether. When considering the conflicting-appearances argument applied to colours, Hylas makes the distinction between true colours and apparent colours without denying that we see the true colours. (When he made the true–apparent distinction for sounds (*DHP1* 182) he also made the mistake of saying that true sounds are motions in the air and thus not immediate objects of hearing.) Philonous replies (*DHP1* 186):

PHILONOUS   . . . I would fain know farther from you, what certain distance and position of the object, what peculiar texture and formation of the eye, what degree or kind of light is necessary for ascertaining that true colour, and distinguishing it from apparent ones.
HYLAS   I own myself entirely satisfied, that they are all equally apparent.

At first Philonous' remark might be mistaken for the epistemic argument that even if there was a distinction between true colours and mere appearances, we could never know which is which. While he is trying to show that materialism leads to scepticism, an epistemic argument at this point would be too weak. What he asks Hylas to provide is a criterion for distinguishing the true from the apparent colours. The epistemic reading would have it that Hylas capitulates because he cannot provide such a criterion; but this is implausible, for there are so many potential criteria he could have offered which we use every day. For example, when shopping we often take clothes into the daylight to see their true colour before buying them. Nor is Philonous simply appealing to indistinguishability here. Rather, the problem Hylas spots is that any criterion he offers is arbitrary. This needs some explaining.

The first move Philonous makes after Hylas has introduced the distinction between true and apparent colours is to point out that, under sufficiently powerful microscopes, things may look to have quite distinct colours from those they look to have with the naked eye. The point of this is not simply to reveal another example of conflicting appearances, but rather to block the move which says that the true colours are those revealed to the 'best' eye, where we have an independent account of which eye is best in terms of acuity. Since microscopes increase acuity, it would follow that all the colours seen by the naked eye are merely apparent. These apparent colours may be the same as the ones revealed by the microscope, but since the naked eye lacks the acuity of the microscope and is thus not equipped to discern true colours, they are still apparent. He then mentions 'inconceivably small animals perceived by glasses' (*DHP1* 185) to remind us that there is no limit to the possible improvements in visual acuity. So there is no eye which cannot be bettered, and by this criterion all colours are equally apparent. The importance of this argument is that acuity presents the best chance of finding an independent criterion of when someone sees the true colours, but it leads to the conclusion that no one does. The next move in the argument is to enumerate all the different changes in the viewer and the viewing conditions which can result in things appearing differently coloured despite there being no change in the object. All these different variables interact with each other: for someone else to see an object the way I see it now, they may have to view it by candlelight, through tinted lenses, or against a special background. But now we see that if Hylas is to give a condition in which we see the true colours, he must specify a value for each of these variables, and the ascription of a particular value to a variable can only be justified if all the others are held constant. For example, one cannot justify saying that something should be viewed in daylight to ascertain its true colour *by reference to the nature of the object* since (*DHP1* 185–6):

upon the use of microscopes, upon a change happening in the humours of the eye, or a variation of distance, . . . [n]ay all other circumstances remaining the same, change but the situation of some objects, and they shall present different colours to the eye.

Thus the justification of any proposed criterion is either circular or stipulative.

This argument does not directly establish that there is no combination of circumstances in which we see the true, mind-independent colours of objects. What it does show is that the claim that there is one set of circumstances in which we see the true colours can never be rationally defended. That being so, the materialist's distinction between true and apparent colours is empty of empirical content.

Spelling out this argument from conflicting appearances in detail, we get:

[1] There are perceptual conflicts.
[2] Reality is self-consistent.
[3] SMP is true.
[4] From [1], [2], and [3], not all experiences are of 'true', mind-independent qualities.
[5] From [4], some experiences are of mind-dependent qualities.
[6] There can never be reasonable grounds for thinking an experience is of a 'true' mind-independent quality.
[7] So, from [6], the materialist's true/false distinction is empty.
[8] From [5] and [7], all experiences are of mind-dependent qualities.

There are here four premisses and four inferences. The only premisses that might be disputed are [3] and [6]. I discuss alternatives to [3] in 3.3. The first inference, [4], is sound. As Russell pointed out, the move from [4] to [5] needs some defending, but this is quite easy once we have seen how the argument turns on considerations of consistency. Generally speaking, the way to avoid apparent inconsistencies, such as someone having a beard and not having a beard, is to limit consistency requirements, in this case removing the inconsistency by relativizing to times, e.g. having a beard one day and not the next. But the facts of perception force one to limit consistency requirements further by reference to perceivers, and this cannot be done if the qualities are only contingently perceived. We can show this by *reductio ad absurdum*. Suppose (under SMP) that the objects of perception are mind-independent. Then constraints of consistency cannot make reference to their standing in the relation of being perceived, since that is contingent and consistency is necessary. But any constraint of compatibility, such as not hot and cold in the same part of the same object, or (for bundle theorists) at the same place and time, is violated by the facts of conflicting appearances. So, given SMP the impossible occurs.

The inferences at [7] and [8] are also pretty solid, so the argument turns upon the premiss [6]. But if we press a little harder, we shall see that the argument for [6] also rests on SMP.

3.2.3 Primary vs. Secondary Qualities

Berkeley does not deny that when we judge something is cobalt or teal or whatever, our judgement is answerable to how the thing would look to suitable observers in suitable viewing conditions, e.g. to someone with normal eyesight in the shade on a cloudy summer's day. What he wants to point out is that we cannot give an objective justification of the choice of these conditions as being the ones in which the 'true' colours are revealed, where true means mind-independent. That we cannot is revealed by the fact that the link between being a certain colour and being judged to be that colour (by appropriate observers in ideal conditions) is not contingent: nothing could reveal that, as a matter of fact, normal observers in ideal conditions are mistaken about the colours of the things they see. No amount of information about the wavelengths of reflected light could ever prove that grass is not green: the evidence of how it looks can only be trumped by how it looks to someone in a better position to judge. Which is to say that part of what it is to have a certain colour is to have a certain sort of appearance. If something is, for example, cobalt blue, then it *must* look a certain sort of way when presented to suitable viewers in suitable conditions. There cannot be an explanation of why this is so which does not make reference to some arbitrary or conventional stipulation, which is why we cannot give an adequate justification for the claim that in these conditions we see the 'true' colours.

What Berkeley says about the colours here, namely that to have a colour is to be disposed to look a certain way, seems correct. It has been challenged by philosophers, but the central intuition is very persuasive. If something did not and could not look, say, scarlet to any normally sighted observers in suitably good viewing conditions, then it just would not be scarlet.

Very appropriately, it is at exactly this point in the dialogue that Hylas introduces the distinction between primary and secondary qualities (*DHP*1 187). In contrast to the case of colours, it would seem that further investigation could reveal whether normal observers in typical conditions do see the true shapes and sizes of objects. Thus one might make a distinction between the qualities for which [6] is true, call them the secondary qualities, and those for which it is false, the primary qualities. This would give us a sophisticated version of materialism according to which only some types of sensible quality are in the mind, since for the primary qualities it is possible to give reasons for thinking that certain conditions are the ones in which the true, mind-independent qualities are perceived.

Berkeley has two responses to this form of materialism. First he claims that the argument for the mind-dependence of the secondary qualities works just as well on the primaries. In the First Dialogue he only runs through steps [1] to [5] (*DHP*1 188–90) for extension and motion, so we shall need to ask whether [6] can be defended for primary qualities. Secondly, he argues that primary qualities are inseparable from secondary (*DHP*1 193–4). This is usually interpreted as a direct objection to the form of materialism we are considering, namely that we cannot conceive of primary qualities without secondary, and thus we cannot understand the suggestion that there is a mind-independent reality with only primary qualities. This argument is vulnerable to the criticism that Berkeley is confusing conceivability with perceivability. However, the position of the argument in the dialectical structure of the *Three Dialogues* suggests that, while he does raise the difficulty of conceiving a world without secondary qualities, what Berkeley really intends is a form of assimilation argument: one cannot perceive primary qualities without perceiving secondary, but since the latter are in the mind, so must be the former.

It is rather ironic that, having listened to Philonous putting forward the first argument, which only shows that some perceived primary qualities are merely apparent, Hylas should wonder (*DHP1* 191): 'why those philosophers who deny the secondary qualities any real existence, should yet attribute it to the primary'. The actual situation seems to be the contrary: why believe that all perceived primary qualities are 'merely apparent', given only an argument that some are? For in the case of the primary qualities we have empirical theories which tell us which are the 'true' qualities and which conditions if any are the ones in which we perceive those qualities as they are, and tell us the latter by making essential reference to the former. Which is to say that [6] is false, for we have a non-arbitrary way of giving a criterion of materialistically interpreted veridical perception.

Berkeley would have rejected this because it is essential to the materialist story that we can give a causal explanation of how, in certain conditions, primary qualities appear as they are. The causal story is necessary, otherwise the selection of those conditions as the ones in which the true qualities appear will be unjustifiable: we cannot just say that those are the conditions in which things appear as they are without committing ourselves to there being some explanation of the difference between those conditions and others. This explanation will not appeal to analytic connections between possessing primary qualities and appearing to possess those qualities, on pain of making all qualities secondary. It is the point of making the distinction between primary and secondary qualities to deny that there are any logical connections between being spherical, for example, and looking spherical. So the materialist must appeal to contingent connections between primary qualities and appearances of primary qualities in order to explain why such-and-such circumstances are the ones in which we perceive the true, mind-independent qualities of objects. However, no such explanation is compatible with SMP (*DHP1* 179, 181–3, 187). For if there are to be contingent, causal connections between the primary quality and how it appears, it must be possible to distinguish that which is perceived from how it is perceived, and this distinction cannot be made from within SMP. There cannot be conditions in which certain qualities contingently appear as they are, because according to SMP everything we perceive necessarily appears as it is. Any causal story about how shapes and sizes affect us and lead to experiences of those very properties confuses the (alleged) cause of an experience with its object. This version of the argument for [6] works equally well against someone who takes the colours and other secondary qualities to be in fact primary. Of course, Berkeley can allow that the empirical theories of sense perception can help to distinguish veridical from illusory experiences, but they do so in a way which is compatible with immaterialism.

So, granting SMP, Berkeley's first argument against the sophisticated materialist works. The second argument also relies upon SMP. The argument is really very simple (*DHP1* 194):

PHILONOUS . . . Besides, if you will trust your senses, is it not plain all sensible qualities coexist, or to them, appear as being in the same place? Do they ever represent a motion, or figure, as being divested of all other visible or tangible qualities?

Philonous does not state the point as clearly as he might, but the idea is a good one. Suppose, to take a specific example, someone suggests that shape is a primary quality and colour a secondary, and that only secondary qualities are mind-dependent. The problem is that we only perceive shape by perceiving boundaries and we can only see these by seeing colour differences. If the colour differences are 'in the mind', then so are the boundaries and the shapes we perceive. This argument can be run for all the primary qualities and each of the senses: we cannot perceive a primary quality except by perceiving some secondary quality.

Now the natural response to this is that the inseparability is a feature of how we represent the world in perception, not of the world we represent. While it is not possible for us to see shapes except by seeing colour differences, it does not follow that we see shapes *as* depending upon colours. That we do see shapes *as* separable from colours is shown by the fact that we can easily imagine the shapes we see as possibly existing even though there were no colour differentiation by which we could see them.

Berkeley would disagree about what is imagined here. On the basis of a thought experiment (*DHP1* 202) about the visual experience of someone congenitally blind whose sight was restored, Berkeley held that visible shape is a distinct quality from tangible shape. Merely having tangible acquaintance with circles and squares, as a blind man might, would not allow one to recognize them visually before one had experienced the correlation between the two experiences. Having made this distinction between visible and tangible shape, he claims that we can certainly imagine tangible shape existing in the absence of colour differences, but to do that is not to imagine visible shape, since in the colourless situation shape would be invisible.

Now Berkeley's claim that there are no cross-modal sensory qualities can be and has been challenged. Berkeley's belief in it is often attributed to an over-simplistic account of concept formation which does not allow us to form concepts of sensory qualities which go beyond their appearances. There are two reasons why this move will not help the materialist here. First, Berkeley does *not* have the over-simplistic account of concept formation, and he can easily allow for *concepts* of cross-modal sensory qualities (*DHP3* 245). What he is denying are objects of perception which can be perceived by more than one sense modality. For example, he can allow that we have a concept of visible-or-tangible circularity, but it does not follow that the very same instance of visible-or-tangible circularity could be either seen or felt. Secondly, SMP provides him with a reason for denying cross-modal qualities, for if there were such things, then there would be no difference to the perceiver between seeing them and feeling them (apart from the allied secondary qualities). The undeniable difference between seeing something round and feeling something round must be explained by a difference in the objects of perception.

Also, since SMP entails that all features of how the world appears to us are fully determined by the objects of our experience, we cannot distinguish between the means of our perceiving the world and how we perceive it to be. Precisely how the sensible things *are* is how we see the world *as*. So if we cannot have a visual experience of shape without colour, then we do see shape *as* inseparable from colour.

3.3 Alternative Models of Perception

In the last section we saw how crucial SMP is to Berkeley's arguments. When I introduced SMP, I argued that we could allow Berkeley his strategy of assuming SMP and then later considering alternatives, on the grounds that SMP had some initial plausibility. But someone of a materialist bent might by now have come to the conclusion that the initial plausibility of SMP is overridden by the implausible consequences it leads us to. So at this point he would conclude that SMP is mistaken and look for alternatives. Not surprisingly, this is exactly how Hylas responds to the arguments Philonous presents: he offers alternative models of perception in an attempt to salvage materialism. Philonous then tries to rebut them. The weakness of Berkeley using this method of argument is that it is open for the materialist to come up with a different model from those suggested by Hylas. However, the two he does suggest are pretty representative of the proposals philosophers have made. They are the Act–Object Model and the Representative Model.

Recall that the Simplest Model of (Sense) Perception (p. 54) is the view that:

'S perceives O (by sense)' describes a two-place relation between a mind and a sensible thing / quality. The relation of *perceiving* or *being aware of* is a pure relation, much like a spatial relation (hence 'before the mind') in that it is not constituted, either wholly or partly, by any concurrent event in or state of one of the relata. . . . The only possible differences between two perceivings are in the identities of the subject or the object (the five senses are distinguished by their objects). . . .

The initial plausibility of this was twofold: it fits the phenomenology of perceptual experience and it offers the best explanation of the character of specific experiences. The forms of materialism we have so far been considering accept SMP in the most important cases, namely when we have veridical experience. They diverge from Berkeley's position by making a distinction between two types of sensible quality, those which are mind-dependent and those which are not. If we try to avoid immaterialism by rejecting SMP, then it looks as if we must introduce an extra element into the perceptual relation, which element can have features which explain the character of experience without those features having to be attributed to sensible things themselves. This extra element is either going to be an event, such as a perceiving by S of O, or an item such as a sense-datum had by S. Hylas makes both these suggestions. At first glance one might think that Philonous' replies address only the very specific models suggested by Hylas, but sympathetically interpreted, the objections have the momentum to undermine a very wide variety of models.

3.3.1 The Act–Object Model

Hylas introduces the first alternative model thus (*DHP1* 194–5):

HYLAS   One great oversight I take to be this: that I did not sufficiently distinguish the *object* from the *sensation*. Now though this latter may not exist without the mind, yet it will not thence follow that the former cannot. . . . The sensation I take to be an act of the mind perceiving; beside which, there is something perceived; and this I call the *object*. For example, there is red and yellow on that tulip. But then the act of perceiving those colours is in me only, not in the tulip.

Now Philonous' response to this looks trivial: he emphasizes that perception is passive and thus cannot be constituted by an act of mind. This could have been easily met by Hylas, had he changed the elucidation of sensation to an event in the perceiving mind. However, in the course of making this point, Philonous says something which suggests a better argument (*DHP1* 196):

PHILONOUS   I act too in drawing the air through my nose; because my breathing so rather than otherwise, is the effect of my volition. But neither can this be called *smelling*: for if it were, I should smell every time I breathed in that manner.

The implication here is that sometimes Philonous draws air through his nose and does not smell anything, but we may wish to question this. Certainly we often report that we do not smell anything ('Is there a gas leak?', 'I don't smell anything'), but someone might say that what really happens is that we do not notice the ordinary and pervasive odours of people, clothes, furniture, etc. Think of the way one can walk into a room and notice that it smells a little stale. An hour later one will not be able to spot that smell without leaving the room and returning. Did one cease to smell the staleness, or only cease to be able to notice it? We cannot

claim that not noticing something *just is* not perceiving it, because
of the well-known phenomenon of only noticing something, such
as a clock ticking, when it stops. To notice it stopping, one must
have perceived it before it stopped.

So Philonous should not assume without further argument that
it is possible to smell nothing. Does this undermine the argument?
Well, suppose that we allow a mental event which occurs when I
smell something, say furniture polish, then according to the Act–
Object Model, whenever this event occurs I have the sensation of
smelling furniture polish. Then the question arises: what causes
this event to occur? Philonous in effect points out that nothing
I do can cause the event, so there needs to be something other
than me and the event if I am to experience the smell of furniture
polish. According to the Act–Object Model, this cause of the event
of perceiving is also the object of perception, and anything which
is the object of a smelling of furniture polish is itself something
which (really or merely apparently) smells of furniture polish. And
it is the existence of something which (really or merely apparently)
smells of furniture polish which ultimately explains why I perceive
the smell of furniture polish. So the mental event has no role to
play. He gives the same argument using the example of vision
(*DHP1* 196):

PHILONOUS   But doth it in a like manner depend upon your will, that
   in looking on this flower, you perceive *white* rather than any other
   colour? Or directing your open eyes toward yonder part of the heaven,
   can you avoid seeing the sun? Or is light or darkness the effect of your
   volition?

Of course he is right about these things not being subject to our control, but the point still holds if we substitute for will and volition the
mental event of perceiving. Nothing I can do is sufficient to cause
the mental event, so there must be another cause. And anything
which is the cause of a seeming-to-see-white event is something
which looks white (either truly or merely apparently). If I have

something which looks white as the object of perception, then the mental event of perceiving is redundant, for SMP can do all the work.

Philonous also has another objection to the Act–Object Model (*DHP1* 197):

PHILONOUS   Besides, since you distinguish the *active* and *passive* in every perception, you must do it in that of pain.

The point here is that the distinction between the pain and the event of feeling pain cannot be made, otherwise there could be unfelt pains and illusions of pain. The important question is whether someone who holds the Act–Object Model of perception *must* say the same about pain. Berkeley's thought here is that if one accepts SMP for pain, then one has no grounds for denying it elsewhere. This seems to ignore the hybrid view which holds that one perceives mind-dependent things such as pains on the model of SMP, but one perceives material things in a different way. However, in the context of a discussion of the merits of materialism, the hybrid view is unjustifiable: the mind-dependence of pains suffices to explain the character of our perception of them, so the only reason why we would need an alternative explanation in the case of the physical world would be if it were *not* mind-dependent. Berkeley then has a point that pains present a problem for the Act–Object Model: if our experience of pain is on the model, then that leads to absurd consequences, but if it is not, then we lack non-question-begging reasons for applying the Act–Object Model elsewhere.

3.3.2 *The Intentional Model*

The Intentional Model is by far the most promising alternative to SMP. It is never discussed by Berkeley. On the Intentional Model, perceptual experiences are mental events which have representational content, much like thoughts. For the parallel to work, the important properties of thoughts are that they can be false and they may lack an object. Thus, to think that Mont Blanc is made of gold is to misrepresent Mont Blanc, and to *see* Mont Blanc as being made of gold is to misperceive it.

There are two sources of difficulty. The first is the vast difference between perceiving something and merely thinking about it. Perceptual consciousness has a distinctive character and is totally unlike even the most vivid thinking, and in perception we usually experience the world with a variety and detail which we could never articulate in thought. Most human beings can adjust their actions in response to the second differential of the velocity of objects they can see. For example, a cricketer running to save a four might slow up as he realizes the rolling ball is decelerating increasingly quickly. This suggests that we have the ability to see the rate of change of acceleration, but it is far from obvious that everyone who has this perceptual capacity also has the ability to think of this aspect of motion. Such expressions as 'getting faster and faster' are ambiguous between high constant acceleration and increasing acceleration.

The second problem is that the Intentional Model must presuppose a theory of thought content. This is problematic because we might think, along with empiricists such as Locke and Hume, that thought content is parasitic upon, or derivative from, perception. But even if someone offered independent accounts of thought and perception, Berkeley would object to the idea of perceptual *content*. He would argue that thinking a thought with a determinate content essentially involves an activity of mind, an activity we might call conceptualization. This is because all thoughts, even simple identities such as 'George Eliot is Mary Ann Evans', involve some general concept, in this case identity, and generality is the work of the mind. Perception, in contrast, or at least the determination of what we perceive, strikes Berkeley as entirely passive, involving no mental activity. In effect, Berkeley would criticize the Intentional Model for confusing perceptual judgements, which are representational, with their grounds, which are not.

To press these objections on behalf of Berkeley would take us far into the theory of content and a long way from Berkeley's thought. Let me instead just raise a couple of small points in his favour. One is that many ordinary perceptual locutions are relational: for example, I saw *the kestrel* or heard *the cat*. The Intentional Model, in its twentieth-century incarnation, is committed to saying that such perceptual statements are true, when true, in virtue of my seeing *that* something or other, and my hearing *that* such-and-such. Every perception must have a representational content, which could in theory be specified. I have no argument that this is impossible, but we should be cautious before assuming that it can be done, even in theory. The seventeenth-century philosopher Antoine Arnauld held a version of the Intentional Model which does not require perceptual content to be propositional, and thus avoids this worry. However, such a view will have to introduce notions of truth and falsity for subpropositional representations. If I think a thought the complete content of which is the subpropositional representation *the kestrel*, then it is hard to make sense of calling that a correct or incorrect representation. But if the Intentional Model is to take seriously the locution 'I saw the kestrel', then the perceptual content *the kestrel* must be either correct or incorrect.

Another worry is linguistic. If the Intentional Model is correct, then the relational 'of' in 'a thought of a golden mountain' and in 'a perception or hallucination of a pink elephant' will be given the same interpretation. But the former can be naturally paraphrased using 'about', though the latter cannot. While this proves nothing, it suggests that we do think of sense experiences as necessarily relational, as always having an object.

3.3.3 *The Indirect or Representative Model*

While Berkeley did not consider the Intentional Model, he did discuss a close cousin, the Representative Model of Perception. According to this model, in ordinary perceptual situations there are two things which might both be called the object of perception.

One is an idea or sensation and the other is an external, mind-independent object or quality. We perceive the external object in virtue of having an experience of an internal object which it causes. How we perceive the external object as being is determined by the character of the internal object, so when there is a mismatch between the internal object and its cause, we undergo illusions or even hallucinations.

The Representative Model comes in two forms, inferential and perceptual. According to the inferential version, only the ideas are actually before the mind, we are conscious only of them, and we infer the existence of their causes. This is not really an alternative to SMP, for it does not introduce the possibility of the *sensible* things being material. In contrast, the perceptual version holds that we have what Hume later called 'a double awareness', for both the idea and the external object are simultaneously before the mind, though we are only ever aware of the latter in virtue of being aware of the former. Filling in the details of this view, and in particular addressing the question of whether it is ever possible to have the same idea before the mind without perceiving the external object, would take us too far afield. The important thought for present purposes is that the perceptual version of the Representative Model holds that having an idea before the mind is a necessary enabling condition of perceiving a material object. If I did not perceive the idea, I would not perceive the object. My relation to the idea and to the object cannot be quite the same, despite Hume's claim of double awareness, since I can stand in the relevant relation to an idea without standing in the relevant relation to an object, but not vice versa. It is this version of the Representative Model which presents a real alternative to SMP.

Berkeley is often accused of paying insufficient attention to the perceptual version, because he assumes a univocal sense of 'perception' such that the only things perceived are those which are 'in the mind', which rules out the possibility that it is the idea which is perceived in the sense of being in the mind, and the object is perceived in some other sense. While Berkeley allows a notion of mediate perception, an idea which is mediately perceived is perceived in exactly the same sense as one which is immediately perceived, the difference lying in the cause of the perception. An appeal to the univocity of 'perceives' looks like what is going on in the first argument Philonous gives against the Representative Model (*DHP1* 203–4). Hylas has suggested, as an analogy for the perceptual version, the way that looking at a portrait allows one to see, rather indirectly, the person depicted. This is true but Philonous thinks it does not help:

PHILONOUS   Tell me, Hylas, when you behold the picture of Julius Caesar, do you see with your eyes any more than some colours and figures with a certain symmetry and composition of the whole?

HYLAS   Nothing else.

PHILONOUS   And would not a man, who had never known anything of Julius Caesar, see as much? . . . Whence comes it then that your thoughts are directed to the Roman Emperor, and his are not? This cannot proceed from the sensations or ideas of sense by you then perceived; since you acknowledge you have no advantage over him in that respect.

One thing that Philonous could be trying to achieve here is to argue, by analogy, that having certain ideas does not allow one to perceive (as opposed to infer) material objects because someone might have the ideas and fail to 'see' the represented objects. In other words, having the ideas themselves is not sufficient, one also needs to make an inference. If this is the argument, Hylas could simply deny that the analogy between ideas and a painting holds at this point: he could say that there is no possibility of someone having the ideas he has when, say, looking at Philonous, and not recognizing what those ideas represent, namely Philonous. One can fail to recognize what a painting is of, but one cannot fail to recognize what one's ideas are of. There is no inference and nothing needs to be learnt: one just sees (or hears or whatever) things by having ideas of them. If we wanted to keep the analogy, Hylas should have insisted that he does see more than just the colours and shapes of the painting, for he sees Julius Caesar, or, more accurately, how Julius Caesar looked (we are making the unlikely assumption that the portrait is accurate). If it is possible for someone not to see what is depicted in the painting, then that is just a point of disanalogy between portraits and ideas of sense. Berkeley's argument then looks like mere denial of the perceptual version of the Representative Model of perception.

However, Philonous' example could be used to make a more subtle point. Suppose someone could not see what was depicted in the portrait of Caesar. Nothing we could point to in the picture could reveal the depiction to him. If he just saw it as colours on canvas, then whatever we pointed to in the picture would just be more colours on canvas. This entails that depiction is not intrinsic, and the point could be made for any way that one object might represent another. However, the perceptual version of the Representative Model is committed to ideas having some intrinsic representational quality. The charge is that this is either mysterious or incoherent. The materialist might respond by retreating to a position intermediate between the perceptual and inferential versions: we have to recognize that our ideas of sense are representations, we have to interpret them as being about the external world, but having done so, we can see the world without inference. Such situations are quite common. Take for an example the graphical representation on the radar screen in an air traffic control room. Here we have a stylized, symbolic representation of the location, height, direction, and speed of several aircraft relative to a part of the earth's surface. If one knows to take the screen as a representation, then, with a bit of practice, one can simply see potential collisions or unusual behaviours of the planes. The intermediate version of the Representative Model holds that at some point we learn to take our ideas of sense as representations of external reality, and from then on we are able to perceive that external reality, or at least those aspects which are represented by our ideas.

When he returns to the matter at *DHP1* 205, Philonous describes the Representative Model thus: 'you say our ideas do not exist without the mind; but that they are copies, images, or representations of certain originals that do'. Since he is here granting Hylas that ideas are representations, we should take his subsequent arguments to be directed at the intermediate version. The first point he raises is that our ideas are 'perpetually fleeting and variable', but the material world is supposed to have 'a fixed and real nature', so how does the former represent the latter? Philonous offers Hylas the response that we should take a lot of our ideas as misleading 'noise', that many are false representations, but he immediately raises the spectre of making sense of this true/false distinction. The point is not a good one in the first place, for it confuses features of the vehicle of representation with features of the content of the representation. If the air traffic controller's radar screen switched continuously between different views, she would not be forced to take it as representing a rotating world. If it refreshed every few moments like a television picture, she would not have to take it that the represented world was refreshing itself!

Philonous then introduces Berkeley's strongest argument. It is assumed that ideas, if they are to represent the external world, must do so in virtue of resemblance. Berkeley does not want to make the point that if ideas are mental then they cannot have physical properties such as colour and shape, and hence cannot resemble coloured and shaped objects. Since he thinks that ideas are not mental and thus do have physical properties such as colour and shape, this argument would be rather confusing. Instead Philonous argues (*DHP1* 206):

But how can that which is sensible be like that which is insensible? Can a real thing in itself *invisible* be like a *colour*; or a real thing which is not *audible*, be like a *sound*? In a word, can any thing be like a sensation or idea, but another sensation or idea?

It is important to see that it is not only the inferential version which holds that the external world is insensible. In the other versions of the Representative Model we do sense the world, but the important point is that we can only sense it in this indirect manner, we cannot see it 'in itself'. The point can be put in terms of appearances. An idea is essentially an appearance (of something external): its character is precisely that which it is experienced as having. The external world, considered in itself, apart from ideas, has no appearance, it is not experienced at all. So the problem is: how can an appearance resemble something unperceivable? They have no qualities in common. In so far as the Representative Model, in any of its versions, is committed to resemblance, it is mistaken. If the perceptual or intermediate versions are committed to representation without resemblance, then they are versions of the Intentional Model, which Berkeley never considers.

3.4 Conclusion

The claim that all the objects of sense, i.e. all the things we can perceive with our five senses, are mind-dependent, that none of them could exist without being perceived, is the keystone of Berkeley's philosophy. This is often called his idealism, as opposed to immaterialism, which is the denial of matter. The First Dialogue contains a sustained argument for idealism. All arguments must start with premises, and we have seen that the substantive premiss doing most of the work in the First Dialogue is the Simplest Model of Perception. If we grant Berkeley this premiss, he has some pretty powerful arguments. If we do not like their conclusions, then we must find an alternative model of perception.

SMP is attractive because it captures the natural thought that sense experience is just openness to the world. There are alternatives to SMP, and Berkeley does try to argue against some of them, but there is only any need to look for alternatives if we find the consequences of SMP unacceptable. The Second and Third Dialogues aim to show that idealism, when combined with the denial of matter, is not as unacceptable as it might at first seem.

Appendix: Perception and Acquaintance

The account of Berkeley's theory of perception, which I called the Simplest Model of Perception, given in this chapter is silent on whether perception is a cognitive relation, on whether to perceive is to know. The silence was because Berkeley does not need perception to be a cognitive relation for the purpose of arguing that the objects of perception are mind-dependent. But the question remains to be addressed. Berkeley's use of the phrase 'perceive or know', with the 'or' of paraphrase, suggests that he did take perception to be cognitive, and if he did that makes it obvious to look for similarities between SMP and Russell's conception of perceptual acquaintance. Can we interpret 'perception' in Berkeley's writings as Russellian acquaintance?

It is worth quoting Russell's account of acquaintance at some length, for the parallels are striking:

> I say that I am *acquainted* with an object when I have a direct cognitive relation to that object, that is when I am directly aware of the object itself. When I speak of a cognitive relation here, I do not mean the sort of relation which constitutes judgement, but the sort which constitutes presentation. In fact I think the relation of subject and object I call acquaintance is simply the converse of the relation of object and subject which constitutes presentation. That is, to say that *S* has acquaintance with *O* is essentially the same thing as to say that *O* is presented to *S*. . . . the word *acquaintance* is designed to emphasize, more than the word *presentation*, the relational character of the fact with which we are concerned. ('Knowledge by Acquaintance and Knowledge by Description', 108)

The most important points of similarity are the contrast between acquaintance and judgement and the dyadic character of the acquaintance relation. To determine whether perception is acquaintance, we need to address two distinct issues. First, is Berkeley's perception a cognitive relation? Secondly, does Russellian acquaintance admit of adverbial modification, by which I mean, can S be acquainted with O in more than one way, so that there can be a variation in the facts about what is perceived even though the same subject and object are involved? The second question is a matter of Russell scholarship, but unless it gets a negative answer, Berkeleian perception is not Russellian acquaintance.

It seems to me, as it does to Winkler (*Berkeley: An Interpretation*, 153–4), that the answer to the first question is an unequivocal affirmative, though this has been doubted (e.g. Pappas, *Berkeley's Thought*, 166–7). On the textual front, I know of no passage in the *Three Dialogues* or the *Principles* which is inconsistent with perception being a cognitive relation, and some positively encourage it. In particular, Berkeley sometimes uses 'know' and 'perceive' as stylistic variants (*DHP1* 202, 206; *PHK* 6). Furthermore, the idea that perception is not a cognitive relation is very strange and unintuitive: seeing, hearing, feeling are ways of finding out about the world.

What we need to make clear here is that it is consistent with Berkeleian perception being a cognitive relation that perceiving something neither involves nor implies the possession of any knowledge *that*. The same is probably true of Russellian acquaintance. For Berkeley, what is perceived is thereby known, but whether one judges it to fall under any descriptive concepts is another matter entirely. Suppose I see an object O. Being seen, it must have some determinate colour, and that must be part of my experience. But then we are tempted to ask whether that colour is a shade of green or not, and to assume that if it is some particular shade of green, then its being that shade of green is part of the content of my visual experience. But Berkeley would not agree, for judging that an object of experience is a certain shade of green commits one to its being similar to or different from other objects, and these similarities and differences are not part of the content of the experience. I just see the colour as it is. If I judge that it is very similar to the colour of grass, then I am going beyond what is given in that experience. It is essential at this point to remind ourselves of Berkeley's nominalism, for he will not allow that experience ever presents us with something as an instance of a universal. Rather, experience just presents us with what is there, namely particulars, and grouping them together into types is the work of the mind.

One way of seeing the point is by a simple thought experiment. Suppose that someone has been brought up in an environment with no red in it. All of the other colours are present as normal, but red is completely absent. Furthermore, the subject is completely unaware of this, for he does not know that human eyes are sensitive to other types of light. So as far as the subject is concerned, the colour spectrum ends with orange, i.e. the colour of a ripe Seville orange. Then one day he is shown a vermilion scarf. In time he will learn to relate this colour to the colours he already knows and thus to form a concept of it, but Berkeley is claiming that long before this, at the very moment he sees the vermilion scarf, he knows something he did not know before. By definition, this knowledge he gains cannot be expressed in words, but once he has acquired it, his view of what there is must change.

When we come to consider Berkeley's epistemology, one striking feature is that he had a concept of 'perfect knowledge'. The subtitle to the *Three Dialogues* begins: 'The design of which is plainly to demonstrate the reality and perfection of human knowledge', and the adjective is used often (relative to the occurrence of 'know' and its cognates, which is pretty infrequent) in the published works. But what can it mean to describe knowledge as 'perfect'? Two suggestions would be 'free from doubts' and 'free from distortions'. Now it would seem that under the cognitive reading of SMP, perception has both of these but judgement has neither. According to SMP, everything perceived is as it seems and seems as it is, for the simple reason that how it seems is to be *identified with* how it is. So doubts and distortions are impossible. But because judgements, however simple, always have commitments beyond the content of one's current perception, there is always room for doubt, and since the concepts from which they are composed are human constructions, there is always room for distortion. So if we do not interpret Berkeley's perceptual relation epistemically, there is no room left for perfect knowledge.

Perfect knowledge is not quite the same as certain knowledge. For a start, it may only be possible to define certainty over propositional attitudes, but more importantly, it would seem that anything that could be known with certainty could also be known, or believed, with less than certainty. But in Berkeley's case, the explanation of why perceptual knowledge is free from doubts makes it clear that it could never be less than perfect knowledge. Acquiring perfect knowledge is not a cognitive achievement over and above simply perceiving, whereas certainty is such an achievement. If Russellian acquaintance involves certainty, then SMP is not acquaintance.

To think that perception in Berkeley is epistemic is not quite the same as to think that it is Russellian acquaintance, for there may be more to acquaintance than is intended in Berkeley's relation of perception. However, there are sufficient similarities for us to be concerned by objections to interpreting perception as acquaintance. One line of objection, suggested by George Pappas, is that Berkeley is explicit that we perceive ordinary objects such as trees and houses, but 'these things are not presented to observers in the way that objects of acquaintance are supposed to be' (*Berkeley's Thought*, 167). In particular, they may appear other than they are, and their appearance to a single person at a time never encompasses all their aspects or features.

The first point is easily dealt with, for Berkeley only allows a distinction between appearance and reality in judgements. If the white house looks pink (to me in this light), it does not follow that it looks other than it is. Rather, it looks, and thus is (to me in this light), such a way that might mislead me into making false judgements. The house really is that colour (to me in this light), but if on the basis of this experience I were to judge that it was pink, I would be committed to its looking pink in certain other circumstances and to other observers, and in so doing I would be mistaken. The real problem is the second point. It seems to be part of the notion of acquaintance that if *S* perceives *O*, then there is no aspect or feature of *O* which is hidden from *S*. Thus, for example, the apple I am looking at may be rotten, but I can perceive the apple without perceiving its rottenness. If perceiving the apple was being acquainted with it, then I could not be acquainted with it unless I perceived its rottenness.

There are three possible responses to this objection. One could deny that Berkeley can coherently maintain that we perceive apples and houses. One could deny that this aspect of acquaintance is part of Berkeley's conception of perception. Or one could find fault with the objection. The first two are forlorn, so I shall take the third. Berkeley thinks we perceive physical objects by perceiving parts of them, and those parts are ideas. There is no problem about being acquainted with ideas, so when we perceive an object we are acquainted with some of the ideas which constitute it. Thus every perception involves an acquaintance and every acquaintance a perception. However, the objection remains that for some substituends for 'O' 'S perceives O' is true but 'S is acquainted with O' is false. The question is then whether this matters, and I think it does not. Perception, for Berkeley, is primarily a relation between minds and ideas, and that relation is very similar to acquaintance. In virtue of that relation holding between a mind and some ideas, we can say that we perceive physical objects, which are not ideas but collections of ideas, even when we do not perceive every element of the collection. The objector points out that an entailment of 'S perceives O' in the primary case does not hold in the secondary case. But it should not be surprising or uncomfortable that when a concept is extended it loses some of its implications. Quite clearly, Berkeley thinks that the relation between a mind and a physical object it perceives is not exactly the same as the relation between a mind and an idea it perceives. When 'O' is an idea, 'S perceives O' entails 'S is acquainted with O', but when 'O' is a physical object it entails 'S is acquainted with some elements of O'.

CHAPTER 4

The Problem with Matter

4.1 The Limits of Thought

Berkeley's strategy in writing the *Three Dialogues* is to divide and conquer: he first argues that the sensible things are not material, i.e. that matter is not perceptible, and then that all alternative conceptions of matter, such as the substratum of sensible qualities or the cause of experience, are flawed (*DHP2* 222–3):

PHILONOUS   Pray tell me if the case stands not thus: at first, from a belief of material substance you would have it that the immediate objects existed without the mind; then that their archetypes; [then a substratum;] then causes; next instruments; then occasions: lastly, *something in general*, which being interpreted proves *nothing*. So matter comes to nothing. What think you, Hylas, is not this a fair summary of your whole proceeding?

It is usual for philosophers studying Berkeley to concentrate on the first two positions in Philonous' list because Berkeley here has arguments, namely the inconceivability of an unconceived tree and that nothing is like an idea but an idea, which, if successful, would make the rest of the argument redundant. What these arguments suggest to the twenty-first-century philosopher who has read Kant and Wittgenstein is that Berkeley is trying to draw limits to what we can think, limits which would leave materialism as literally unthinkable. It is not hard to see that this interpretation is anachronistic, even though it undoubtedly results in interesting philosophy. If materialism were in this sense unthinkable, then the correct project would be to show that we cannot really understand what the materialist is saying. Berkeley, in contrast, is concerned to show that it is false (*DHP1* 173):

PHILONOUS   How cometh it to pass then, Hylas, that you pronounce me a *sceptic*, because I deny what you affirm, to wit, the existence of matter?

This is something he can do only if he understands the thesis in the first place. Philonous later makes it clear that he is denying the possibility of matter, which he takes to require proving its impossibility (*DHP2* 225). And this is where some confusion might set in, for in one sense we must be able to conceive the impossible, such as a round square window, otherwise we could not understand the claim that it was impossible, but in another sense we say that we cannot conceive a round square window. When Berkeley claims that a materialist thesis is inconceivable, it is in the second sense. Thus, for example, Philonous concludes the tree argument by saying (*DHP1* 201):

PHILONOUS   And yet you will earnestly contend for the truth of that which you cannot so much as conceive.

The original challenge was to '*conceive it possible* for . . . any sensible object whatever, to exist without the mind' (*DHP1* 200, my emphasis). This is analogous to saying that we cannot conceive it possible for a house to have a round square window, though we understand the claim well enough to deny it. It is very different from the Kantian claim that we cannot have meaningful thoughts about what he called the transcendental object, the thing in itself, because all our concepts can only be legitimately applied on the basis of experience, which is always experience of the phenomenal object, the thing as it appears to us and never the thing in itself. Materialism is not unthinkable, it is just impossible.

So if we want to understand *Berkeley's* metaphysics, to know what *he* thought was wrong with materialism, we should avert our eyes from these potential uses of some of his arguments. In this chapter we shall concentrate on his objections to forms of materialism which accept the mind-dependence of the immediate objects of perception.

4.2 A Material Substratum

The idea of a material substratum is the idea that sensible qualities need to be had by something. There cannot be a free-floating quality, say an instance of cobalt blue, which is not an instance of *something* being cobalt blue. That thing is distinct from the quality but stands in a relation to the quality—the quality *inheres* in it. As Hylas says (*DHP1* 197):

... considering [sensible things] as so many modes and qualities, I find it necessary to suppose a material *substratum*, without which they cannot be conceived to exist.

The point is simply that a mode is always a mode *of something*, a quality always a quality *of something*. One cannot conceive of there being a quality instance which was not a quality of something. The point is familiar both in the scholastic philosophy and in Berkeley's immediate predecessors like Locke (e.g. *Essay*, II. xxiii. 1), though how best to interpret and apply it is a highly contested matter. However, as Berkeley was well aware, it is rather odd to claim that this something, whatever it is, which has the sensible qualities is material when the sensible qualities which inhere in it have been proved to be immaterial. Berkeley often compares the idea of a sensible thing having a material support to the suggestion that unthinking things can feel pain, 'it being too visibly absurd to hold that pain or pleasure can be in an unperceiving substance' (*DHP1*

191), and he has a point here. If pain has a subject, that subject must be a mind or mental substance (*DHP1* 176), and so too for all the qualities or sensations we perceive. However, the issue is not as simple as that, for we have seen how, in accepting the mind-dependence of the sensible qualities, Hylas was led to think of them as 'merely apparent': they are mind-dependent because they are appearances and there is nothing more to how they are than how they seem. Now, while appearances have to appear *to* someone, they also have to be the appearances *of* something. This makes a little more sense of Hylas' thought that there can only be sensible things perceived by minds if there is something else, as it were, lying behind or under the appearances.

There are three distinct views about matter which it might help to separate at this point. One is that the material world is the cause of our ideas. The second is that matter is some strange, qualityless substratum which is needed to 'ground' the qualities we perceive, and the third is that there are material objects, such as books and trees, which have the qualities we perceive. Given the arguments of the last chapter, all three views have in common the introduction of something over and above what is given in perception, and it is that which is Berkeley's main target. But at the moment we are considering arguments to do with the second and third views, and only after those have been dismissed does he turn to the first.

Berkeley tends to conflate these two different senses of substance because he assumes that anyone wanting to distinguish between a quality and the subject of that quality would do so by introducing something logically distinct from the qualities it supports. Thus his attacks on material substratum are sometimes attacks on the idea of something without sensible qualities lying behind or under the sensible world, and sometimes attacks on the more general idea that qualities must inhere in or be instantiated by something non-mental. He also uses the terms 'substance' and 'substratum' interchangeably, where we might want to use 'substance' for any subject of qualities and reserve 'substratum' for the occult stuff that lies under them. While Berkeley accepts the general idea that there cannot be a quality without a substance, he thinks that this requirement is met by their being perceived. He offers the same objection to the two conflated alternatives, namely that he cannot make sense of the relation which is meant to hold between quality and either substance or substratum.

The attack on material substratum relies upon our not being allowed to conceive it as Cartesian matter, which is essentially extended. If we were able to do this, then we could understand the qualities of extension, such as particular shapes, sizes, and motions, as being modes or manners of the existence of extension. The substratum would be extension, of which all the qualities are just forms. But this conception of matter is not available: primarily because extension has been shown to be mind-dependent (*DHP1* 189), so something essentially extended is not material, and also because we cannot conceive of extension without conceiving of some specific form of extension (*DHP1* 193). So it is quickly granted that we have only a relative conception of the substratum. A relative conception of something is a conception of it as related to something else by a specified relation. Thus if someone knows me but not my father, when we talk of my father that person has only a relative conception of who we are talking about. Clearly one can only have a relative conception of something if one has a conception of the relation, so Philonous attacks Hylas' claim to have a relative conception of the material substratum by questioning the relation between quality and substratum. All Hylas' metaphors are spatial—it stands under or supports the qualities—and thus inadequate to give a conception of something which cannot stand in a spatial relation to the qualities, since extension is one of the qualities it is meant to support.

Hylas later (*DHP3* 249–50) tries to turn the tables on Philonous: if Philonous can explain the spatial metaphor of qualities being *in* the unextended mind, then Hylas can do the same with his claim that qualities are *in* a material substratum. But Philonous explains qualities being in the mind as their being perceived by the mind, which clearly does not help. Now this takes us to the heart of Berkeley's objection to material substances: he has a totally clear way of understanding the requirement that a quality must exist in a substance, namely that it must be perceived by a mind, whereas the materialist cannot explain what he means by qualities inhering in matter or any other substance.

Jonathan Dancy has raised a very astute objection to Berkeley: not all the things we want to say about minds can be accounted for in terms of those minds perceiving ideas. For example, we want to say that 'some are cleverer or more imaginative than others . . . some are confused or worried on occasion' (Editor's introduction to the *Three Dialogues*, 24). It is implausible to say that being worried is having an idea of worry, or having one or more of the set of worrying ideas; after all, some people can worry about anything, and without realizing it. But if we want to say that minds have these properties, and their having them is different from their having ideas, then we appear committed to a relation between a property and a substance which is not the relation of perception. This would appear to give us enough material to form a relative conception of material substance.

However, there is an important asymmetry between our conception of mental substance and any conception of matter that may be formed after the proofs of the mind-dependence of sensible things. The mind is essentially active, and we can know this. But when we think of the mind as essentially active, then we can see that to say it is worried or clever is to say it acts in a certain manner. More precisely, we should say that to be worried or angry or happy or unintelligent is to have one's mental activity *constrained* in a certain way. It is a familiar point that people who are angry are not able to control their thoughts, and we should be able to see that all the emotions create some degree of lack of control over one's thoughts. Berkeley nowhere gives a theory of the emotions, but it would be possible for him to say that emotions and other mental states which do not consist in perceiving an idea consist in a specific constraint upon mental activity. This view has the advantage of forging a connection between the emotions, or passions, and action. The limits to mental activity created by the emotions are always temporary, but other mental qualities, such as lack of intelligence or imagination, impose more permanent but still contingent limitations. For Berkeley the mind is essentially active, so he must deny that ideas, being passive, are mental modes. But he can accept all the other modes of mind described by Descartes, so long as he can understand them in terms of mental activity. The properties Dancy mentions are modes of the mind's action and thus do not need to be thought of as qualities inhering in the mind, like sensations.

Before leaving the subject of substance and substratum, we should ask whether Hylas was right to agree so quickly that we could not form a conception of material substance 'by reflexion and reason' (DHP1 197). One of the traditional reasons for distinguishing between substance and quality was to explain change: a beloved teddy bear loses its eyes, its fur rubs off, maybe some limbs detach, the stuffing comes out, it is stitched and repaired until it may even be unrecognizable as a teddy bear at all, let alone as the pristine gift that was gleefully unwrapped all those years ago. Throughout all the changes I have just described, we keep referring to 'it', to the thing which changes. That is why we can talk of change rather than destruction, and it had seemed obvious to most philosophers before Berkeley that the 'it' must refer to something distinct from the changing qualities, which thing they tended to call a substance. But Berkeley saw clearly that there was an alternative (DHP3 245–6):

your preconceived notion of (I know not what) one single, unchanged, unperceivable, real nature, marked by each name . . . seems to have taken its rise from not rightly understanding the common language of men speaking of several distinct ideas, as united into one thing by the mind.

Here Berkeley also slips in one of his own prejudices, namely that the unity of an object is the work of the mind, despite having admitted that distinct ideas can 'have some connexion in Nature, either with respect to co-existence or succession' (*DHP3* 245). Still the point remains that we can explain change, while allowing the object to be nothing more than a bundle of qualities, in terms of an organizing principle which unifies diverse qualities. Whether the organizing principle is subjective, and whether it really can explain persistence through change, is the subject of Chapter 8. For present purposes it will suffice to note that the fact that we take our sense impressions to be of persisting, changeable objects does not alone compel us to accept the existence of substances distinct from their qualities.

4.3 The Scientific World-View

When Berkeley was a student, one of the most influential philosophical works was Locke's recently published *Essay concerning Human Understanding*. In this Locke put forward a view which is now so familiar that we forget how radically in conflict with common sense it was, and still is. The view is that science, particularly physics, reveals the true nature of the world, and in so doing it has shown that the world is, in many respects, very unlike the way we take it to be on the basis of experience.

Berkeley has already rejected Locke's specific account of ultimate reality as revealed by science, which was that the world contained only primary qualities (which in certain combinations had the power to produce in us experiences not only of themselves but also of the secondary qualities). He argued that the primary qualities are as mind-dependent as the secondary, and also questioned our ability to conceive of a world extended but uncoloured (see 3.2.3). But this still leaves in place the more general idea that science can, and perhaps does, reveal the nature of reality to be quite different from how we experience it to be. If in doing this the scientist uses concepts such as size and shape which apply in everyday experience, then Berkeley can use the same arguments he used against Locke: ultimate reality so revealed would still be mind-dependent.

There remains the possibility, which the physics of the twenty-first century makes plain, that science might not use concepts which apply in experience. Thus the scientists' claim to be describing a mind-independent, unperceivable reality would not fall foul of the arguments of the First Dialogue. The physical world of atoms and subatomic particles is not observable and is not described (except perhaps for expository purposes) in terms of observation concepts. Even the concepts of extension, position, and motion are rejected or reshaped.

The crucial issue is then the claim that science describes the world as it really is, and correlatively, that sense experience can and often does mislead. Someone would be endorsing this view if she said that science has shown us that the table I am writing on is not really solid, but consists largely of empty space lying between millions of unobservable particles which are constantly in motion at great speeds. Alternatively, she might hold the weaker view that the scientific story about the motions of particles does not contradict the sense experience of a solid table, but gives an account of the true underlying nature of solid objects. Of course, if she is to avoid the objections to Locke, she must admit that her talk of motion is merely a metaphor to help us grasp what science reveals and that the thesis can be stated in terms not applicable within sense experience. Berkeley is, of all the modern philosophers, the one most strongly opposed to such claims. He is not being reactionary here, he does not need to deny the enormous practical benefits of theoretical science, nor its excellent intellectual credentials, rather he is challenging the interpretation of it as revealing the true nature of reality.

Berkeley's solution to the tension between the experienced sensible world and the world revealed in science is to deny the reality of the latter. What science does is to predict what happens in the sensible world, and to explain these phenomena. The aim of science is (*DHP3* 242):

PHILONOUS ... to shew how we come to be affected with ideas, in that manner and order wherein they are imprinted on our senses. Is it not?

Scientific theories are instruments for predicting and explaining experience, and it has turned out that the best instruments involve the fiction of there being such unobservable entities as electrons and quarks. We should respect the instrument for the job it does, without confusing its fictions for reality by believing what it says about unperceivable entities (*DHP3* 243):

PHILONOUS And yet for all this, it will not follow, that philosophers [i.e. scientists] have been doing nothing; for by observing and reasoning upon the connexion of ideas, they discover the laws and methods of Nature, which is a part of knowledge both useful and entertaining.

The ingenuity of this response is impressive, and, in so far as science deals in unperceivable entities and qualities, it looks like the only option for the immaterialist who does not want to reject science. Berkeley is putting forward a view of science now known as *instrumentalism*, but Philonous does not come to it directly. His first claim (*DHP3* 241–2) is that no 'demonstrations', i.e. experimental proofs, require the existence of matter. It is an interesting passage, not least because our high-school familiarity with Newton's laws allows us to see how inaccurate and confused Hylas' presentation is. That aside, Philonous' reply misses the important point, which is that Newton's law $F = ma$ is framed in terms of mass rather than weight. Weight is a sensible quality, mass is not, and there are grounds for thinking that mass is the 'real' property and weight a mere appearance: if one takes an object to a different gravitational field its weight changes but the object itself undergoes no change (except in location). If we want to say that transporting things around the universe does not change their true nature, then we must say that their true nature is to have a mass, not a weight.

Berkeley's response to this argument would be that objects patently *do* change as you move them around the universe; for example, Neil Armstrong discovered that they are lighter on the moon. Mass is a concept introduced to facilitate prediction of these changes, but it does not pick out anything real in the object. This combination of complete trust in the senses and instrumentalism does lead to a slightly different understanding of the world. Specifically, Berkeley has to say that bringing objects closer to each other can change their qualities. That sounds rather odd to us, but it is not much stranger than gravity. Also, most of us have so thoroughly absorbed the scientific world-view that we distrust our senses (when Neil Armstrong landed on the moon he was *perceptibly* lighter than on earth) in favour of general principles about how changes are caused in objects. What we take to be common sense, namely that objects do not change their natures by being brought closer together, incorporates both some scientific theory, which may at some time be rejected, *and* a particular interpretation of it. The scientific thesis is that objects do not change their *mass* by being brought closer together. But they do change their weight, so we can only infer that they do not change their real natures if we add the interpretation of science (rather than perception) as revealing the truth about the world. Instrumentalism only appears obviously false because common sense often contains hidden commitments to a realist interpretation of science.

We must now ask whether instrumentalism is a tenable philosophy of science. There are two main lines of objection. One is that instrumentalism is inconsistent with the actual details of physics, that physics does not work under an instrumental interpretation. I am not qualified to judge this matter, but we should note that the objection only works if the *true* physics is not amenable to instrumentalist interpretation, and hence the objection is always in hock to future developments. And the details may cut the other way, for we might come across theories to which it is impossible to give a realistic interpretation. The jury is still out on whether a realistic interpretation of quantum mechanics is possible. In fact there is an asymmetry here: since instrumentalist interpretations are subject to fewer constraints than realist ones, we can expect every realistically construable theory to have an instrumentalist construal but not vice versa.

The second line of objection is that the instrumentalist needs to draw a line between scientific theory, about which he is not a realist, and non-scientific everyday knowledge, about which he is a realist, and he cannot reasonably disentangle the two. Michael Dummett has given an excellent example of this ('Common Sense and Physics', 18). Thomas Aquinas thought that if one added a small quantity of water to wine, the water *became* wine—the water changed its nature. This was because he thought of liquids as homogeneous, so that if someone mixes two liquids, the product is a single substance, which may or may not be identical to one of the ingredients. In contrast, we think of liquids as granular (but with very small grains), so if one mixes a little water in some wine, what one produces is wine with a small proportion of water in it. (Since wine is a mixture anyway, and water is one of its components, we find that mixing a little water with wine does produce wine, but for reasons different from Aquinas's.) We think of the mixing of liquids in this granular fashion because the discovery of the molecular composition of liquids has infiltrated into our everyday conception of things. But molecules are imperceptible, by most standards and certainly by Berkeley's, so it looks as if our everyday account of what happens when we mix two liquids must fall on the side of theory, and so must Aquinas's account, which was just based on a different theory. The crucial question then becomes whether we can formulate a description of what is to be observed when we mix water and wine which is complete, accurate, and neutral between the two explanations. The problem with this is that Aquinas needs to say that the water disappears, that after stirring we can see wine but not water, whereas we would want to say (prescinding from the fact that wine contains water anyway) that we see wine-and-water. Both parties agree in denying that after the mixing we see some wine and we see some separate water, but they disagree over what we do actually see.

This is just one example, but the objector to instrumentalism thinks it is typical. If so, the division between pure observational fact and fiction-laden theory leaves little, if anything, on the side of fact. To meet the objection we need to look at how Berkeley would draw the division. The obvious suggestion is that he would take an instrumentalist attitude to anything involving imperceptible entities or qualities, and here he can fall back on his discussion of sensible qualities at *DHP1* 174–5. Now one response would be that this leaves too little, since only colours and shapes, smells, sounds, tastes, and textures are sensible. However, it does not immediately follow that he must take the instrumentalist attitude to everyday objects such as trees and houses, since he is going to claim that they are combinations or congeries of sensible qualities, and we can perceive those by perceiving their parts. There is, however, a different problem which will lead Berkeley into a very radical rejection of realism.

Sensible qualities are fully given in sense experience, which means that one needs nothing more to answer the question of whether something has a given sensible quality than to have an appropriate experience of it. It follows that one needs nothing more than an appropriate experience of two things to determine whether they both have a given sensible quality: perceptual indistinguishability is sufficient for sameness of sensible quality. Unfortunately this leads to paradox, since perceptual indistinguishability is not transitive. It is relatively easy to find triples of colours or tastes such that the first and the second cannot be distinguished, the second and third cannot be distinguished, but the first and third can. In the face of this fact of experience one simply has to give up the thought that one can tell whether two objects share a sensible quality simply by looking, or feeling or smelling or whatever, which amounts to saying that there are no sensible qualities in Berkeley's sense. The problem only occurs for sensible quality types, not for tokens. Two distinct things can be of the same type, but by their very distinctness they are different tokens. Cobalt blue, for example, is a quality type of which there can be many tokens, such as the colour of that rug, the colour of this book, etc. When we ask whether the book and the rug have the same colour, we are asking about a type, for they are trivially different tokens. Token colours are specific to a time and place, they cannot have several instances like types. They are, in other words, concrete individuals. The relation between particular ideas and types of idea is explored more fully in Chapter 7. Now Berkeley can admit that quality types are not immediately perceivable without having to deny that sensible quality tokens can be immediately perceived. So he can say that the contents of our sense experiences are such things as the particular blueness of this book, the particular smell of this coffee. Any judgement we make about what we perceive, if it is to be more than just a list of names for token sensible qualities, will necessarily use general words or concepts, words for types of quality. Therefore it follows from the non-transitivity of perceptual indistinguishability that every judgement about what we perceive goes beyond the content of the immediate experience. Given Berkeley's very strict conditions on what is sensible, quality type is not sensible, so all judgements of quality type are actually judgements about the insensible and thus ones towards which we should take an instrumentalist attitude.

So it turns out that Berkeley needs to be an instrumentalist about science, but he does not face the main problem for instrumentalists, namely drawing a distinction between fact and fiction, because he should also take an instrumentalist, or non-realist, attitude towards *all* judgements of fact. However, this is perfectly consistent with his being a staunch realist, though not a materialist, about the actual objects of sense experience, the token sensible qualities.

There has been some scholarly dispute about whether Berkeley really was an instrumentalist about corpuscles, which were the elementary particles of contemporary physical theory. The mechanistic physics of Berkeley's time appeared to explain why various things occurred by an appeal to natural necessity. Once one properly understood the working of a watch, one saw that the small hand simply had to move once for every complete revolution of the big hand. Corpuscularians like Boyle and Locke took this mechanical explanation one step further and posited minute insensible parts of physical objects, which, if we knew about them, would allow us to see that the perceptible properties of those objects arose mechanically and with natural necessity from the behaviour of their parts.

Now Berkeley was quite happy to allow still undiscovered mechanistic explanations of natural phenomena (*DHP2* 211; *PHK* 60–5), but he had two disagreements with the corpuscularian hypothesis. One is that mechanistic explanations revealed how phenomena arose by natural necessity from the behaviour of their parts. Since the whole physical world is composed of ideas, and ideas are inert, mechanistic explanations could not provide that sort of understanding. Rather, it is contingent that there is a mechanistic explanation of any given phenomenon to be found, and where that explanation is found, it is contingent that the mechanism gives rise to the phenomenon. However, we have some reason from theology and the progress of science to believe that God chose to produce our experiences in accordance with a limited number of basic physical laws applying to the scientifically discoverable parts of things ('So fixed, so immutable are the laws by which the unseen Author of Nature actuates the universe'—*DHP2* 210–11). So Berkeley can agree with the mechanists that (*PHK* 62)

There are certain general laws that run through the whole chain of natural effects: these are learned by observation and study of Nature, and are by men applied as well to the framing artificial things for the use and ornament of life, as to explaining the various phenomena.

However, this explanation is not a demonstration of natural necessity, rather it (*PHK* 62)

consists only in shewing the conformity any particular phenomenon hath to the general Laws of Nature, or, which is the same thing, in discovering the *uniformity* there is in the production of natural effects; as will be evident to whoever shall attend to the several instances, wherein philosophers pretend to account for appearances.

Berkeley is arguing that explanation is merely subsumption by laws, and since the laws themselves are contingent, this does not provide an insight into phenomena arising by some sort of natural necessity. These passages, which clearly point the way forward to Hume's account of causal necessity and the laws of nature, allow Berkeley to endorse the practical benefits of mechanistic science. But this does not commit him to the second strand of mechanism, the corpuscularian hypothesis.

Daniel Garber ('Locke, Berkeley, and Corpuscular Scepticism') has argued that according to Locke, corpuscles are in principle observable and it is just a human limitation that prevents us from seeing them as clearly as we see the workings of a watch. Berkeley certainly allows that there can be things too small for us to see (*DHP1* 185):

PHILONOUS Besides, it is not only possible but manifest, that there actually are animals, whose eyes are by Nature framed to perceive those things, which by reason of their minuteness escape our sight.

Furthermore, Garber thinks that Berkeley allows that there might be mechanisms subsuming phenomena under the laws of nature, but which we are unable to discover. This is one reading of 'secret' in Philonous' long speech at the beginning of the Second Dialogue (*DHP2* 211):

Yet all the vast bodies that compose this mighty frame [the stars and planets], how distant and remote soever, are by some secret mechanism, some divine art and force linked in a mutual dependence and intercourse with each other.

However, given that no one in Berkeley's time understood how gravity worked, the use of 'secret' may only imply that we do not yet know, not that we cannot know. What is clear is that Berkeley will allow that there are mechanisms which we have not yet discovered, and that there are mechanisms which we shall not discover but other creatures might discover. He may even allow that God has put in place mechanisms underlying various phenomena which we could discover but will never know about owing to our own free choices. What is less clear is whether Berkeley can allow that, perhaps for the sake of completeness and simplicity in the laws of nature, God created mechanisms undiscoverable by us or any other finite creature. Assuming for simplicity that we are the only finite creatures capable of understanding and predicting the world, this suggestion would have to attribute to God a motive for creating the world one way rather than another, a motive which was not anthropocentric. To decide that issue would take us into theological territories which I would rather avoid. On more philosophical ground, Garber's interpretation commits Berkeley to there being ideas which are part of the physical world but which are unperceivable by any finite creature. This only makes sense if Berkeley holds that existence unperceived is to be understood in terms of ideas existing in God's mind. I reject this interpretation of Berkeley in Chapters 5 and 8. Also, the Garber interpretation is inconsistent with Berkeley's radical nominalism, which is discussed in Chapter 7. If God were to produce a secret or hidden mechanism, in order for it to conform to the laws of nature, the ideas which it comprised would have to be of determinate types. At the very least, sameness of type requires similarity, but since there is no such thing as objective similarity, according to the Berkeleian nominalist, the only way God could create an idea of determinate type would be to create an idea which is *subjectively* similar to other ideas of that type. An idea which we cannot experience cannot be subjectively similar to one we do experience.

4.4 Explanation

The substratum of sensible qualities, the theoretical entities of science, the cause, instrument, or occasion of experience (*DHP2* 215, 218, 220), are all notions of matter introduced to fill a perceived explanatory gap in immaterialism. The Second Dialogue is a wonderful piece of writing which captures, in Hylas' increasingly desperate proposals, the common feeling that there is 'something missing' from immaterialism. Philonous takes the debater's strategy of waiting to see what suggestions are made about what needs to be added to the immaterialist's catalogue of what exists and then arguing against each in turn. This succeeds in leaving Hylas in the ridiculous position of insisting on the existence of 'something entirely unknown' (*DHP2* 221) which can only be conceived in terms of what it is not. Dialectically this strategy is powerful but unpersuasive: to be shown that you cannot coherently formulate your concerns rarely, if ever, gets rid of those concerns. Unfortunately, Berkeley never deals directly with the source of the unease, he never digs out why immaterialism is thought to be inadequate or incomplete. He simply has Philonous offer a challenge which goes unanswered (*DHP2* 224):

PHILONOUS ... I challenge you to shew me that thing in Nature which needs matter to explain or account for it.

The reason for this insouciance may be that he found in his predecessors, especially Locke but to some extent also Malebranche, a simple acceptance of our inability to explain how matter could cause us to have ideas. If it is an integral part of the materialism he was attacking that something inexplicable happens whenever we have sense experiences of the world, e.g. *DHP2* 210, then, far from creating an explanatory gap, immaterialism plugs one.

4.4.1 *Russell's Argument*

Several philosophers have since responded to Philonous' challenge
to find something in Nature which needs matter to explain it. I
shall take Russell as an example because what he writes is both
representative and elegant (for 'sense-data' read 'sensible qualities',
since both are names for what is immediately perceived):

> If the cloth completely hides the table, we shall derive no sense-data
> from the table, and therefore, if the table were merely sense-data, it
> would have ceased to exist, and the cloth would be suspended in empty
> air, resting, by a miracle, in the place where the table formerly was.
>
> . . . When ten people are sitting round a dinner-table, it seems preposter-
> ous to maintain that they are not seeing the same tablecloth, the same
> knives and forks and spoons and glasses.
>
> . . . I bought my table from the former occupant of my room; I could
> not buy *his* sense-data, which died when he went away, but I could and
> did buy the confident expectation of more or less similar sense-data.
>
> . . . If the cat appears at one moment in one part of the room, and at
> another in another part, it is natural to suppose that it has moved from
> the one to the other, passing over a series of intermediate positions. But
> if it is merely a set of sense-data, it cannot have ever been in any place
> where I did not see it; thus we shall have to suppose that it did not exist
> at all while I was not looking, but suddenly sprang into being in a new
> place.
>
> If the cat exists whether I see it or not, we can understand from our own
> experience how it gets hungry between one meal and the next; but if it
> does not exist when I am not seeing it, it seems odd that appetite should
> grow during non-existence as fast as during existence.
>
> . . . Thus every principle of simplicity urges us to adopt the natural view,
> that there really are objects other than ourselves and our sense-data
> which have an existence not dependent upon our perceiving them. (*The
> Problems of Philosophy*, 9–11)

This sort of argument is initially immensely persuasive, but it does
not stand up to closer inspection. Let us take Russell's five examples

one by one. First, it is not obvious that Berkeley has to say that, when covered by a tablecloth, the table ceases to exist. He may be able to accommodate existence unperceived by distinguishing between the physical object and the sensible qualities of which it is composed, but more to the point, Russell is confusing seeing with perceiving. A visually occluded table may still be felt as we lean our elbows on it, and perhaps even smelt by those with a sharp nose for mahogany. That aside, it is certainly not miraculous, in the sense of surprising or unexpected or in conflict with the laws of nature, that the tablecloth stays in place, for it is a familiar experience. So the thought must be that it lacks an explanation, but here Russell misdescribes the case. A tablecloth suspended in empty air certainly cries out for special explanation, but the tablecloth placed over a table is not suspended in empty space: if the immaterialist is not allowed to say there is a table underneath the cloth, then he is no more allowed to say that there is empty space. What he should say is that the cloth takes the shape and position of the table and maintains that shape and position until there is a suitable cause for change, such as the meal being cleared away. The omnipresent force of gravity will not cause it to fall because gravity only does that to cloths suspended in empty space, which we have already said this cloth is not.

The point about tables, knives, and other cutlery being public objects is inconclusive. Certainly we need an answer to the question of what makes it true that we both see the same glass, and there being a persisting, public material glass would provide an answer, but it is not the only answer. A similar charge is made by Hylas at DHP3 247. Berkeley does not have to deny that there are public physical objects, for they are collections of ideas perceived by several people at several times.

As to the purchase of his writing table, Russell makes it clear that what he pays for is future sense-data. He clearly thinks he has done this by buying a material cause of sense-data, but it would be as natural to say that he paid the former occupant of his room not to do certain things which would prevent his having those desired sense-data.

We certainly do believe that cats do not spring in and out of existence. On the one hand, this is not a datum of experience but a belief based on experience which needs justifying (and Hume showed how hard *that* was), and on the other, the immaterialist can and does try to account for existence unperceived. Of course, one may argue that Berkeley ultimately fails to provide for the cat's continuous existence, but that leaves us with a straight choice between rejecting our belief about the cat and rejecting one of the premisses of the argument for immaterialism.

Finally, it is simply false that we understand the cat's hunger from our own experience. We learn about the needs of animals by observing them; if we try to extrapolate from our own experience we more often than not do our pets a great disservice. Furthermore, we are quite used to going to bed well fed and waking several hours later quite hungry, without having experienced our own existence in the meanwhile. This is probably the only pattern of hunger that babies experience. The behaviour of cats, like that of cloths and tables, follows regular and predictable patterns which are only disturbed in certain sorts of way, and we can learn all these patterns and their exceptions from experience of the things in question. Once we have discovered these patterns, the phenomena Russell points out are neither surprising nor unnatural, nor difficult to understand.

So Russell's conclusion does not follow for two reasons: his examples are not as neutral as he thinks, and his claim that the existence of matter is the best explanation rests upon false claims about what the immaterialist must leave mysterious. But showing this does nothing to remove the sense of unease with immaterialism. To remove that feeling we need to show not merely that immaterialism can deal with all the data of experience, but that it provides the *best* explanation.

4.4.2 *What is to be Explained?*

There are two important features of our experience which the materialist claims are best explained by the existence of matter. One is the fact that our experience comes from outside us, that it is beyond our control. As Berkeley puts the point (*DHP2* 214):

> PHILONOUS Nor is it less plain that these ideas or things by me perceived . . . exist independently of my mind, since I know myself not to be their author, it being out of my power to determine at pleasure, what particular ideas I shall be affected with upon opening my eyes or ears.

This is, I take it, uncontroversial. It is presented by Philonous not as a datum in need of explanation but as a premiss in a proof of the existence of God. If, following the proof, one accepts that God exists and causes all our sense experience, then, as Philonous points out at great length in the Second Dialogue, the further supposition of matter is redundant. However, there are other premisses in the argument for God's existence which *are* 'less plain', such as that only minds are active and able to cause things, which will be challenged by a materialist. Berkeley's official proofs of God are far from conclusive, so for the purposes of discussing the issue of explanatoriness we shall diverge from the *Three Dialogues* and not take the existence of God to be independently established. Rather, we can consider whether a package with God but without matter provides the better explanation of the facts of experience.

This first fact which needs explaining could be described as the fact of our having sense perceptions at all, as opposed to merely imaginings and dreams. When put like this, it is obvious that the content of those perceptual experiences needs explanation as well. This will be the second explanandum. If experiences were random, they would not need further explanation, but they are shown not to be random by the regular patterns we discover and the successes of our past predictions (which is not to gainsay Hume's doubts about our justification for believing that they will not suddenly *become* random). This is what Berkeley calls the 'fixed order of Nature' (*DHP3* 258):

PHILONOUS   we ... place the reality of things in ideas, fleeting indeed, and changeable; however not changed at random, but according to the fixed order of Nature. For herein consists that constancy and truth of things, which secures all the concerns of life.

It is important to see how much is included here. Mackie, for example, when discussing the question of explanatoriness, thinks that the main thing needing to be explained is the similarity between what we experience before an interruption in our perception (such as sleeping or moving to a different place) and what we experience afterwards (*Problems from Locke*, 60). Berkeley's fixed order of nature includes both the similarities between what I experience before and after sleep, and the differences, such as daylight and bird song. It includes both the natural regularities, such as the changing seasons and the gravitational effects of the earth, and the man-made ones, such as a watch keeping time or this computer responding to my typing. Of course these regularities are based on more fundamental regularities in the succession of ideas, but since all regularities are inherently general, we shall see in Chapter 7 how the difference is only one of degree.

One explanation of these phenomena is that there exists a mind-independent material world which has a continuous existence, changes by the interaction of its parts according to strict (but not necessarily deterministic) laws, and causes us to have the perceptual experiences we have. Call this [M]. The alternative Berkeley is proposing is that apart from us and our ideas there exists another, vastly more powerful, mind which acts upon us to produce the train of sense experiences we have. Call this [I].

4.4.3 *Which is the Better Explanation?*

If we admit the validity of the question, there are really no alternatives to [M] and [I]. [M] includes the view that the very objects of perception are material, but it is only the indirect version of materialism, which holds that we immediately perceive ideas but material things also exist, which is a rival to [I]. This is because, as was argued in the last chapter, the direct version of materialism fails to account for conflicting appearances, and thus does not explain a prior datum. To appreciate fully the strengths of Berkeley's system we need to keep in mind that different arguments have different specific targets. It is not legitimate at this stage in the argument to object that the data of experience already commit us to the existence of matter. The inference to the best explanation only gets off the ground when we have established the independence of experience from matter (and concomitantly its dependence on mind).

So for present purposes we should regard [I] and [M] as supplements to a basic picture according to which in sense perception we confront the *sensible* world as it really is. It would almost do for the immaterialist to leave things at that, except for the need, pressed by the materialist, to explain the involuntariness and regularity of experience. The materialist thinks that we can only do the explaining if we supplement the basic picture with material objects causing our experiences, whereas Berkeley thinks that the only supplementation needed is another, infinite mind. Given that both explanations are adequate, we should choose the simpler.

4.4.3.1 *Ontology, ideology, and coincidences*

If theory choice is to be based on considerations of simplicity, then simplicity needs some more careful elaboration. A first suggestion, following Ockham's razor, might be that the theory which postulates fewer entities is the simpler; but this is not always so since reducing the number of entities may require adding large amounts of complex conceptual apparatus to the theory. For example, prior to Rutherford's discovery of the structure of the atom, chemical theory had hundreds of basic entities, namely the atoms of each of the elements. Rutherford discovered that atoms of every element were composed of just three types of entity—electrons, neutrons, and protons—in various combinations. This looks like a great on-tological simplification. However, this discovery also meant that solid objects were not made up of solid parts, but of large amounts of 'empty space'. This required considerable reconceptualization of many parts of physics. The reconceptualization eventually paid off in new discoveries, but the initial cost was huge, for it required physicists to work with a completely new, and considerably more complex, ideology (the term comes from Quine, 'Ontology and Ideology', and refers to the conceptual apparatus of a theory). Simplifying the ontology complicated the ideology, so straight on-tological comparisons between theories are not decisive.

However, in the case of [M] vs. [I], it *is* relevant to count entities because [I] is both ontologically *and* ideologically simpler. To see this remember that the data to be explained commit us to the existence of both minds and ideas. The theory that God, a spirit, causes us to have the sense experiences we do introduces no new type of entity and is thus ontologically simpler than the theory which says that material bodies, which are neither minds nor ideas and are not presupposed by the data to be explained, are the cause of our sense experiences.

We can see the ideological simplicity of [I] by considering that the data include the claim that our sense experiences are involuntary. This would only make sense if it was at least possible for us to have voluntary experiences, which we do have when we imagine. So the data presuppose that a mind is capable of causing experiences, which is exactly what [I] says about those of our experiences which are not caused by us. [M], in contrast, says that our involuntary sense experiences are caused by material bodies. This requires a new ideology according to which something non-mental is able to cause a mental event (*DHP2* 215):

PHILONOUS   . . . how can any idea or sensation exist in, or be produced by, anything but a mind or spirit? . . . But on the other hand, it is very conceivable that they should exist in, and be produced by, a spirit.

Not only does [M] introduce this new relation of matter causing ideas, but also its ability to explain regularities relies upon a
new conception of non-randomness. From our own experience,
we know that voluntary actions are not random but are performed
in the light of practical reasoning as a means to some end. In so far
as our goals and intentions are consistent, our actions will show a
discernible pattern. So if our experience is willed by God, it must
be willed as a means to some end and, given that God is rational,
we can expect that his willings will not be random or serve inconsistent ends. If experience is the product of God's will, then there is
an a priori reason to think it will not be random but display considerable systematicity. On the other hand, there is no a priori reason
to think that the effects of mindless matter will not be random.

So far there is a prima facie case for the relative simplicity of
[I], but John Mackie has argued (*Problems*, 62–7) that the most important criterion of simplicity in theory choice is not ontological
or ideological parsimony but the number of unexplained coincidences. He gives as an example theories of planetary motion. If
one assumes that the earth is stationary and the planets in motion
around it, then the motions of distinct planets will all involve at
some point an unexplained 365-day cycle. We would have to accept this as a coincidence, as something which just happens to be.
However, if we drop the assumption that the earth is stationary and
instead say that the earth and all the planets revolve around the sun,
then we can explain the appearance of 365-day cycles as a product
of our observing the planets from the earth, which takes 365 days
to orbit the sun. The apparent coincidence of there being 365-day
cycles in the motion of each of the planets has been explained by
the fact that it takes the earth 365 days to orbit the sun. We have
simplified the theory.

The argument for [M] must then proceed by pointing out how,
every time I briefly close my eyes, whatever I am looking at, when I
open them the scene before me is the same or very similar to what
I saw before. This phenomenon is not limited to the sense of sight,

but to perception in general: the world not only changes in a regular and patterned way when I am perceiving it, but also between the gaps in my perceptions. [M] explains this by the existence of material objects which are independent of my perceptions, which change according to fixed laws and which cause my perceptions. It appears that literally millions of coincidences have been given a unitary explanation.

If [I] entailed that each time I reopen my eyes or reach again to touch something, God remembers how it looked or felt to me before and gives me sense impressions which fit in with that, then it would be a considerably worse explanation: for each gap in anyone's perception, God would have to decide separately to keep up the regularity, and there is no explanation why he makes this decision every time. It is far from clear that his being benign would help here. But [I] need not make such claims, for God could form general intentions about how perceptions vary over time, including over gaps in perception, which general intentions would explain all the numerous particular cases. And now we can compare the theories for simplicity: where [I] has general plans or intentions of God's, [M] has the laws of matter. Both regard these plans or laws respectively as unexplained brute fact. Each is equally good at reducing unexplained coincidences, but [M] also has to introduce the extra ontological and ideological complexity already discussed.

It is also worth noticing that a criterion of simplicity in terms of unexplained coincidences is not quite straightforward. Some coincidences are bigger coincidences than others. Thus, for example, if I meet a long-lost friend by a coincidence such as our both happening to go on holiday to the same place at the same time, that is less of a coincidence than if I had also been reminded of him just before the holiday by accidentally coming across an old photograph. So it might seem that we have not really improved on a theory which has many small coincidences when we give an alternative which has one big coincidence. Coincidences are, of course, cumulative, but how they accumulate is very sensitive to how one describes them.

What Mackie overlooks is that the existence of matter, in a form which enables it to explain away the coincidences he finds in our perceptual experience, is itself due to some very big coincidences at the beginning of the universe. Of course, if we accept the existence of stable matter and then discover that its existence depends upon a huge coincidence in the initial conditions at the start of time, then we may be able to live quite happily with that coincidence. But if we are comparing immaterialism with a theory which says that, owing to a very big coincidence at the beginning of time, matter exists, then materialism introduces more unexplained coincidence than it removes.

4.4.3.2 Seven objections and replies

We shall see much more of the power of the immaterialist position here if we consider it in the light of some objections that might reasonably be made. The seven I shall consider seem to cover all of the major sources of concern and the replies make clear how to respond to any further objections.

(1) *The existence of God is independently implausible.* If one starts from an inclination towards atheism, [I] is considerably less plausible than [M]. Crudely, someone might think that the existence of God is so improbable that any difficulties encountered by alternative explanations are easily outweighed.

This objection underestimates Berkeley in two respects. First, the Berkeleian inference to the best explanation is simultaneously trying to prove immaterialism and theism: it is giving us an independent reason to believe in God which should undermine our atheism. Secondly, the objection takes inference to the best explanation as inference to the most probable explanation, but this is to get things precisely the wrong way around. Such inferences are ways of *assessing* the relative probabilities of various explanations: if those probabilities were antecedently fixed, then the inference would amount to no more than the redundant 'x is most probable, therefore x is most likely to be true'. Rather, inference to the best explanation must take some other features of each explanation and from these deduce their relative probabilities. So the objection amounts to the expression of a preference for an atheistic world-view, but Berkeley is giving an argument for a theistic one. The possibility of immaterialism without God is discussed in 4.5.

There is also the possibility of turning the objection against the materialist. Physics, realistically construed, tells us that of all the possible universes, very few would be such as to support persistent physical objects such as planets, let alone human life. The existence of this universe is extremely improbable, when one considers the alternatives. It has been argued that this raises the question of why this universe exists, rather than any other, a question which [M] is incapable of answering. The hypothesis of matter with a certain law-governed character cannot explain the existence of that matter.

(2) *Goes against scientific disenchantment of nature.* During the century before Berkeley was born, the scientific understanding of the world had become prominent by its startling success. Modern science had been born, and nature had become disenchanted: to answer the question of why some event occurred, we must look to its causes; consideration of the possible purpose or effects of a natural event is irrelevant. Surely [I] is incompatible with this, because it suggests that everything which happens in the natural world is willed by some rational being as a means to his (possibly inscrutable) ends?

While I suspect that Berkeley himself intended to fight a rear-guard action against the disenchantment of nature, it is possible for the Berkeleian to avoid this charge. The disenchanted picture is one of mindless objects or events blindly following causal laws. To say that every happening is willed by God for some specific pur-pose *would be* to re-enchant nature, for then understanding of the natural world would not best progress by the search for causes and causal laws, but rather by consideration of and speculation about God's purposes. But the Berkeleian need not say this, as we have already seen, for he can say that God's volitional strategy was to introduce certain laws governing the perceptions of humans. He does not need matter to enact these laws since, having willed the laws and being logically omniscient, he knows and thus wills all the consequences. Given [I], the success of modern scientific method is evidence that God has chosen to cause our experiences in this law-governed manner, rather than piecemeal.

(3) *Nothing could explain regularities better than matter, which is essentially stable and subject only to law-governed change.* This objection arises as a response to the argument that we can expect actions to display a pattern, but we cannot in the same way expect matter to be law-governed. The objector claims that matter is essentially stable and law-governed, that is part of its nature.

If such a philosopher meant by 'matter' *whatever has sufficient stability to explain the regularities in experience*, then matter would be stable, but there would be no reason to believe that it is not mental, i.e. that it is unthinking. So let us assume that matter is by definition unthinking. Now we face a dilemma, for either matter is, also by definition, stable or we need evidence that it is stable. The only evidence that it is stable could come from the regularities in experience, but the status of that as evidence depends upon the contested hypothesis that matter is the cause of experience.

So we are left with the hypothesized source of experience being by definition unthinking and stable. But now the immaterialist is in a very good position, for we have (introspective) evidence that there are thinking things with consistent, stable volitional strategies, but we have no evidence at all that there are or could be things which fulfil the materialist's definition of matter. To see why this makes immaterialism a better explanation, compare two explanations of noises in the night. One explanation would be ghosts, i.e. bodiless, non-physical agents, while the alternative would be the effects of temperature change on the materials of which the house is made. We know that there are materials which expand and contract in response to sudden temperature changes, the contraction of which on a cold night could cause noises. However, we have no independent reason to believe that there is or could be anything which fulfils the definition of a ghost.

(4) *Minds are material.* One objection which is unlikely to have occurred to Berkeley is that he has illegitimately assumed that minds are immaterial. If minds are part of the material world, then the data to be explained already commit us to the existence of matter. But we must again be careful what we mean by matter here. If it is just 'unthinking . . . substance' (*DHP2* 216), then there is no need to prove that minds are immaterial. If matter is meant to include the brain, then that is an object of perception (idea), not a perceiver (spirit), and Berkeley does have reasons why we cannot identify the two (*DHP2* 209). Which is not to say that the fixed order of nature cannot include regular connections between what happens in brains and what people experience. We know that it does.

Suppose that the mind is material in some other sense, then Berkeley has no objection to saying that ideas are caused by matter in that sense, because such matter is mental. Of course, someone might say that we do not need to assume that because some matter is mental, all is. Berkeley has overlooked the possibility of a view which holds that there is just one kind of substance, namely matter, but only some of it thinks. However, that possibility does not help [M], since (*a*) for the reasons outlined above, it is still a better explanation that our experiences are caused by thinking rather than unthinking 'matter', and (*b*) we have no evidence that anything is or could be the same sort of substance as a mind and yet *not* think.

(5) *There is no justification for talk of God, with all the associated theology.* Berkeley thinks that God explains 'the constancy and truth of things, *which secures all the concerns of life*', but to explain this

we need to attribute to God not only power and rationality, but also benevolence towards mankind, and [I] does not license those further claims. Now Berkeley himself may not have thought that introducing the Christian God added anything to the idea of a being omnipotent with respect to the physical world: to prove the existence of one was to prove the existence of the other. But we can clearly see the possibility of a malevolent being in complete control of the physical world.

The immaterialist ought simply to accept that [I] alone does not provide grounds for belief in the Christian God. So the counterfactual commitments of [I] need only be that any possible course of experience will follow some pattern, which pattern may or may not be detectable by human beings and may or may not be conducive to their well-being. Any stronger claims ought to fall within the realm of natural theology, not metaphysics. The existence of some sufficiently powerful, rational mind is a matter for inference to the best explanation. Further claims as to the nature of that being need further evidence. There is no reason for the theism involved in [I] to have any religious consequences.

(6) *We cannot form a coherent conception of a spirit capable of causing ideas in us.* This is the most serious objection. It appears that in our own experience we only encounter a mind causing itself to have ideas by exercising the imagination, and on the basis of this, according to Berkeley, we form a conception of an all-powerful mind capable of putting ideas into other less powerful minds like ours. It is crucial to the claim of ideological parsimony that [I] explains experience in terms understandable from our own case. The objection is analogous to Wittgenstein's concern that we could not form a conception of pain purely from our own case as something others might experience:

If one has to imagine someone else's pain on the model of one's own, this is none too easy a thing to do: for I have to imagine pain which I *do not feel* on the model of pain which I *do feel*. That is, what I have to do is not simply to make a transition in imagination from one place of pain to another. (*Philosophical Investigations*, § 302)

The objection Berkeley faces is that to conceive of another mind he has to do more than conceive of himself doing something different. He has somehow to conceive of ideas he is not aware of on the model of ideas he is aware of.

What Berkeley seems entitled to in describing our own case is a distinction between the voluntary and the involuntary, between what we do and what happens. What we do includes imagination, which is bringing ideas before our own minds, and action. God's putting ideas in our minds cannot be understood on the model of imagination, for imagining is essentially private: we have no understanding of what it would be to imagine something so that someone else experienced it. Even the idea of direct knowledge of what someone else is imagining is dubiously coherent, but what Berkeley would need is something even odder than that.

So we have to understand God putting ideas into our minds on the model of our acting. Now, it is true that I can put ideas into other people's heads. For example, if I now type ORANGES, you will think of oranges. And if I take something out of my pocket in front of an observer, then I give the observer some ideas of, say, a pen. But the materialist will object that in all these cases I can only put ideas into the heads of others *by doing something else*. If God can only put ideas into our heads by doing something else, then [I] collapses into [M], for what he does must be to cause something other than ideas in minds.

It is also far from clear that Berkeley is entitled to talk of our putting ideas into other minds by doing something else. The obvious thing we might be doing is putting ideas in the mind of God, which he then puts in others' minds. We are able to put ideas into God's mind because he is omniscient and knows what we are trying to do. But this would have the consequence that we are never actually able to do things ourselves: that we try and God does it for us.

There is here a general difficulty about how Berkeley is to account for action. In order to distinguish doing something from merely imagining it he needs to say that action, unlike imagination, is public. When I imagine drinking coffee, I have the ideas of lifting the cup to my lips and tasting the warm, bitter fluid. When I actually drink coffee, not only do I have these ideas, but so do other people. They see me lift the cup and perhaps hear me swallow.

There are two obvious problems: (a) no one else has the experience of the taste of the coffee, yet it was not imagined, and (b) as a matter of fact, I am alone in my study and no one saw me drink. On the first point, Berkeley will refer us back to his discussion of the act–object model of perception, where it was made clear that tasting the coffee is not something I do, for it is having a perception and perceiving is entirely passive (*DHP1* 194–7). On the second point, he could appeal to an omniscient God, but this God would know just as well what I have imagined as what I have done. Better would be to find a distinction between sense perception and imagination which would allow him to say, without circularity, that in acting I cause perceptions in my mind and others. The others would still be needed to cover the full scope of what we are able to do.

Whether Berkeley is able to give a cogent account of action will be discussed in more detail in Chapter 6. For present purposes we can summarize that discussion by saying that if he is able to give an adequate account of action, it will have the consequence that we *do* have the ability to put ideas into other minds directly, i.e. not just by doing something else. It will also allow him to solve the problems of other minds and free will. We know about other minds because not all our perceptions come from God: some come from other humans. If we have such an ability to act, then God's will does not fully determine everything that happens in the physical world. This is not in conflict with there being laws of nature, i.e. exceptionless generalizations, since God's intentions could be of the conditional form: if x does such-and-such, then y will happen.

(7) *We cannot form a coherent conception of an omnipotent being.* First, we should note that [I] commits us only to a being omnipotent with respect to the physical world, but that still causes problems. It has sometimes been argued that there is a fundamental incoherence in the concept of omnipotence, but I want to concentrate on an objection specific to Berkeley. He thinks that he can form a conception of an omnipotent being on the basis of his own experience of his limited agency. The objection is that our ability to act is necessarily limited by the fact that we act with our bodies on our spatially and temporally local environment. God, in contrast, has no body and no location, but far from explaining his omnipotence, this makes it puzzling how he can act at all, since what we understood by agency in our own case essentially involved a located body. The important point here is the connection between action and spatial location. And it follows from this connection that our agency is necessarily limited: because we must act at a point in space, what we are able to do is constrained by our spatial location. The objection is then that if we try to form a conception of omnipotence by removing the constraint, then we also lose the idea of acting at a place and thus of acting at all.

What the objection assumes, which the immaterialist will question, is that our conception of ourselves as located is independent of our agency. If the concept of agency is going to involve the concept of spatial position, then the concept of spatial position had better not depend upon agency. In an earlier book, the *New Theory of Vision*, Berkeley simply denied this, arguing that no single sense modality gives spatial information, that we regard seen things as located in space purely in terms of whether we can or cannot touch them. The notion of what we can touch clearly presupposes action. For the account of spatial position to be non-question-begging, such actions as reaching out and walking towards must be given non-spatial interpretations.

Abstracting from the details, which are going to be tricky, the response is that there is a conceptual connection between action and spatial position, but it does not constrain our concept of action in the way the objector envisaged. Action is not determined by location, but location is determined by action. The objection has usefully drawn our attention to a commitment of [I], namely that human action is only contingently limited, that the will is of its nature able to do anything but in practice constrained by God to operate within a limited sphere.

There is a tendency of Berkeley's critics to push objections (1) and (3), but this is a mistake because he is on strong ground here. Much more troublesome are (6) and (7). What they reveal is that, although Berkeley is not a solipsist, for he does believe in the existence of more than just his own mind and what he experiences, he is limited to the conceptual resources of the solipsist. In the next chapter we shall look at Berkeley's official argument for the existence of God, and the role that God plays in his metaphysics. This will allow us to fill in more details of the system before returning, in Chapter 6, to the question of whether the responses to objections (6) and (7) can really be made to work.

4.5 Immaterialism without God?

Despite all the arguments just presented, there is still a resistance to Berkeley's philosophy merely on the grounds that it is theistic. It seems that in our secular age many people would simply *prefer* to believe in a godless universe. Of course, we should not confuse what we want to be true with what we have grounds to believe, but nor should we ignore these stubborn inclinations. On the one hand, they sometimes help us take a more critical view of our assumptions, and on the other, philosophy does not only answer to our rational natures. So it is worth asking whether an atheistic immaterialism is possible, and it turns out that the price of atheism is solipsism.

The question of choosing between [I] and [M] was set up so that there were no other alternatives, but the atheist might avoid both [I] and [M] by denying that we need to supplement the basic picture at all. He might simply say that the involuntariness and regularity of experience are brute facts which have no explanation.

4.5.1 *The Regress of Explanations*

It does not take much reflection to see that if we explain some phenomenon by citing a fact, then the explaining fact becomes itself something in need of explanation. All we can do to explain the explanans is to cite another fact, and we have set off on a regress which threatens to be infinite.

There are various attitudes one can take to this regress. One is to point out that if the past is infinite, we might expect there to be an infinite series of explaining facts. Then no explanation is or ever could be complete, but this is not a problem unless we assume that explanations, to be any good, must be complete. Even if we can never give a complete explanation, it does not follow that all attempts at explanation are pointless; in fact some partial explanations are better than others, and any partial explanation is better than none.

This is a perfectly reasonable attitude to take, but it rests on two assumptions. The obvious assumption is that the past is infinite, that for every past moment there is an earlier moment. Less obviously, it has also been assumed that all explanations proceed by citing prior facts, presumably causes. But this is not true of much of the explanation we seek. For example, one explanation of why the sun rises in the east and sets in the west is that the earth rotates anti-clockwise, roughly on its north–south axis. This is a small-scale example of explaining regularities by citing other regularities.

It is explanatory because the fact of the earth's rotation accounts for more than just where the sun rises. The search for ever more fundamental physical laws is a paradigm of this sort of atemporal explanation. Appealing to the infinite past does not solve our difficulty about a regress here.

If the past is finite, if there is a first moment of time, then there are some facts without explanations. The second attitude to the regress says that it stops with brute facts which have no further explanation. These brute facts may be the initial conditions of the universe at the beginning of time, or the most fundamental laws of physics, or both. The problem here is that if one explains a phenomenon in terms of the ultimately inexplicable, then one does not seem to have done any explaining at all.

The third attitude stops the regress not with the inexplicable but with the self-explanatory. The exact character of the self-explanatory can be debated, but it is not hard to see that it must exist necessarily and either be uncaused or self-causing. In other words, it will be very much like God. For those who find the first and second attitudes unacceptable, the third provides a familiar route to the existence of God.

Now [I] and [M] are both neutral on how to react to the regress of explanations. The God of [I] is physically omnipotent, which means his existence cannot be explained in physical terms, but this falls short of being self-explanatory. The matter of [M] may have an infinite history, may be brute, or may be explained by a self-explanatory necessary existent. (Hylas piously takes the third option.) The most promising route for an atheistic materialism is to take the second attitude to the regress of explanations, so we should now explore what happens if the immaterialist takes this attitude.

4.5.2 Suppose This is as Good as it Gets

A proponent of [M] might well accept that the regress of explanations stops when we find the most fundamental laws of matter.

Perhaps $e = mc^2$ and there is no further explaining this fact: the universe could have been different, but that is how it is. But then we can ask why it is that the involuntary and patterned nature of our sense experience needs explaining, but the basic laws of physics do not.

This attitude is more plausible with respect to the regularities and patterns in experience than its source. The immaterialist says that in sense perception we experience the physical world, which is as it seems and seems as it is. The character of the physical world is contingent, and if we are forced by the regress of explanations to accept that some contingent facts are inexplicable, that the best we can say is that they could have been different but are not, then we might as well accept the bruteness of the patterns we encounter in experience. If I close my eyes and then open them again, the scene I see is almost unchanged. It *might* have changed in all sorts of ways, but the world turns out not to be like that. Each time I open my eyes I am going to see something (even if it is just total darkness), each time I reach out I shall feel something (even if it is just empty space). The suggestion we are considering is that if what I see or feel conforms to my expectations based on past experience, then that is just a contingent fact about the world which we cannot explain.

It does not follow that science is redundant. We quickly discover that the patterns in experience are subtle and complex, that apparent exceptions to the regular order are actually consistent with some deeper regularity. Describing these deeper regularities may require us to talk of things other than the objects of experience, but as we saw in 4.3, the immaterialist can and must take an instrumentalist attitude towards such talk. If we want to explain the existence of regular patterns in experience, then we need either matter or God, but if we are prepared to accept the contingent nature of the physical world as brute fact, then an atheistic immaterialism looks promising.

We are left with the involuntariness of experience. The equivalent attitude here is that we cannot control our sense experience because when we perceive we simply perceive what is there to be perceived. Perception is a relation to something, and we can only stand in that relation to what exists. The difficulty for the immaterialist here is that what exists, the sensible things, are mind-dependent, they are necessarily perceived. So perception is not a relation to what is there anyway, rather what is there to be perceived comes into existence at the moment of perception, and yet its being perceived does not cause its existence. If we accepted this as brute, we would be accepting 'the repeated springing into existence of complex groups of appearances remarkably like other groups which had passed out of existence before' (Mackie, *Problems*, 65). If the sensible things do spring in and out of existence, then there is no more problem in accepting as unexplained fact that they do not do so randomly than there is in accepting regularities in matter. The real problem is that we do not find continuous existence in need of explanation, but we would like, if possible, to explain things coming into existence. The best line for an atheistically inclined immaterialist to take is simply to reject this intuition: the continuous existence of matter is just as much or as little in need of explanation as the coming to be of sensible things.

It is interesting to note that Berkeley appears to follow Descartes, Malebranche, and 'the Schoolmen' (*PHK* 46) in thinking that continuous existence is just as much (or as little) in need of explanation as creation (see the first letter to Johnson, paragraph 3, which is discussed in Chapter 5).

4.5.3 *Solipsism*

By simply denying that the phenomena discussed in 4.4.2 need any explanation, it is possible to be an atheist immaterialist. Of course, without God the immaterialist cannot account for existence unperceived by us in terms of what God perceives or intends. Such an attitude also seems to lead to a form of solipsism, for if we deny the need to explain natural events as the actions of another (infinite) spirit, then it is groundless to explain human behaviour as the actions of another (finite) spirit.

The only way for the atheist to avoid this solipsism is to argue that those parts of our experience we classify as human behaviour have a special character which distinguishes them from the natural world and licenses the inference to their being actions, without requiring us to see every event as an action. It is hard to see what this could be, for even contra-causal free will will not do the trick. Suppose it was discovered that human behaviour produced exceptions to the physical laws. While it would be very tempting to explain this by saying that the human behaviour is caused by the will of a free agent, we could equally say that it has turned out that physical laws have localized exceptions, that this is a contingent but ultimately unexplainable fact about the nature of the physical world. To find agency we would have to appeal to an argument by analogy: from my own case I know that some of the exceptions to the physical laws are caused at my volition, so I can reasonably suppose that others have the same explanation. If this is an inductive argument, it is incredibly weak, being a generalization from a single case, and if it is intended to be an inference to the best explanation, then it will not appeal to an immaterialist who has already rejected such arguments when used to introduce either matter or God.

4.6 Conclusion

The major premiss for Berkeley's arguments against the existence of matter is his idealism, namely the thesis that the objects of sense perception are mind-dependent. Materialist explanations of sense experience are very tempting, but when we look hard at them, they do not look like very good explanations at all. Or to be precise, they do not look very good on certain formal measures, compared with Berkeley's explanation in terms of a mind more powerful than ours. At this point in the debate, we reach a parting of ways. Some people find the postulation of a superior intelligence explanatory, and others fail to see how it can explain anything. The latter group are the ones who find the workings of human minds deeply puzzling and in need of explanation. If it is mysterious how a mind can act on the physical world at all, then postulating God will not help to explain our sense experiences. What the Berkeleian arguments force the materialist to accept is that postulating matter will not explain much either. For on the one hand, any mystery that surrounds the ability of mind to act on the world will also surround the ability of matter to cause experiences in minds (*DHP2* 210), and on the other, the ability of matter to cause things is not well understood itself. If we refuse to accept mentalistic explanations, then we may have to accept that there is no explanation at all of our sense experiences. The deep attraction of Berkeley's position is that it takes the intelligibility of our own agency, which is something we rarely question, as given and then shows how we can use it as a model to explain our sense perceptions. And by doing this he avoids all pressure to accept the existence of a material world of which our experiences are a mere shadow, a claim which he sees as inevitably leading to scepticism of one sort or another. And he has equally, but separately, argued that we do not have any reason to believe in a material substance or substances in which sensible qualities inhere.

Appendix: The So-Called Master Argument

Students of Berkeley's philosophy often devote much time and intellectual energy to the argument which appears at *DHP1* 200 and *PHK* 22–3 to the effect that it is impossible to conceive an unconceived tree. Since a famous paper by André Gallois, this has been known as the Master Argument. The reasons for all this attention are that (*a*) the stakes are high, since Berkeley says 'I am content to put the whole upon this issue', and (b) the argument seems obviously wrong, but it is hard to pin down the exact mistake.

The first thing to note is that Berkeley only ever explicitly endorses a single conditional relating conceivability and his immaterialism:

> If you can conceive it possible for any mixture or combination of qualities, or any sensible object whatever, to exist without the mind, then I will grant it actually to be so. (*DHP1* 200)

> [I]f you can but conceive it possible for one extended moveable substance, or in general, for any one idea or anything like an idea, to exist otherwise than in a mind perceiving it, I shall readily give up the cause. (*PHK* 22)

The 'Master Argument' aims to show that the antecedent of this conditional is false, and thus has no implications whatsoever for the consequent. As it stands in the texts, it is not an argument *for* immaterialism, but a reply to an objection. Berkeley probably did think that what was inconceivable was impossible, and thus that proving the inconceivability of sensible things existing without the mind was sufficient to prove the impossibility, but he chose never to make that inference in print, preferring always to argue for his immaterialism in different ways. So if that were his master argument, it would also be his secret or hidden argument. Furthermore, the argument only aims to show that one cannot conceive of *sensible* things existing without the mind, and thus has no bearing on forms of materialism which hold that matter is imperceptible. Arguments against that form of materialism are reserved for the Second Dialogue.

Yet the stakes are still high, for if the antecedent is true, then Berkeley's immaterialism is, by his own word, shown to be mistaken. If we are to understand why Berkeley found the argument so convincing, we must begin with a small clarification. What he is alleging cannot be done is conceiving a sensible thing, i.e. an idea or a collection of ideas or a part thereof, which is 'without the mind', and by that phrase he must mean an idea (or collection of ideas) which is not present to a mind, which is not sensed or imagined or dreamt, or desired or willed or feared or in any other way related to a mind. If this is taken as arguing for the inconceivability of an *unperceived* thing, then perception must be being taken as encompassing more than just sense experience. In particular, an idea which is imagined or conceived is perceived in the relevant sense.

It is sometimes claimed that Berkeley's argument simply collapses or runs together conceiving and perceiving. As we shall see, Berkeley's argument does address a notion of conceiving which is very similar to his notion of sense perception, but he would be grossly inconsistent if his argument involved the claim that conceived or imagined ideas are perceived by sense (see Pappas, *Berkeley's Thought*, 135). Sensation is involuntary, imagination and conception are voluntary. Therefore, any idea which is imagined is under my voluntary control and by definition not perceived by sense. So whatever might be wrong with his argument, it is not the mistake of saying that conceiving something always involves perceiving it *by sense*. Rather, conceiving something involves having the ideas before the mind, and is thereby a species of perception on the broadest understanding of that term.

The infamous argument runs thus (*DHP1* 200):

PHILONOUS   How say you, Hylas, can you see a thing which is at the same time unseen?

HYLAS   No, that were a contradiction.

PHILONOUS   Is it not as great a contradiction to talk of *conceiving* a thing which is *unconceived*?

HYLAS   It is.

PHILONOUS   The tree or house therefore which you think of, is conceived by you.

HYLAS   How should it be otherwise?

PHILONOUS   And what is conceived, is surely in the mind.

One immediate worry about this is that the analogy with seeing is a sophism. 'See' is a success verb: it is a matter of definition that you cannot see what is not there, but surely you can seem to see what is not there. So suppose I have a hallucination in which I seem to see my dog, and my dog is in fact alone and unseen at the time. Then I seem to see something which is unseen. Since I can equally conceive something which is not true, e.g. that it is now sunny, surely the correct analogy is with seeming to see, and not with seeing?

Unfortunately this plausible line of reasoning forgets the philosophical context in which Berkeley presents the argument. In particular, it forgets that Berkeley held that the content of a sense experience, i.e. *how* things seem to us, is fully determined by the object of that experience, by *what* we experience. As I argued in Chapter 3, he thought that this was the obvious, default understanding of perception, any deviations from which needed to be justified. So to see something *as red* just is to see something *that is red*. There is no other way of seeing something as red, or tasting something as sweet, except by seeing something which is red or tasting something which is sweet. Furthermore, if the thing you see, the object, is red, then you see it as red (though you may pay little or no attention to its colour), and if it is sweet, then you taste it as sweet. It follows that if I seem to see my dog, then there is a dog, or rather a cluster of dog-like qualities, which I do in fact see. My mistake would be to take those qualities to be part of the collection which is my dog, and that is a mistake of judgement, not perception. So, if one wants to say that one can seem to see (as opposed to judging that one sees) something which is unseen, one must reject everything Berkeley says about perception.

Let us grant Berkeley that in sense experience the object perceived fully determines the content of the experience, how it is perceived. We can then define a notion of conception, call it *d*-conceiving (for direct conception), for which a parallel thesis is true: the content of a *d*-conception is fully determined by the properties of the object (i.e. idea) *d*-conceived. If one is to *d*-conceive something red, then one must have a red idea in mind, and similarly for any other qualities. So if one is to *d*-conceive an object which is not 'in the mind' or perceived, then the idea one has in mind in that act of *d*-conceiving would have to have the property of being 'without the mind' or unperceived. One cannot perceive an idea which is not perceived, hence one cannot *d*-conceive something which exists without the mind. If all conception were *d*-conception, then Berkeley's argument would be sound.

There is much conception and thought which is not *d*-conception, namely conceiving that such-and-such is the case. The content of *t*-conceiving (for conceiving *that*) is not fully determined by the ideas before one's mind (see Williams, 'Imagination and the Self'). So surely Berkeley's argument fails in full generality, since we can easily *t*-conceive something which exists without the mind? To which Berkeley's answer ought to be 'No and Yes'. We cannot *t*-conceive that an *idea* exists unperceived, for that is a simple contradiction. But we can *t*-conceive that a physical object exists unperceived, for that is just the common-sense belief that the table in my study continues to exist when I leave the room.

On one interpretation of Berkeley's metaphysics, the table only exists while I am out of the room in virtue of God perceiving it. In Chapter 5 I argue that there are many problems with giving this role to God, but if it could be made to work, then Berkeley would have had a motive for arguing that one cannot *t*-conceive that the table continues to exist when unperceived by any mind. One of the major problems I note in that chapter is that the criterion of real existence for Berkeley is sense perception, and even if God perceives the table, he does not perceive it by sense. In Chapter 8 I give an alternative conceptualist account of physical objects which enables Berkeley to hold that the table continues to exist when unperceived by us, without committing him to its being perceived by God in those intervals. Roughly put, the idea is that our concept of a table is one that allows it to exist in certain conditions even when none of its component ideas exist. If that is right, then Berkeley does *not* want to deny that we can *t*-conceive that the *table* exists when unperceived by any mind. So the argument is not addressing that point at all.

We can see that Berkeley's so-called Master Argument is nothing of the sort. It is merely a response to an objection. Berkeley is prepared to admit that if the objection worked, it would be conclusive against him, so the stakes are high. The objection he has in mind is that we can *d*-conceive a sensible thing existing unperceived, i.e. without the mind. He is right that such a *d*-conception is impossible. The *t*-conception that an *idea* should exist unperceived is too obviously impossible to be worth discussing. What of the *t*-conception that a physical object exists unperceived by any mind whatsoever? On my interpretation of Berkeley he should allow that *t*-conception is possible, but on other readings he should not. This matter turns on the details of God's role in Berkeley's world, which is a subject he hardly discusses at all in the *Principles* and does not touch on until the Second Dialogue, where he proves God's existence. Put briefly, if we are looking for points of lasting interest in Berkeley's philosophy, we shall not find them in the 'Master Argument', and if we are looking to prove him wrong, we would do better to look elsewhere.

PART 3

CHAPTER 5

God: Causation and Dependence

5.1 The Puzzle

This chapter is about a puzzle that is produced by the introduction of God into Berkeley's metaphysics. The Inference to the Best Explanation (IBE) discussed in the last chapter, while certainly endorsed by Berkeley, is not his official argument for the existence of God. We find the official argument summarized thus (*DHP3* 240):

From the effects I see produced, I conclude that there are actions; and because actions, volitions; and because there are volitions, there must be a will. Again, the things I perceive must have an existence, they or their archetypes, out of my mind: but being ideas, neither they nor their archetypes can exist otherwise than in an understanding: there is therefore an understanding.

Now there appear to be *two* arguments here, for the use of 'again' suggests that Philonous is proving the same conclusion twice, but in two different ways. The first is a causal argument with the major premise that all causation is intentional action. This is much stronger than the IBE, but has a similar effect: God's role is to cause us to have sense perceptions. The second argument turns on the premiss that the objects of sense perception have an existence independent of my mind. This independence argument ascribes to God, rather than us, the role of sustaining or supporting sensible things.

It is this second argument which creates the puzzle, for it seems to commit Berkeley to the thought that sensible things are independent of being perceived by us, though dependent upon being perceived by God. The main arguments of the First Dialogue, in contrast, are directed towards the conclusion that sensible things depend upon being perceived by us.

This last point needs some defence, for *Philonous* never says that they depend upon being perceived by us but only upon being perceived by some mind. For example, at *DHP2* 212 he says:

To me it is evident, for the reasons you allow of, that sensible things cannot exist otherwise than in a mind or spirit.

So someone might argue that only *Hylas* is committed to the claim which conflicts with the argument for God's existence. At the one point where Philonous states the Berkeleian conclusion of the First Dialogue and then proceeds to argue for God's existence, he avoids saying that the sensible things he perceives depend upon being perceived by him. So perhaps there is no puzzle for Berkeley: the things we perceive are independent of us but dependent upon God.

While the text supports this interpretation, the logic of the arguments does not. In the passage just quoted, Philonous is accepting mind-dependence for the reasons that Hylas allows. So one of the things he is saying is that he accepts at least some of the conclusions that Hylas draws from the First Dialogue. Hence, the best way to investigate Berkeley's position is to look carefully at what exactly should be concluded from those arguments. In Chapter 3 I described the conclusion as the mind-dependence of sensible things. We now need to ask: dependent on which mind?

There were two main arguments in the First Dialogue, the Assimilation Argument and the Argument from Conflicting Appearances. According to the former, if a very great heat is a pain, then the heat I feel depends upon being perceived by me if and only if the pain I feel depends upon being perceived by me. It is my intuition that this very pain I feel could not exist if I did not feel it, that a pain felt by someone else, however similar, would be a different pain. From which it would follow that the heat also depends upon being felt by me. Such intuitions are not decisive, since some people disagree. What is really needed is a theoretical ground for relativizing sensations and sensible qualities to the subject, and that is provided by the Argument from Conflicting Appearances. Suppose that the sensible qualities I perceive are necessarily perceived by God but only contingently perceived by me. I perceive the water of the famous example to be both hot and cold. If the heat and the cold are only contingently perceived by me, then (assuming SMP) there exists, independent of me, some hot-and-cold-at-once water. But hot-and-cold-at-once water is impossible, so not even God could have created it. To put it bluntly, God's ideas cannot contain contradictions. Suppose, instead, that the sensible qualities perceived by me are necessarily perceived by me. Then what God creates is not impossible, for he makes it the case that *I feel* the water to be hot and cold at once. The qualities he creates are hot-for-me-now and cold-for-me-now, which being relativized to me are necessarily perceived by me.

The arguments of the First Dialogue do lead to the conclusion that sensible qualities are dependent not just upon some mind, but upon the mind which is the subject of the experience. Yet in the Second Dialogue, when arguing for the existence of God, Philonous keeps emphasizing that sensible qualities do not depend upon us who perceive them. So there *is* a puzzle.

There are two well-walked routes out of this puzzling situation. One is to say that the second, independence, argument is irrelevant to Berkeley's real position. In favour of this interpretation, we can note that only the causal argument appears in the *Principles*. Further, it has been alleged that the second argument contains an illicit slide from causal independence to some other form of independence. However, against this interpretation we can cite a number of references to the independence of sensible things which appear to have nothing to do with causation.

The second route out of the puzzle is to deny the importance of the arguments of the First Dialogue. In doing this, one might either say that Berkeley's apparent realism about sensible things leaves him with no decent argument for their mind-dependence, or that his real argument for mind-dependence is not based on the perceptual considerations of the First Dialogue but on thoughts about abstraction and conceivability. In favour of the claim that Berkeley does not in fact have an argument for mind-dependence we can again look at the *Principles*, which *begins* with the claim that the 'objects of human knowledge' are ideas, which implies mind-dependence. In favour of saying that Berkeley's argument is not based on perceptual relativity but conceivability, we can again look at the *Principles*, which has a lengthy introduction about abstraction and contains several apparent references to the relation between materialism and mistakes about what is conceivable. The reasons for rejecting this interpretation have been rehearsed in the last chapter. I discussed whether we should treat Berkeley, as opposed to Philonous, as committed to the soundness of the First Dialogue arguments in 2.2.

What is striking about these ways of escaping the puzzle is that they both take the *Principles* to be the primary text and the *Three Dialogues* to contain an internal inconsistency, which is presumably explained as a by-product of its populist objectives. The second route out of the puzzle goes so far as to take the arguments of the First Dialogue to be entirely *ad hominem*. Before resorting to such interpretations, we should explore the possibility that the *Three Dialogues* is the more mature work, which, though not doctrinally different, may include insights missing from the *Principles*. We shall see that this is exactly what has happened here, for in the *Three Dialogues* Berkeley operates with two types of dependence, which we can call perceptual and ontological dependence. This distinction gives him a new argument for God's existence. To reveal this aspect of Berkeley's thought, we need to address the following questions:

1. Do our perceptions depend upon God in some way other than merely being caused by him?
2. Do sensible things caused by God also depend upon being perceived by finite spirits?
3. How do sensible things differ from material things, which, if they existed, would equally be caused by God?

5.2 Causation

The core of the causal argument for the existence of God is the inference from 'I am not the cause of the ideas I perceive by sense' to 'Some other mind is the cause of my sense perception'. We know the premiss is true by contrasting sense perception with imagination, of which I am the cause. Berkeley makes the inference by using the major premiss that only minds are capable of causing anything. His reasons for holding this are not at all clear, for this seems to be one issue on which Hylas capitulates too early, perhaps through a misplaced sense of piety. Furthermore, an influential essay by John Stuart Mill has served to confuse the matter. Mill's essay credits Berkeley with 'clearly discerning this fundamental truth . . . that all we can observe of physical phenomena is their constancies of co-existence, succession, and similitude', but criticizes him for not extending the insight:

No one, before Hume, ventured to think that this supposed experience of efficient causation by volitions is as mere an illusion as any of those which Berkeley exploded. ('Berkeley's Life and Writings', 462)

Mill's thought seems to be that Berkeley, like Hume, failed to perceive any causal relations between the objects of sense perception, but, unlike Hume, claimed to observe a causal efficacy between minds and their actions. Apart from ignoring Malebranche, who thought that neither bodies nor finite spirits were true causes (*Dialogues* VII), this does an injustice to Berkeley by assuming that he would agree with Hume on the inability of *reason* to discern causal powers. Berkeley's philosophy blends elements of empiricism and rationalism, and this is one element of empiricism he does not endorse. Hume's argument is, roughly speaking, that causal relations are contingent and hence it cannot be a priori that *A* is such as to cause *B* (*Treatise*, I. iii. 3–6). It is only once one has rejected the thought that it is a priori that *A* has a given causal power that the point about the unobservability of causal powers is relevant. Unlike Hume, Berkeley never appeals to the observability or otherwise of causal powers, yet still takes the inefficacy of ideas to be obvious, which suggests that he does think it an a priori matter. Berkeley agrees that all relations between physical objects are contingent and that there is no observable causal efficacy between ideas. However, he does not accept the more general claim that causal relations, if there are any, are all contingent. On the contrary, it appears that he sides with Malebranche in thinking that causal relations, where they exist, are necessary. Berkeley disagrees with both Malebranche and Hume, because he thinks that the relation between a volition and an action is not contingent. Hume tries to persuade us that there is nothing about a cause, considered on its own, that allows one to predict the effect: we have to wait and see if bread is nourishing, if one billiard ball will bounce off another or stick to it, and so on. This is less plausible with respect to minds or spirits, because minds act by willing something to happen. If I form the volition to type a 'p', then we do not have to wait and see what the effect of this is. We know, a priori, that, subject to certain enabling conditions, the effect will be my typing a 'p'. All Hume's attacks on the ability of reason to discern causal efficacy are aimed at the physical world, and as such fail to address Berkeley's understanding of the causal efficacy of spirits. Once we realize this, the question of whether we have an introspective observation of our own causal power is irrelevant.

Malebranche thought that the connection between a human volition and the ensuing action was contingent because it might fail. If God wills something, it inevitably happens, but if I will something, it may not happen. Malebranche requires a cause to be logically sufficient for its effect, where Hume thinks that there is no logical connection whatsoever. Berkeley takes the intermediate position of thinking that a cause is sufficient for its effect, *ceteris paribus* (i.e. unless there are defeating circumstances). If there is to be mental causation, a volition must be sufficient for an action, so long as no other stronger cause intervenes to prevent the action.

So, according to Berkeley, it is not the unobservability of physical power that counts against physical causation, but the contingency of all physical relations; and it is not the observability of mental power that counts in favour of the causal efficacy of the mind, but the non-contingent relations between volition and action.

While Berkeley certainly has a point here, it does not in fact get him the conclusion he wants. It is true that the relation between a person's intentions or volitions and their actions is not contingent, for the intentions *rationalize* the action, they make it intelligible; but to draw the conclusion that only minds have causal efficacy would require Berkeley to assume that this rationalization or intelligibility makes the volition sufficient for the action, *ceteris paribus*. Good evidence for the sufficiency of volitions or intentions would be that one could predict someone's behaviour on the basis of what they were thinking and intending, and it looks as if we can and do make such predictions all the time and with a great degree of success. For example, if A intends to meet B over lunch, and A knows that B goes to the sandwich bar at 1 p.m., then we can safely predict that A will go to the sandwich bar at 1 p.m. In making this prediction we are relying on a general thesis to the effect that people usually do what they intend to do. It is essential to Berkeley's account of causation that this is not contingent. The usual argument to show that it is not contingent is that in cases where there are no defeating circumstances and yet someone fails to do what they apparently intended to do, we deny that they had the intention in the first place. If someone said that they intended to give up smoking straight away, and then two minutes later lit a cigarette, we would, all else being equal, deny that they ever had the intention in the first place. Since Berkeley is committed to saying that we do not always succeed in forming the volitions we try to form (6.1), he would probably have been prepared to argue for this claim.

In a slightly later work, *De Motu*, which was an essay entered for a competition on the causes of motion, Berkeley hints at a different reason for thinking that all causation is action by some mind or other. The premiss of this argument is the reassuringly empirical Newtonian principle that action and reaction are always opposite and equal. This principle, now known as Newton's 3rd law, appears to commit one to causal agency in physical objects, but Berkeley suggests that, properly understood, it does quite the reverse:

I, for my part, will content myself with hinting that that principle could have been set forth in another way. For if the true nature of things, rather than abstract mathematics, be regarded, it will seem more correct to say that in attraction or percussion, the passion of bodies, rather than their action, is equal on both sides. For example, the stone tied by a rope to a horse is dragged towards the horse just as much as the horse towards the stone; for the body in motion impinging on a quiescent body suffers the same [degree of] change as the quiescent body. . . . And that change on both sides . . . is mere passivity. It is not established that there is force, virtue, or bodily action truly and properly causing such effects. (*De Motu*, 70)

In Newtonian mechanics change is brought about by either percussion or attraction. When one body impacts upon another, then, holding mass constant, both bodies change degree and direction of motion. The changes are exactly proportional. Newton and Torricelli disagreed on whether there was a transfer of force from one body to the other, or whether the force in one was destroyed and a new force created in the other, but Berkeley wisely pointed out that these two theories were empirically equivalent (*De Motu*, 67). In our normal experience of attractive forces such as gravity, the difference in mass between the two interacting objects (my body and the earth) is usually so great as to obscure the 'equal and opposite reaction'. It would seem that my body is attracted to the earth, but not the earth to me. There is no practical way of preventing me from moving, which is what would be necessary to prove that the earth is attracted to me. However, in Newtonian mechanics the choice of inertial frame is purely pragmatic, so if we take my body (or its centre of gravity) as stationary, we can see that the earth *is* gravitationally attracted towards me.

It follows that, whenever two physical objects are related in such a way as to bring about change in one, there is just as much change brought about in the other. Thus, any physical-change relation, such as percussion or attraction, is *symmetric*. This is the empirical premiss of the argument. Next Berkeley claims that 'change on both sides is mere passivity'. The thought here is that causation, or causal agency, is not symmetric, that if *A* acts on *B*, it does not follow that *B* acts on *A*. If we grant this a priori premiss, we can validly conclude from Newton's laws that physical objects do not, in fact, causally affect each other.

Now Berkeley is certainly right that learning Newton's 3rd law comes as something of a surprise to most of us. But a little reflection quickly makes it plausible: if one billiard ball hits another, the first does not just continue as if nothing happened; the iron bar is pulled towards the magnet, unless we hold the bar stationary, in which case the magnet is pulled towards it; when hot and cold are brought into contact, the hot object cools and the cold one warms; and so on. We are so easily convinced by such examples, that it cannot be part of our concept of causation that when *A* causes a change in *B*, *A* never changes as a result.

However, Berkeley only needs a weaker claim, for the Newtonian principle is that there is *always* a reaction which is *equal* and opposite. Mundane examples do not establish either the universality or the equality. The 3rd law is contingent, so the issue is whether our concept of causation allows the *possibility* of equal and opposite reactions. And here Berkeley has a point: the causal relation is not completely symmetric.

Berkeley's implicit proposal is that the only way to understand the asymmetry between cause and effect is that the effect changes more than the cause. But there are two alternatives: the cause precedes the effect, or the effect is counterfactually dependent upon the cause but not vice versa.

To distinguish cause from effect by temporal order entails that backwards causation, and hence time travel, are logically impossible. This suggests one line of Berkeleian defence, though hardly one we can imagine Berkeley pursuing. The proposal also rules out simultaneous causation. However, in Newtonian mechanics the concept of a rigid rod, like that of perfect inelasticity, is coherent, and with a rigid rod we can easily construct examples of simultaneous causation. Finally, we need to ask what determines temporal order. Berkeley held that it was the subjective order of experiences. If that is correct, we can easily construct counter-examples to the claim that the alleged physical cause always precedes the alleged physical effect. Nor can the advocate of this proposal determine the temporal order by the causal order.

The proposal that cause is distinguished from effect by counterfactual dependence is also beset with difficulties. First, the counterfactual 'the effect would not have occurred had the cause not occurred' is only true if we hold the laws of nature and initial conditions constant. But then the converse counterfactual is also true. Consider, for example, switching on an electric light by pressing a button to make a connection. Given the laws and the initial conditions, the light would not have gone on had the connection not been made. But given those laws and those initial conditions, we can deduce from the light going on that a connection had been made, so the counterfactual relationship works in the other direction as well: were it the case that the light had remained off, then it would have been the case that there was no connection.

So, while Berkeley's main arguments about causation rest on the strong principle that all causes must entail their effects (*ceteris paribus*), he has another argument, based on Newtonian physics, that only needs the principle that causation is asymmetric. The conclusion of this argument is that if Newtonian mechanics is correct, there is no physical causation. The further conclusion that spirits do have causal powers needs an extra step. To make this further step we would need to show that Newton's 3rd law does not apply to the activities of mind. This has some plausibility for imagination, which gives the mind some efficacy, but perhaps less so for action.

The causal argument for the existence of God needs Berkeley to do a lot of work on the nature of causation. It is rather surprising that he does so little to defend his strong claim that only spirits have causal powers, since the philosophers he was most concerned to refute either thought that things other than spirits had causal powers (Descartes and Locke), or that spirits did not (Malebranche). And common sense, it would seem, sides with Descartes and Locke.

5.3 Independence

As well as the causal argument, we saw that Berkeley has a second proof. There are several passages in the Second and Third Dialogues where Philonous states or summarizes his argument for the existence of God without mentioning the key premiss of the causal argument, namely that only minds are active, are capable of causing anything (*DHP2* 212, 212–13, 214; *DHP3* 230, 240). The first statement of this argument is also the first argument for God's existence (*DHP2* 212):

PHILONOUS . . . To me it is evident, for the reasons you allow of, that sensible things cannot exist otherwise than in a mind or spirit. Whence I conclude, not that they have no real existence, but that seeing they depend not on my thought, and have an existence distinct from being perceived by me, *there must be some other mind wherein they exist.*

The argument expressed here is:

[1] Sensible things are mind-dependent. (Premiss)
[2] Sensible things depend not on my thought. (Premiss)
[3] Sensible things have an existence distinct from being perceived by me. (From [2])
[4] There is some other mind on which they depend. (From [1] and [3])

I take [2] to be the claim that perception is involuntary. The puzzle we face is how to interpret [3] so as to entail [4] but also be consistent with the First Dialogue's claim that sensible qualities perceived by me are necessarily perceived by me.

The first point to make is that [3] is not the modal claim that it is possible for the qualities I actually perceive to exist without my perceiving them. It may entail that modal claim, but is not itself such a claim, because it is unclear how one might justify the modal claim without, in the end, resorting to either matter or God. The involuntariness of perception alone does not prove modal independence. The move from my lack of control over what I perceive to its modal independence assumes that whatever determines what there is for me to perceive does so independently of whether I am in a position to perceive it or not. This would be true if matter caused our perceptions, since it is a deep feature of materialism that the existence and character of matter are indifferent to whether it is perceived or not, but not if God caused them, at least not if the interested, personal God of Christianity was the cause. While it is conceivable that an infinite spirit could cause our perceptions with a total indifference to this effect of his actions, that is hardly an assumption Berkeley wants to make in the course of arguing for the existence of God.

One non-question-begging ground Berkeley might have for asserting modal independence would be that when I cease to perceive something, sometimes others continue to perceive it. But this confuses physical things, which are undoubtedly independent of me, with the sensible qualities which compose them. That others continue to perceive the same object as me, e.g. a tree, does not entail that the sensible qualities I perceive when I perceive the tree have a continued existence. Even if, as Berkeley thinks, the tree is composed of sensible qualities, it can continue to exist even though some of its components do not. So [3] is not a modal claim.

It is, however, clear that Berkeley thinks his distinctness claim [3] follows from [2], for there are at least two other places where the argument is formulated in exactly the same manner (*DHP2* 214; *DHP3* 230):

Nor is it less plain that these ideas or things by me perceived, either themselves or their archetypes, exist independently of my mind, since I know myself not to be their author . . .

. . . it is plain they have an existence exterior to my mind, since I find them by experience to be independent of it.

These transitions presuppose that an effect is somehow not fully distinct from its cause. Sometimes this is described as an inference from causation to causal dependence, but it is a little misleading to talk of causal dependence, because all we can mean by that is simply *causation*. Causation is a process, which may take time but does not persist like the state of dependence, and once the process is over, the cause can cease to exist without changing the relation between cause and effect. So Berkeley's thought is that, *as well as being caused by them*, sensible things are also *dependent* in some other manner upon their causes, and that this dependence persists throughout their existence. We might say that, as well as being brought into existence, they need sustaining. This thought is strange to us, for we tend to think that most physical things are self-contained, that once caused to exist they have, as it were, a life of their own. The only contemporary models that we have for continual dependence are either biological or psychological, neither of which form of dependence seems to be a simple consequence of causation and in neither case is it bare physical existence, as opposed to life or health, which is dependent. But among Berkeley's philosophical predecessors it was commonplace that causation, in the sense of the creation of things, also involved dependency relations. We find a clear statement of this in part 1 of Descartes's *Principles of Philosophy* (§ 51):

By substance we can understand nothing other than a thing which exists in such a way as to depend on no other thing for its existence. And there is only one substance which can be understood to depend on no other thing whatsoever, namely God. In the case of all other substances, we perceive that they can exist only with the help of God's concurrence. . . . In the case of created things, some are of such a nature that they cannot exist without other things, while some need only the ordinary concurrence of God in order to exist.

The thought here is that only God fully satisfies the definition of substance because only God is self-causing. To be caused, to exist contingently, is to be a dependent being. Berkeley has simply extended this thought from substances to sensible qualities or ideas, which is not a particularly significant move for Berkeley, since he thinks of sensible qualities as particulars. Let us call the dependence of a thing created upon its creator ontological dependence, in contrast to the modal dependence discussed above. The transition from [2] to [3] is the obverse of the transition from createdness to ontological dependence.

Thus the contrast between the voluntary ideas of imagination and the involuntary ideas of sensation gives us two thoughts which each lead Berkeley to God. On the one hand, ideas of sense need a cause, which must be another mind, and on the other, since they have a cause distinct from myself, they must differ from ideas of imagination in ontologically depending on something distinct from me.

The second argument can be summarized: in experience we are aware of certain items (ideas) which are ontological dependants (not being self-creating), but are not dependent upon me, therefore there exists something else on which they depend. Since we are talking about ideas, which are mind-dependent, the only thing they could depend on would be a mind. Being a little more precise, we can see that the independence argument has the following structure, which is exhibited perfectly in none of its many statements but can best be seen at *DHP2* 214–15:

[1] Sensible things are mind-dependent/can only exist in a mind. (Premiss)

[2] Sensible things are ontologically dependent entities. (Assumption)

[3] My ideas of sense, unlike my ideas of imagination, are not ontologically dependent upon me/depend not on my thought. (Premiss)

[4] My ideas of sense are ontologically dependent upon something other than me. (From [2] and [3])

[5] My ideas of sense are dependent upon another mind. (From [1] and [4])

[6] Not all ideas depend upon finite minds. (Premiss)

[7] There is an infinite mind on which (some or all) ideas of sense depend. (From [5] and [6])

[8] God exists. (From [7])

There are three points we should question in this argument: the assumption [2], the inference to [5] and the inference to [8]. Against [2] we should ask whether things which contingently exist, such as sensible qualities, need be ontologically dependent on anything at all. Is it true that only a necessary existent does not presuppose the existence of something other than itself? Against the inference to [5] we should question whether the mind-dependence of sensible things established in the First Dialogue suffices to show that they can only be *ontologically* dependent upon minds. Perhaps sensible things depend upon minds in some ways, but not others; to be specific, perhaps they ontologically depend upon matter. And against the inference to [8] we should question whether Berkeley has established uniqueness, let alone the other theological qualities.

The assumption that contingent existents are dependent beings is common to Berkeley's argument and countless other proofs of the existence of God. Hume is often credited with being the first to challenge this assumption when he argued that it is not a necessary truth that everything has a cause. However, it may be a contingent truth, so it is not the assumption that our perceptions have a cause which we should question, but the assumption that in having an external cause, they are somehow dependent upon that cause. Talk of causal dependence gives us the impression that we understand this claim, but the dependence involved is more than mere causation. As I have already pointed out, causation is a process, but dependence a state. Of course everything is counterfactually dependent upon its cause, but that adds nothing to the thought that it has a cause. However, ontological dependence is also clearly distinct from perceptual or experiential dependence, as the case of pain makes clear. Pains, I take it, are perceptually dependent upon their subjects: there cannot be a pain if no one *feels* pain, and though God knows about our pains, he does not feel them, for that would be an imperfection (*DHP3* 240–1). So God's knowing about pains, even his perceiving them voluntarily, is not sufficient for there to be pains. Yet pains are not caused by ourselves (except indirectly) and thus, by the above argument, cannot be ontologically dependent upon us. If they are ontologically dependent upon anything, it must be God. What the example of pain shows is that perceptual dependence is not sufficient for ontological dependence, given that the latter can be inferred from the causal relation. It may, however, be necessary, which would account for Berkeley's reference to the ideas we perceive 'existing in' God's mind, a phrase he also uses to mean 'perceived by'. At *DHP2* 212 he appears to paraphrase the argument in a way that suggests that God must perceive everything:

sensible things do really exist: and if they really exist, they are necessarily perceived by an infinite mind: therefore there is an infinite mind, or God.

However, we shall see below that there are serious problems with this suggestion, so it is better to read this passage as using 'perceive' very loosely to include 'know about'. That God knows about our experiences looks like a fairly uncontroversial consequence of their being caused by him.

Given that ontological dependence is neither causation nor perceptual dependence, it is unclear what ontological dependence could be. The problem is that the secularized twenty-first-century conceptual scheme leaves no place for ontological dependence. In which case it is hardly surprising that there are connections between that concept and the existence of God, but such connections will not constitute a persuasive argument for God's existence. We would need to be given a reason to embrace a conceptual scheme which allowed for ontological dependence, and none has been given. This, I think, fairly precisely locates the source of the thought, common to many contemporary readers of Berkeley, that he takes the existence of God for granted. The truth is that Berkeley takes for granted a conceptual scheme in which there is a well-fitting niche for God. Berkeley makes explicit that his understanding of the dependence of the sensible world upon God is part of a long tradition in his first letter to Johnson. Within the context of a theological point about whether it is a greater sign of perfection to create a machine which runs on its own as opposed to one which needs continual attention, Johnson had put forward the modern conception of causation, and Berkeley responds by saying that created things are dependent in such a way as to need conservation (25 November 1729, numbered paragraph 3):

For aught I can see, it is no disparagement to the perfections of God to say that all things necessarily depend on Him as their Conservator as well as Creator, and that all nature would shrink to nothing, if not upheld and preserved in being by the same force that first created it.

And a few sentences beforehand: 'I am not . . . singular in this point itself, so much as in my way of proving it.' This notion of dependence on something as 'Conservator', as opposed to mere causal creation, generates ontological dependants. It is only if one can find grounds for applying such a concept at all that one will find a proof of the existence of God.

The second point to question in the independence argument is the inference from the mind-dependence of sensible things to their being ontologically dependent upon minds. To see that there is a slide here, remember that the mind-dependence of sensible qualities, as established in the First Dialogue, amounts to their being necessarily perceived. Now it is a premiss of the independence argument that sensible things perceived by me are *not* ontologically dependent upon me, which gives even more evidence that ontological dependence is distinct from perceptual dependence, and thus blocks the quick inference from perceptual dependence always being dependence on a mind to ontological dependence always being dependence on a mind.

There are two ways that Berkeley might justify this transition. First he might say that things are ontologically dependent upon their causes, and only minds are active, so sensible things can only be ontologically dependent upon minds. But this requires him to invoke the major premiss of the causal argument, making the dependence argument virtually redundant. Secondly he could argue the more specific point that it is unintelligible that unperceiving matter should be the cause of ideas, which are necessarily perceived. This point is rather cleverly raised by Philonous at the beginning of the Second Dialogue, in an otherwise rather weak discussion of 'the modern way of explaining things' (*DHP2* 210), and is restated at *DHP2* 215:

But how can any idea or sensation exist in, or be produced by, any thing but a mind or spirit? This indeed is inconceivable . . .

It is a fair point but weaker than Berkeley thinks, since the inconceivability here is just unimaginability, and we know from plenty of experience that new discoveries can allow us to imagine what was previously unimaginable. What Berkeley needs, if he is to have a demonstrative proof of the existence of God, is the claim that it is incoherent that there should be something other than a mind which produces ideas in us. Without that claim, the independence argument, though more elaborate, is no more persuasive than the inference to the best explanation discussed in the last chapter.

The main difference between Berkeley's independence argument and other philosophers' use of ontological dependence to prove the existence of God is that Berkeley does not invoke the impossibility of an infinite regress, since he thinks that ideas of sense are directly dependent upon God. However, he does need to say something to establish a *unique* being upon whom the sensible world depends. He appears to be offering a plug for this gap in the Third Dialogue (*DHP3* 230–1):

When I deny sensible things an existence out of the mind, I do not mean my mind in particular, but all minds. Now it is plain they have an existence exterior to my mind, since I find them by experience to be independent of it. There is therefore some other mind wherein they exist, during the intervals between the times of my perceiving them: as likewise they did before my birth, and would do after my supposed annihilation. And as the same is true, with regard to all other finite created spirits; it necessarily follows, there is an *omnipresent eternal Mind*, which knows and comprehends all things, and exhibits them to our view in such a manner, and according to such rules as he himself hath ordained, and are by us termed the *Laws of Nature*.

The reference here to the 'intervals between the times of my perceiving them' has fuelled speculation that Berkeley has here a third argument for God from existence unperceived. However, the argument comes in two stages: first it is argued that there are other finite minds, and then that there is an infinite mind. For Berkeley to allow that there are sensible things unperceived by me but perceived by other (finite) minds is just to make clear that he is no solipsist. At the second stage we see how, to prove the existence of God, he needs to claim that there are some sensible things which are not merely independent of me, but independent of all finite minds. However, this step does not require there to be existence unperceived by all finite minds, since what I am currently perceiving does not ontologically depend on me, and being alone in the room I have good reason to believe that it does not depend upon any other finite mind either. When he says 'the same is true, with regard to all other finite created spirits' he could be referring to the existence of sensible things during the intervals in my perceptions, before my birth and after my death, or he could be referring to their existence exterior to my mind. If the latter, then the argument does not take existence unperceived as a premiss and is just another version of the independence argument. Furthermore, it would be an obvious fallacy to infer from there being some things unperceived by finite minds which need a different mind to perceive them to the conclusion that that mind is 'omnipresent'. But omnipresence would plausibly follow from the premiss that all finite minds find their perceptions to be independent of them.

On neither premiss is the argument valid, for in both cases a plurality of non-human minds would do the job the argument assigns to a unique God. When I am alone, my ideas of sense do not depend upon me or upon any other finite minds *which I can recognize*, but that does not show they depend upon a unique, infinite mind. Equally, that there might be sensible things before the first and after the last human being does not entail that there are sensible things at times when no finite spirits exist. Quite simply, the most that the argument can prove is that there is at least one mind distinct from the human and animal minds which I recognize on normal empirical grounds.

5.4 Continuity

It has been suggested that the possibility of continuous existence of sensible things is a *consequence* of the independence argument. In a famous limerick Berkeley is taken to hold that when no human is about to see the tree in the quad, it still exists owing to God's perceiving it. This, as we shall see in Chapter 8, is a mistake, but the suggestion we need to consider now is whether the distinctness of sensible things commits one to their possible continuity unperceived. Clearly, if the premiss of the dependence argument was the *modal* independence of sensible things, then, assuming that our ceasing to perceive the tree does not cause its demise, it will continue to exist in the quad when no one is about. But the correct interpretation of the argument had ontological independence as a premiss, so we only get the conclusion of continuity if ontological independence entails modal independence.

This entailment has some plausibility when we are considering substances. Taking humans as an example, they are usually both ontologically and modally independent of each other. In the cases in which there *is* modal dependence, for example a 23-week foetus or Siamese twins with shared vital organs, it looks as if, in so far as we understand it, we should say that there is ontological dependence as well. However, Berkeley's argument does not focus on relations of ontological dependence between substances, but on the onto-logical relations between spirits and the qualities they perceive. In this case ontological does not entail modal independence. To make the point clear, consider pain. Berkeley would certainly hold that it is ontologically independent of the humans who feel it, because we do not create our own pains (except indirectly). Yet, as has already been remarked, it would be strange to think that my headache is modally independent of me, that it could exist without me.

The example of pain looks to be a special case which will not generalize when we remember that most sensible things, being persistent public objects like trees and chairs, are more like substances than qualities. However, Berkeley has argued (*DHP1* 174–5) that we only ever perceive qualities, so sensible things must be composites made up of sensible qualities. Sensible qualities, like the apparent colour of this handkerchief, are fleeting, qualitative particulars, and pain is a good analogy for them. The-look-of-the-handkerchief-to-me-now, regarded as a concrete particular, could no more exist without me than could my headache.

Furthermore, when contraposed the inference looks even less plausible: modal dependence does not entail ontological dependence, quite simply because there could be other explanations of modal dependence. For example, there are relations of modal dependence between mathematical objects and properties which carry no implication of creation or being sustained.

It is also of the first importance not to confuse physical objects with the qualities that make them up. The ontological independence of sensible qualities does not entail their modal independence, but that leaves wide open the question of whether we can truly say that there are physical objects unperceived by all finite spirits. A possible position would be that the sensible qualities actually perceived by finite spirits are modally dependent upon those finite spirits, but their ontological independence entails that the physical objects which they compose are modally independent of us.

5.5 Perceptual Dependence

So far we have established that apart from a purely causal argument for the existence of God, which, like the IBE, only invokes his role as the cause of our experiences, Berkeley also has an argument which turns on the independence from us of the things we perceive. This gives God a further role, of somehow supporting or sustaining sensible things. We have also seen that this ontological dependence is distinct from perceptual dependence and not inconsistent with sensible qualities also being necessarily perceived by us. God creates ideas, and thus ideas depend (ontologically) upon

God, but it is also of the essence of ideas that each is perceived by a particular mind or spirit at a particular time. What God creates is the green-of-the-grass-for-me-now, *not* the green of the grass which I happen to perceive now. We should probe the relation of perceptual dependence a little further. We know from the First Dialogue that sensible qualities must be dependent upon being perceived by a mind, but we do not really know why this is the case. This is made especially pressing when we see that ideas are not created by, are not ontologically dependent upon, the finite spirits that perceive them. If God creates ideas, i.e. sensible qualities, and they ontologically depend on God alone, what is there to stop him creating an idea which is unperceived? If we simply define 'idea' so as to make this impossible, the question becomes: why are we only able to perceive things which fulfil that definition? If God created something which was like an idea but did not fulfil that definition, why would that be necessarily imperceptible?

We get a better understanding of perceptual dependence when we remember that the perceptual relation is supposed to replace the inherence relation between a substance and a quality. The need for a quality to subsist or inhere in a substance was what lay behind one of the reasons for introducing matter (4.2). There are three main philosophical motivations for the traditional substance–accident distinction: to explain continuity through change, to give an account of predication, and to distinguish qualities belonging to the same object from ones merely coincidentally instantiated together. Berkeley is sympathetic to these motivations, but thinks that it is a great mistake, and a mistake which leads to materialism, to try to give a single solution to all three problems. With respect to physical objects but not minds, Berkeley has very innovative solutions for the first two problems: he is a conceptualist about identity and thinks that predication is a membership relation (see Chapter 8 for the details). Neither of these invokes a notion of substance even remotely similar to the traditional one. But Berkeley still needs to account for the difference between qualities belonging to a single object and qualities occurring unrelatedly.

Locke introduces substance thus:

> Because, as I have said, not imagining how these simple *Ideas* can subsist by themselves, we accustom our selves, to suppose some *Substratum*, wherein they do subsist, and from which they do result, which therefore we call *Substance*. (*Essay*, II. xxiii. 1)

Berkeley accepts the premiss, but finds that material substance sheds no further light upon how sensible qualities exist, given that they cannot 'subsist by themselves', since we do not have any clear grasp of how they subsist in matter. What is needed, rather, is spiritual substance which perceives the sensible qualities:

> That ideas should exist in what doth not perceive . . . is repugnant. But it is no repugnancy to say, that a perceiving thing should be the subject of ideas, (*DHP3* 233—1734 edn. only)

> Farther, I know what I mean, when I affirm that there is a spiritual substance or support of ideas, that is, that a spirit knows and perceives ideas. But I do not know what is meant, when it is said, that an unperceiving substance hath inherent in it and supports either ideas or the archetypes of ideas. (*DHP3* 234—1734 edn. only)

> It is therefore evident there can be no *substratum* of those qualities but spirit, in which they exist, not by way of mode or property, but as a thing perceived in that which perceives it. (*DHP3* 237)

As these passages make clear, Berkeley thinks that, setting questions of ontological dependence aside, there is no more that needs to be said about the nature of sensible qualities when it has been specified that they are perceived. The last is often read as a rejection by Berkeley of the thought that qualities exist in a substance, but in fact it only rejects material substrata and the inherence relation. The first 'but' should be read as 'except' rather than 'instead'.

We can re-express Locke's underlying thought by saying that if there were free-floating qualities, say a patch of yellow and a smell of rose (note I do not say 'a patch of yellow *here* and a smell of rose *there*'), we would not be able to describe the world. The qualities would be completely unrelated to each other, but just about any proposition worth expressing is going to state some relation between sensible things. Without the qualities being tied down to some frame of reference which allows them to be related, we simply cannot say whether there is, for example, a yellow rose or not. One option would be to tie them to places and times, but this is not an option for Berkeley, for whom space is an empirical construct out of experience, rather than something that could be given in experience and thus ground our judgements. Another, fairly hopeless, option is to tie them to unperceivable material substances. Berkeley's suggestion is that they are tied to perceivers and subjective time. If I see the yellowness and I smell the rose, then I can work out, by reference to what else I perceive, whether there is a yellow rose or not. If I see the yellow, and you smell the rose, we can go through a similar, though more complicated, process.

Free-floating qualities would not be qualities of anything, and it is this which Locke could not imagine. The traditional response, which Locke endorses, is to posit substances which both tie down the free-floating qualities by the inherence relation and are also the things which the qualities are qualities of. Berkeley finds the inherence relation unintelligible and has a different account of the objects of which these qualities can be predicated. So he ties down the free-floating qualities by relating them to the perceiving mind by the much less mysterious relation of perception. Because he is giving separate accounts of how the qualities are tied down and what they are predicated of, Berkeley is not committed to the absurd conclusion that the yellowness perceived by a mind is a quality of that mind (*DHP3* 237).

In Berkeley's thinking about dependence we find another reason for the structure of the *Three Dialogues*. In the First Dialogue it is argued that sensible qualities are dependent upon the minds that perceive them, that they are necessarily perceived. In the Second

Dialogue it is argued that sensible qualities depend upon God. This is clearly a different sort of dependence from that identified in the First Dialogue, and I called it ontological dependence. So this leaves us wondering about the nature of perceptual dependence. In the Third Dialogue we discover that sensible qualities, being qualities or attributes, must inhere in a substance, and they inhere in the mind that perceives them in virtue of being perceived by that mind. A world of unperceived ideas would be a world of free-floating qualities unrelated to each other.

5.6 The Existence of the Physical World

God causes ideas or sensations in us, which ideas perceptually depend upon us and ontologically depend upon God. That is one role for God. But as well as an agent, God is also a subject who has or perceives ideas. Since it is Berkeley's view that to be is to be perceived, we can ask whether God's status as a perceiver also plays a role in determining what exists.

One thing to note about the slogan 'esse is percipi' (PHK 3) is that Berkeley is talking about the existence of things other than minds, for minds are not themselves perceived. A second thing to note is that we should regard this as a thesis about real existence, as opposed to merely imagined existence. In which case it would seem that 'perceive' is being used to apply to sense perceptions, for an imagined unicorn does not thereby exist. Of course, if one imagines a unicorn, one must have ideas in mind, and those ideas must exist, but if one sees a unicorn, the ideas one has before one's mind have a rather different status, for they make up part of the physical world. It is the existence of things seen (and heard and felt) which Berkeley is concerned with, for there is no question that the existence of imagined ideas consists in their being imagined. So the slogan is best understood as saying that existence in the physical world consists in being perceived by sense. However, this may not apply for things perceived by God, in so far as they go to make up the physical world as well. There are several different ways one might elaborate on the slogan in order to make clear the role of God as a potential perceiver of the physical world.

(*a*) THE DISJUNCTIVE VIEW: *To be is to be perceived by us or by God*

Each idea can only be in one mind. So the ideas we perceive are not also perceived by God. Objects are composed of ideas 'actually imprinted' on our senses, but not perceived by God, and also of ideas had by God alone, which no finite spirit perceives.

(*b*) THE EXHIBITION VIEW: *To be is to be perceived by God and sometimes also by us*

Each idea can only be perceived by one *finite* mind, but God perceives all the ideas he causes in us. Objects are composed of ideas in the mind of God, some of which are shown/exhibited to us at God's will.

(*c*) THE REPRESENTATIVE VIEW: *To be is to be perceived by God*

Ideas can only be in one mind. The real world exists in God's mind and the ideas we perceive are not part of that world. Rather, God gives us ideas which represent those ideas or archetypes in his mind.

(*d*) THE REDUCTIONIST VIEW: *To be is to be actually or counterfactually perceived by us*

Truths about the physical world can be analysed or reduced to truths about how things seem to various people at various times, i.e. to which ideas are perceived. Claims about the unobserved must be reduced to claims about hypothetical observations. Only God's actions, not his perceptions, play any role in determining physical existence.

(*e*) THE POSSIBILIST VIEW: *To be is to be a possible object of our perception*

God creates the ideas which comprise the physical world, but while he knows about them he does not perceive them. All of them are possible objects of our perceptions. He does not determine which of those ideas we actually perceive, but leaves that to be a consequence of our free actions.

(*f*) THE SIMPLE VIEW: *To be is to be perceived by sense*

God has a general volitional strategy which entails, in conjunction with our free choices, what we will perceive at any given moment. God knows all the consequences of his volitions, so he knows what we perceive, though he does not perceive it himself. Thus God creates those ideas we actually perceive, but not those we might have perceived had we acted differently.

The first three views all hold that God perceives some or all of the ideas which constitute the physical world, whereas the last three all deny this. Rather they take the criterion of existence to be perception by us, the fourth and fifth supplementing our perceptions either with counterfactual truths or possible objects. These are clearly phenomenalist in their nature. The sixth view, the Simple View, neither appeals to God nor to possibilia to supplement our perceptions and thus appears to lack an account of existence unperceived by finite minds. There are places in the texts where Berkeley states that God has knowledge of the ideas which make up the physical world (e.g. *DHP2* 212; *DHP3* 230–1, 253). There are also passages which support the phenomenalist interpretation (e.g. *DHP3* 251; *PHK* 3). However, we shall see that there are also serious problems with these accounts.

There are two problems that the first three views, which we might call the theocentric views, have in common. First, God does not perceive by sense, for the criterion of sense perception is that it is involuntary (*DHP3* 235), but (*DHP3* 241):

such a being as [God] can suffer nothing, nor be affected with any painful sensation, or indeed any sensation at all.

Imagination, in contrast, is voluntary, and all God's perceptions are under his voluntary control. So when these views mention God's perception, they mean simply the voluntary having of ideas by God, which is imagining. But God's imaginings will presumably include not only the way the world actually is, but also the myriad ways it might have been. So what is to stop these being equally real? The only difference for God between the actual world and the merely possible worlds is that we perceive some of the actual world. We are substances and thus not composed of ideas so there is not a parallel problem about our actuality, hence being perceived by us will be sufficient to denominate the ideas we perceive as actual. On interpretation (c) that does not help at all, and on (a) and (b) there is still the problem of distinguishing the actual but unperceived by us from the merely possible but unperceived by us.

Another problem common to all three theocentric views is epistemological. How can we know about God's ideas? In particular, they all agree that for the table to exist unperceived is for God to have some suitable table ideas, for what they disagree on is whether God needs also to perceive it when we do. But whether God has some table ideas while I am out of the room is entirely up to him, and not something I could infer from my own experiences. We gain the reality of unperceived (by us) sensible things at the cost of total scepticism about them.

(b) faces the further problem that it needs us to make sense of a particular idea being in or being perceived by more than one mind. If, as I have argued, an idea is a relativized quality, such as the-green-of-this-grass-to-me-now, then God cannot stand in the same relation to it as the finite subject of that idea. Furthermore, if an idea can be perceived by more than one mind at once, it is hard to see how the relation of perception between an idea and a substantial mind could play any of the philosophical roles that the relation of inherence between a quality and a substance was supposed to play. (b) does not hold that ideas are types, different tokens of which are perceived by us and God, but that the very same token idea is perceived by more than one mind. And if perception is meant to replace inherence, Berkeley would be left with a situation analogous to the materialist saying that the very same property instance, say my weight right now, inheres in two material substances at once. Which is nonsense.

(c) is certainly not the view of Berkeley given the interpretation I have put forward here. Berkeley several times claims to hold a direct theory of perception, most prominently in the conclusion to the *Three Dialogues* (*DHP3* 262), and that is what has been articulated as the Simplest Model of Perception. But (c) attributes an indirect theory of perception to Berkeley, for the real world consists of ideas in God's mind which we never perceive ourselves. When discussing the creation, Berkeley does allow that one might want to talk of archetypes in the mind of God (*DHP3* 248), but never suggests that our ideas *represent* those archetypes. That would be completely inconsistent with his views on perception. Rather, the archetypes should be understood in terms of God's intentions or volitions for us to perceive ideas. The archetypes may be or involve ideas, but our ideas are not representations of them, rather they are consequences of them.

All the theocentric views are flawed, but attributing (a) to Berkeley at least has the virtue of maximizing the internal consistency of his views. However, before doing that, we should explore alternative views which are not theocentric. Views (d) and (e) are phenomenalist, in the sense that they (1) deny any role to God's perception of the physical world, and (2) hold that we should understand physical existence disjunctively in terms of either what finite spirits actually perceive, or what they would have perceived in slightly different circumstances. This appears to be exactly the view Berkeley is expressing at the beginning of the *Principles* (*PHK* 3):

The table I write on, I say, exists, that is, I see and feel it; and if I were out of my study I should say it existed, meaning thereby that if I was in my study I might perceive it, or that some other spirit actually does perceive it.

As ever, the text is not decisive as to which interpretation is correct.

First, in the context it is clear that Berkeley's concern here is to delineate the 'esse is percipi' view by making it clear that he does not hold that existence unperceived is existence without the mind. He is merely pointing out that saying the table exists while he is out of his study does not immediately commit him to the existence of matter. The sentence illustrates two ways to avoid that conclusion, but it does not endorse either. Secondly, though we can read the 'or' in this sentence as a genuine disjunction, we could also read it as introducing a paraphrase. Berkeley could be telling us that he understands the conditional 'if I was in my study I might perceive it' to be equivalent to 'some other spirit actually does perceive it'.

The two phenomenalist views differ over what makes the conditional true. The reductionist holds that the conditional 'if I were in my study I would perceive the table' is made true by there being certain patterns in our actual experience. Crudely put, I learn from experience that if I see a table at one time and have no reason to believe that someone has interfered with it, then at any later time which I choose to look in the study, I will see a table. When enough evidence supports this generalization, then the counterfactual conditional is also true: had I been in the study now, I would have seen the table. On this view, existence unperceived is a by-product of what we actually perceive. Given that God created the ideas we perceive in a certain way, it simply follows that were I in my study, I would see a table, and that is what it takes for there to be a table in my study which no one perceives.

The Possibilist view (e) patches a problem for the Reductionist. Do the patterns of our experience *entail* that had I been in my study, I would have seen the a table, or is the support for this consequence merely inductive? If the former, then it would be logically impossible for the table spontaneously to cease to exist when unobserved. While such spontaneous creation and annihilation of physical objects is something to which we are very resistant, it does appear to be a logical possibility: given that the causal relations between physical objects are not a priori, which was precisely Berkeley's reason for rejecting them altogether, no set of actual experiences, however large and varied, entails anything about non-actual experiences. So the Reductionist must hold that our actual experiences give at best inductive or probabilistic support for the counterfactual conditionals about existence unperceived. But if our actual experiences do not determine the truth of the counterfactual, what does? If there is a possible world on which we have all these experiences but the counterfactual is false, then what makes it true on this world? The Possibilist answers this by saying that God creates not only the actually perceived ideas, but also those that we would have perceived had we acted differently. Like the theocentric views, the Possibilist interpretation of Berkeley finds a role for God above and beyond causing our perceptions, but unlike the theocentric views, this role does not require God to perceive some or all of the physical world. He merely needs to create it.

It is unlikely that Berkeley held the Possibilist view, since he explicitly rejects it in the Third Dialogue (*DHP3* 234):

And what is perceivable but an idea? And can an idea exist without being actually perceived? These are points long since agreed between us.

Berkeley might have held the Reductionist version of phenomenalism, for he did not have any of Hume's later scruples about inductive reasoning and thus might allow that generalization from actual experiences could determine the truth of counterfactual claims about possible experiences. However, there is a deeper problem. Physical objects are collections of ideas. According to the Possibilist, they are collections of ideas some of which are actually perceived and others of which are only possibly perceived. But there is no such thing as an idea which is not perceived, so that cannot be correct. According to the Reductionist, physical objects are collections of actual and possible ideas. For if there being an unperceived table in my study consists in the fact that if I were in my study, I would perceive a table, then the table is in part composed of the merely possible idea I would have had in that situation. However, this is equally hopeless, for how can merely possible experiences determine actual, as opposed to possible, existence?

The only consideration against interpreting Berkeley as holding the Simple View is that it appears to leave him without an account of existence unperceived. This is an objection to the interpretation only if (1) it matters to Berkeley that he should have such an account, and (2) the Simple View really is inconsistent with the existence of unperceived physical objects. Both these conditions will be challenged in Chapter 8, where we shall see that the best account of existence unperceived for Berkeley brings him very close to phenomenalism, but not to either of the varieties we have been discussing.

5.7 Conclusions

We can now return to the three questions at the end of 5.1 and see how they have been answered.

1. Do our perceptions depend upon God in some way other than merely being caused by him?

   Yes, they ontologically depend on God.

2. Do sensible things caused by God also depend upon being perceived by finite spirits?

   Yes, as was proved in the First Dialogue. This relation replaces the materialist's conception of qualities inhering in a substratum.

3. How do sensible things differ from material things, which, if they existed, would equally be caused by God?

   Sensible things depend both on us and on God, the former perceptually and the latter ontologically. Material things would ontologically depend upon their cause, but would not perceptually depend upon anything. Were we to perceive them, we could not use the independence argument to deduce God's existence.

Finally, it is worth commenting on Berkeley's favourite biblical quotation: 'in God we live, and move, and have our being' (Acts 17: 28). To some commentators this has seemed to sit best with the Exhibition View, but it is interesting to note that one place the quotation occurs is precisely when Berkeley is trying to distinguish himself from Malebranche's view that we see all things in God (*DHP2* 214). Berkeley does not hold that what we perceive somehow exists in God's mind, rather it directly depends upon God's will: except when we interfere by doing something against God's wishes, our sense experiences are a direct expression of God's will for us. I have denied that Berkeley's arguments are strong enough to introduce the God of Christian theology that he wanted, but he thought they did, so it is easy to see why he was proud of the way his metaphysics makes us, in day-to-day experience, intimate with God.

Appendix: Official vs. Real Arguments

It has been argued by Margaret Atherton ('Berkeley without God') that Berkeley does not in fact use two arguments for the existence of God in the *Three Dialogues*. But Atherton fails to distinguish the demonstrative arguments Berkeley offers from the considerations he mentions which motivate an inference to the best explanation. In fact, she goes so far as to call the causal argument an inference to the best explanation (p. 233), which is clearly a mistake, since she accepts that one of the premises of the argument is 'Ideas can only be caused by a mind', which rules out the possibility of any *alternative* explanation. There is a big difference between a probabilistic argument from effects to causes and a demonstrative argument with an a priori premiss about the nature of causation.

Atherton also notes, in evidence for her interpretation, that in the *Principles* Berkeley mentions laws of nature when laying out the causal argument, but attention to his theory of action shows that the purpose of this is to distinguish an inference to the existence of God as cause from an inference to the existence of other finite minds as cause. As I argue in Chapter 6, God does not cause all our ideas, for other spirits cause some by their free actions, and this fact needs to be integrated into the causal argument. However, the picture Atherton gives of Berkeley's argument for the existence of God is very similar to the IBE presented in Chapter 4, so I do agree that we have textual grounds for thinking that Berkeley *would have* endorsed this probabilistic argument as a reason for believing in the existence of God. It is just that in the *Three Dialogues* he actually offers two, rather different, demonstrative arguments.

There may be a methodological disagreement here as well. If Atherton is addressing the question of what Berkeley, the historical figure, took as the best reason for believing in the existence of God, then she may well be right. But my concern in this book is the narrower question of what arguments are presented in a particular text; see p. xi above. While Chapter 4 argued that the best reconstruction of the Second Dialogue was as an inference to the best explanation, it cannot be denied that the *Three Dialogues* also contains two explicit arguments for the existence of God, and it is the interpretative problems raised by these which were addressed in the present chapter.

CHAPTER 6

Action, Other Minds, and the Self

6.1 The Volitional Theory of Action

A philosophical theory of action tries to say what an action is. This slightly nebulous project is usually made more precise by giving an account of which things, among the vast class of happenings or events, are actions and which are not. The volitional theory of action is one answer to this question. The theory states that actions are happenings or events which are willed by persons or minds. An event is willed if someone wills that it happen, and we can call this act of will 'forming a volition'. Since some things which happen are willed but still not actions (for example, I might will that the sun shine this afternoon, and even if the sun does shine, making the sun shine is not something I did), the volitional theory adds a further condition, namely that the volition actually cause the event to happen. Furthermore, since my volition can only cause anything to happen by first causing my body to move, the proper statement of the theory is: actions are bodily movements caused by acts of will, called volitions. Thus, when I pick up the glass three things happen: I form a volition, my hand moves, and the glass moves.

The volition causes my hand to move and that causes the glass to move.

Now Berkeley does not hold exactly this view of actions for two reasons. First, he thinks that *all* happenings are actions, so he cannot define an action as an event caused in a certain way. Secondly, and following from the first point, he does not think that my hand moving causes the glass to move, since my hand is composed of ideas and all ideas are inert. So he cannot analyse our saying that I move the glass *by* moving my hand as: I move my hand and that causes the glass to move. However, Berkeley does in fact think that everything we do, all our actions, are caused by our volitions. Thus we find Philonous saying (*DHP1* 196):

In plucking this flower, I am active, because I do it by the motion of my hand, which was consequent upon my volition . . . I act too in drawing the air through my nose; because my breathing so rather than otherwise, is the effect of my volition.

What is distinctive about the volitional theory of action is the structure it imposes upon actions. All our physical actions, according to the volitional theory, have two components, one mental and one physical, namely the volition and the bodily movement, which are causally related. It would seem that anyone who is committed to a dualism between mind and body is committed to finding such a structure in actions, because actions bridge the mind–body divide and thus must have a foot in each camp, and also, being distinct, mind and body can only interact causally. Since Berkeley does make a very sharp divide between the mental and the physical, some sort of volitional theory of action is certainly appropriate and may even be necessary.

The volitional theory suffers notorious problems. It has been said that I can no more cause my hand to move *just by willing it* than I can cause the glass to move just by willing it. That is to say, if I *just* will my hand to move, it will not move. To get it to move, not only must I will it to move, but also I have to move it.

Phenomenologically, this is true: I can move my hand, in a way that I cannot move the glass, and this is distinct from willing either of them to move. Willing something to happen, even something I can easily do, is not the same as doing it. However, it is not clear that this is an unanswerable objection, since it does not show that there is not always a willing or volition which causes the things we do. What it does show is that this volition is not the same as the rather ludicrous activity of willing a glass or a hand to move, which would better be described as a wish.

Another related problem is that many of our actions are automatic and do not seem to involve volitions. For example, as I am typing I depress the space bar between words. While I intend to type the words, I never form an intention or volition to depress the space bar; it is, as we say, something I do without thinking. Similarly, when I am driving I may be concentrating on a conversation but still respond to the road and traffic conditions. Berkeley's most natural response to this objection is that the cases will either fall into the category of reactions, which he may not want to class as actions, or will be parts of complex actions which are willed.

It is also alleged that the volitional theory is subject to an infinite regress because the willing is itself something we do, an act of mind, so must be caused by another volition, and so on. But there is no good reason why someone should hold the volitional theory about acts of mind. One attraction of the theory in the first place, and especially to Berkeley, is that it breaks physical actions down into a mental and a physical component. There is no need to find such a component structure when we are talking of such mental actions as imagining or hoping. If we were to ask Berkeley what makes a physical event an action, he would answer that it is caused by a volition. The physical world is in itself inactive, so this sort of explanation is necessary. However, with respect to the mental, the question is pointless, since there is no other way to conceive of a mental event other than as an action.

Finally, the causal component of the volitional theory has been thought to face problems owing to the fact that my volitions might cause my behaviour without that behaviour counting as acting. For example, if I decide to shoot a feared enemy, my forming the volition might make me so nervous that the gun goes off in my hand 'accidentally' and kills him. If we accept that in this case the death was an accident, that I did not commit a murder, then we need to be more precise about *how* the volition causes the effect which is my action. This turns out to be rather difficult.

It is not my intention here to defend the volitional theory, so I shall not say anything more about these very general objections. They are discussed and disputed at length in the philosophical literature on action. Nor will much turn on the fact that Berkeley endorsed the theory, or on the details of his version. Rather, the problems we face lie deeper than this and are peculiar to Berkeley, for he needs to distinguish, not between actions and mere happenings, but between imagining something and actually doing it.

6.2 Doing and Imagining

Initially the difference looks to be that in imagining all we change are our ideas but in acting we do something more. The materialist has an obvious account of what else happens when we act, which is not available to Berkeley, namely that there is some change in the extra-mental world. Berkeley faces the difficulty that the physical world is composed of the same sorts of entity as the imagined world, namely ideas. Both doing something and merely imagining it have the same result, in Berkeley's world, for they both produce a change in our ideas.

6.2.1 *Distinguishing Action and Imagination*

One option would be for Berkeley to distinguish ideas of imagination from ideas of perception, to say there are two different kinds of mind-dependent entity. At first sight, this seems to be what Philonous is saying in the following exchange (*DHP3* 246–7):

HYLAS ... Pray are not the objects perceived by the senses of one, likewise perceivable to others present? If there were an hundred more here, they would all see the garden, the trees, and flowers as I see them. But they are not in the same manner affected with the ideas I frame in my imagination. Does not this make a difference between the former sorts of objects and the latter?

PHILONOUS I grant it does. Nor have I ever denied a difference between the objects of sense and those of imagination. But what would you infer from thence? You cannot say that sensible objects exist unperceived, because they are perceived by many.

Hylas' objection is that the objects of perception are public and therefore not mind-dependent. The reply is to grant the publicity of sensible things but deny that their being public is inconsistent with their being mind-dependent. This response can be interpreted two ways. Philonous could be saying that some ideas, i.e. sensible qualities, are perceived by more than one (finite) mind. Ideas of imagination, in contrast, are private, and this is the difference between them. Or he could be saying that physical objects, such as gardens, trees, and flowers, are public, though the ideas of which they are composed are private to each of the several people who have them. The difference then between sense and imagination on the second interpretation is that an imagined object is exactly as I perceive it, but a sensed object has more qualities than I perceive since it is composed not only of my ideas but also of other people's ideas. (Berkeley would also need to distinguish fiction or fantasy, which can be a collaborative creation, from imagining.)

The first interpretation sits more naturally with the text, because it does not require a fine distinction between two sorts of objects of sense or imagination, namely ideas and the things they combine to compose, a distinction which is not being treated with any care at this point in the text. The first interpretation also commits Berkeley to two types of idea, those which are private and those which are potentially shared. The distinction between acting and imagining could then be the difference between affecting only private ideas and affecting the other sort of public idea.

An initial objection to this view is that God knows what we imagine, since he is omniscient. But God does not in fact present a problem for the privacy of imagined ideas, since his relation to our ideas of imagination does not need to be the same as our relation to them. Knowing what someone is imagining is very different from imagining the same thing as them. To allow for a distinction between knowing what someone else is imagining and imagining it for oneself, Berkeley needs to distinguish three species of the perceptual or mind–idea relation. There is sense perception which is involuntary, imagination which is similar to sensing but voluntary, and knowing about or understanding, which is like imagination in being voluntary, and like perception in grounding, or providing evidence for, judgements, but unlike it in being subject to error. The possibility of error arising in the understanding derives from the fact that ideas of the understanding, while actually perceived by me now, are sometimes understood with reference to other perceivers and times. This is exactly the same reason why imagined scenarios can correspond to or diverge from reality: if we imagine something, we imagine it *as perceived*. We may or may not imagine it as perceived by a specific person at a specific time, but if we do, then our imagining can correspond to reality. An idea of the understanding must be understood as perceived by someone at some time, and thus always corresponds (or not) with perceived reality.

To see what is really wrong with interpreting the ideas of sense / ideas of imagination distinction as a public/private distinction, we need to ask whether ideas of the imagination are essentially private, or just contingently so. Suppose ideas of imagination are only contingently private. It would seem to follow that they are 'perceivable to others present', so the difference must amount to ideas of sense, in contrast to ideas of imagination, actually being perceived by others. But this rules out the possibility of completely private actions: anything one did which no one else perceived, one would have really only imagined.

If, instead, we suppose that ideas of imagination are necessarily private, then we seem to have two completely different categories of ideas. This gives Berkeley a position structurally like that of the materialist. The problem with this position is how to interpret the perceptual dependence of ideas on spirits. It was argued in the last chapter (5.5) that sensible qualities are relativized to a subject at a time, so they perceptually depend upon that subject. It would be possible to relativize them to more than one subject—for example, one might talk of the green of the grass for *us* now—but since the grass does not look green to everybody, there would need to be some means of specifying who is included in 'us'. This is difficult to do, because the group cannot be specified as all those who have the same experience as such-and-such, on pain of circularity, since what we are trying to do is, in effect, define sameness of experience. Furthermore, if an idea, i.e. a sensible quality, could be perceived by more than one spirit, then we cannot understand their dependence upon being perceived in terms of perception being the substance–quality relation, because a quality can inhere in only one substance. This last point is not stipulative, but follows from the account of why qualities *must* exist in a substance at all.

So, we should not construe the difference between the objects of sense and of imagination in terms of the privacy of ideas of imagination. Of course, we still want to respect the intuitive distinction between two people imagining the same thing and their seeing the same thing, but this can be done without denying the privacy of ideas. Rather we should follow the second interpretation above and distinguish between the objects of sense and of imagination by the fact that my imagining completely determines the (possibly indeterminate) character of the imagined object. Suppose I imagine an orange, then nothing anyone else could imagine (or perceive) could reveal that the orange I am imagining is, unknown to me, rotten or made of plastic. Whereas, if I have a sense perception of an

orange, other people's sense perceptions are relevant to the character of the orange I perceive. For Berkeley, this is because a physical
orange is composed of ideas perceived by many different people
at many different times, according to a principle of composition
which maximizes accurate predictions of future sense experiences.
So imagined objects are private in a way that sensed objects are
not, but this is more to do with what we might call their ownership
than with who perceives what. Unfortunately, this distinction does
not help with the problem of distinguishing acting from imagining,
since both sorts of object are composed of a single kind of thing,
namely ideas.

The key to the distinction between acting and imagining is not
a difference in the objects of sense and imagination, but the effect
of the agent's will on other minds. When I imagine something I
only affect the ideas that I have, but when I do something physical,
then I affect the ideas in other (finite) minds. There are two ways I
might affect the ideas of others. If they are suitably situated, such
as in the same room, in good light, awake and looking at me,
then in taking my pen out of my pocket, I am giving them certain
sense experiences, I am causing them to perceive certain pen-like
qualities. Here I am directly affecting the ideas other people have,
but I can also indirectly affect them. For example, if I leave the
pen on the table, then that changes everyone's pattern of possible
experience. Before I put the pen on the table, it was true of (just
about) everyone that, had they come into the room, they would
have seen uninterrupted brown. But now, were they to come into
the room, they would see a red cylinder on the brown surface.

For the materialist, both the effects are indirect, are results of
my actions. I give you sense experiences *by moving the pen*, I change
what is available to be seen *by leaving the pen on the table*, where
the pen is a mind-independent object. Clearly Berkeley cannot say
this, but neither does he distinguish between your having certain
ideas and the (real) pen moving. The pen, according to Berkeley, is
partly constituted by your ideas, so the pen's moving *just is* certain

people having certain ideas, and further, my moving the pen *just is* my giving the relevant ideas to the relevant people. If putting the pen on the table in a room with no other people is to be an action of mine, then we have to allow that determinism is false, at least to the extent of making sense of the question 'How would things have been had I not acted?' Then we can say that, before I acted, the laws of nature (i.e. God's intentions) entailed certain conditional claims about what would be perceived, and after I acted they entailed different ones. My action consisted in making this change.

My imaginings do not affect other minds in either of these ways. The difficulty arose because both imagining something and doing it changed what ideas the agent had. The present suggestion is that doing something also changes the ideas of (finite) spirits other than the agent, or at least potentially changes them. This is a much more satisfactory solution than distinguishing two types of idea, those of imagination and those of sensation, for the simple reason that the agent may not perceive his actions, but he has still acted for all that.

So Berkeley's combined theory of action is:

> An agent does x IFF the agent wills x and this causes (1) any suitably situated finite spirits to have ideas constitutive of x, and (2) the course of future experiences (which is a function of the past and the laws of nature) to be modified from one which did not, to one which does, include x.

This account will be developed further in the light of three objections.

6.2.2 *Three Objections*

(1) *The account at* PHK 147

In the *Principles*, while discussing our knowledge of God, Berkeley makes the following claim about human agency (*PHK* 147):

For it is evident that in affecting other persons, the will of man hath no other object, than barely the motion of the limbs of his body; but that such a motion should be attended by, or excite any idea in the mind of another, depends wholly on the will of the Creator.

If it was not for the 'wholly', we might see this as the claim that our volitions are necessary but not sufficient for the creation of ideas in others' minds; but as it stands, the second part of this sentence goes flatly against the analysis of action presented in the last section. I propose to deal with this by ignoring it, on the grounds that it is simply a mistake on Berkeley's part which is not repeated in the more mature work (though neither is it excised from the later editions of the *Principles*).

The main reason for thinking it is a mistake is not the problem it causes for giving an adequate account of action, though it certainly does raise such a problem, but inconsistency with Berkeley's metaphysics of physical objects. Charity in interpretation should make us favour an overall coherent position. The biggest problem is simply that, according to *PHK* 147, when one person acts by moving an arm, no other person perceives the motion of that arm but merely some ideas attendant upon that motion. This flatly contradicts Berkeley's insistence that we do directly perceive the physical world (on the reasonable assumption that human bodies are part of the physical world). Furthermore, Berkeley's account of public, persistent objects makes essential use of the claim that objects are composed of ideas in the minds of more than one person. Combining this with *PHK* 147, we would get the unacceptable conclusion that our bodies are not persistent, public objects. Berkeley's considered view is that the motion of my arm consists in part in the ideas others have of my arm moving. Then there is no distinction between the 'object' of will, namely the 'motion of the limbs of his body' and the attendant ideas 'in the mind of another', and Berkeley cannot contrast our efficacy with respect to the former and God's with respect to the latter.

If the compatibilism I urge below is correct, then the whole of *PHK* 147 is a bit of an exaggeration, for in fact we come to know God through the natural regularities which science reveals, but we come to know of others more immediately through our everyday experience. Though he himself may not have approved, it seems right that we should interpret Berkeley to the benefit of his philosophical coherence at the cost of his theological attractiveness, for however theologically attractive his philosophy may be, it is of no service to theology if it is not coherent. Finally, unless he were to make the implausible claim that the only bad things are the motions of bodies and never the effects of those motions on other minds, he faces a version of the problem of evil, and his response to the problem of evil at DHP 237 is to emphasize human agency.

(2) Mind control

The first purely philosophical objection comes from Christopher Taylor, who originated this interpretation of Berkeley on action. He wrote:

Surely one would have to be God to control the sensory states of others just by one's will. ('Action and Inaction in Berkeley', 220)

This objection attempts to show that the blend of the volitional theory and Berkeley's account of physical action produces an absurdity. The absurdity is that I should have some sort of direct control over your mind such that I can affect your sensory states at will and not by doing anything else. Obviously it is not absurd to say that I can affect your sensory states indirectly, e.g. by shouting or waving a pen in front of your eyes. Taylor's intuition is that it is only by doing something physical, by making some physical change, that we (as opposed to God) can affect the sensory states of others.

As we saw above, it is a common objection to the volitional theory that we cannot do anything, not even move our arms, just by willing it to happen. This is true but irrelevant, for the volitional theory was not committed to the thought that genuine volitions and mere attempts at telekinesis are the same mental operations.

Rather, the view is that if I formed a genuine volition that your arm moved, and that caused it to move, then your arm moving would have been something I did, in exactly the way that when I form the volition to move my arm, and it moves, that is something I did. Forming a volition is also an action, though a mental one, and there need be no implication that whenever I try to form a volition I shall succeed. Thus we can explain the oddity of trying to move a glass directly, just by willing that it move, by my failure even to form the appropriate volition. Berkeley can (and must, as I explained in Chapter 4) insist that the constraints on action are all contingent: as we explore the world we discover which things we can do, which we can try to do but cannot do, and which we cannot even try to do. For example, some people can wiggle their ears at will. I cannot, and I do not even know how to try, whereas there are some people who cannot succeed in wiggling their ears, but are clearly trying to.

So Berkeley should not rule out a priori that someone can 'control the sensory states of others', just by will. But Taylor will insist at this point that you and I cannot form the volition, that we do not even know how to *try* to control the sensory states of others directly, and yet we can clearly perform physical actions. To which the correct reply is: of course, you cannot form *that* volition, but nor do you need to. What Taylor is pointing out is that on a particular understanding of sensory states and physical objects, Berkeley's proposal is absurd. However, this is not Berkeley's account of sensory states or physical objects.

According to the Simplest Model of Perception, to be in a sensory state is to be directly confronted with a sensible quality, which is distinct from the mind which is aware of it. (Of course, Berkeley goes on to argue that these sensible qualities are mind-dependent, but that is quite another matter.) If this is the correct account of sensory states, then to control the sensory states of others would be to control which sensible qualities they were related to in this way. 'Control' is probably too strong a word here, since the perceptual relation can always be broken by an act of the perceiving subject, so let us concentrate on affecting the sensory states of others. Given SMP, all one needs to do in order to do this is to affect the sensible qualities in such a way as to make it the case that the other perceiver is, if co-operating, suitably related to the qualities of one's choosing. The materialist thinks that manipulating parts of the physical world *causes* changes in the sensory states of others, but according to SMP, there is nothing to be so caused. Rather, manipulations of parts of the physical world, namely ideas or sensible qualities, can *constitute* a change in the sensory states of others.

Behind Taylor's objection lies a conception of the physical world and sensory states as distinct but causally related. He tries to motivate the absurdity by claiming that, 'using our ordinary concepts', we say:

> I can cause it to seem to you that my hand is moving by moving my hand within range of your vision. . . . But we should find quite baffling the assertion that I produce that effect [i.e. its seeming to you that my hand is moving] just by willing that that effect should be produced. ('Action and Inaction in Berkeley', 219)

Crucial to this passage is the distinction between it seeming to someone that my hand moves and my hand moving. The question is whether the relationship between these is causal or constitutive. To assume that it is causal is question-begging against Berkeley.

By taking SMP seriously, Berkeley must take the existence of a sensory state as a pure relation between a mind and a sensible quality, from which it follows that if one can control/affect the sensible qualities, one can thereby directly control sensory states. Since a sensory state is a relation, to change or otherwise affect one relatum is to affect the relation. Further, physical action involves making changes to the physical world, and the physical world, for Berkeley, is composed of sensible qualities, so physical action involves changing sensible qualities. Taylor's objection assumes that we can only affect sensory states by affecting the physical world, and hence only indirectly. What this overlooks is that Berkeley takes 'affecting sensory states' and 'affecting the physical world' to be two descriptions of exactly the same process, namely manipulating ideas or sensible qualities. It is agreed that if someone wants to imagine a pen or an orange, they can just do it. Taylor's objection is that if someone wants others to perceive a pen, they cannot *just do it*, rather they must do something else which causes others to perceive a pen. Similarly, if one wants to perceive a pen oneself. The response is that in so far as I am able to control the pen, say by taking it out of my pocket, thereby I control the sensory states of those watching me. My producing the pen does not cause them to see a pen, for their seeing a pen consists in there being a pen for them to see, and the single thing I did, which we can describe as taking a pen out of my pocket, can also be described as making it the case that there was a pen for them to see, and thus, if they co-operate, as affecting their sensory states.

Berkeley's reply to this objection has three elements. First, while I can control or affect the sensory states of others just by my will, there are severe but contingent restrictions on this capability. For example, I can no more bring it about that you have a sense experience of a pink giraffe than I can create a pink giraffe just by my will. Secondly, two apparently incompatible statements are both true:

(1) I cause you to experience a red pen just by my will.
(2) I cause you to experience a red pen by putting my pen on the table.

This is because there is no difference between the event of my putting my pen on the table (in good light, in front of your open eyes) and the event of your coming to perceive a red pen. They are one and the same thing, and according to the volitional theory, I do one just by my will, therefore I do the other just by my will. Finally, that I did something just by my will does not entail that doing that thing was the content of my volition. Only someone convinced of Berkeley's theory of action could intelligibly form the volition to change someone else's sensory states directly. Normal agents would form the volition to put the pen on the table, knowing that this would result in others having certain experiences.

What the discussion of this objection clarifies is that the difference between imagining and doing is that in imagination I only create sensible qualities which I perceive, whereas in doing something I also create sensible qualities which others perceive. Since the sensible qualities in my imagination are not real things, but those sensorily perceived by myself and others are real things, it is not surprising that the imagination is easier and less constrained. Nor should the ability to create and change real things be at all mysterious, for even the materialist must say that that just happens to be one of my causal powers. I yawn and make a noise. Both Berkeley and his objectors accept that that noise is something in the physical world which I caused to exist, in accordance with the laws of nature. Berkeley just adds that it is necessarily perceived by someone.

(3) *Perceiving my own actions*

The third objection is much more problematic. Above I quoted a passage in which Philonous allows the objects of sense to be public and those of imagination to be private. We saw that this would not help him in the project of distinguishing imagining something from doing it, because ideas, whether of sense or imagination, are all private. It is the objects which ideas of sense compose which are public. If both are private, what is there to distinguish ideas of sense from ideas of imagination? As the passage suggested, Philonous was referring back to an earlier exchange (*DHP3* 235):

HYLAS   But according to your notions, what difference is there between real things, and chimeras formed by the imagination, or the visions of a dream, since they are all equally in the mind?

PHILONOUS   The ideas formed by the imagination are faint and indistinct; they have besides an entire dependence on the will. But the ideas perceived by sense, that is, real things, are more vivid and clear, and being imprinted on the mind by a spirit distinct from us, have not a like dependence on our will.

Philonous is here asserting that it is a necessary condition of an idea being perceived by sense, not imagination, and thus being a real thing, that it is not dependent upon our will, as ideas of imagination are. But now we have a problem, for when I act, my actions are real things and I sometimes perceive them by sense. It seems to follow that we are impotent to change the physical world: either the ideas I perceive when I act, which constitute the physical changes I am trying to bring about, are actually caused by God, not by me, or they are caused by me but are not part of the real world.

The problem here is an interesting consequence of the response to the first objection. There it was emphasized that the ideas that are perceived by myself and by others when I act are not caused by my action, but constitute it. But then, being something I do, those ideas are under my direct voluntary control, so they cannot be classified as real, rather than imaginary, by their involuntariness, by their independence from my will.

This difficulty was noticed by Michael Ayers, who wrote:

... no coherent explanation could be offered [of the difference between voluntarily imagining one's leg moving and voluntarily moving one's leg], since in the latter case the ideas that constitute the leg-movement would have to be both voluntary and, being 'real', involuntary. (Introduction to Berkeley, *Philosophical Works*, xix)

However, the objection is not quite as simple as he states it, for if the ideas which constitute my leg movement are your ideas, they can be both voluntary (for me) and involuntary (for you), since 'voluntary' just means 'under the control of' and is clearly relativized to minds. The distinction between doing and imagining essentially involved ideas in the minds of others. It is certainly true that Berkeley will have a problem with the distinction if he wants to draw it on a purely first-personal basis; however, he nowhere commits himself to that sort of methodological solipsism. Yet Ayers is right that there is a problem, since we undeniably do perceive our own actions, and it is the ideas we have in so doing which are both voluntary and involuntary in a contradictory way.

Sometimes, when giving grounds for believing in the existence of God, Berkeley talks as if everything real that happens is caused directly by God. This would have the consequence that we are, in fact, impotent, that we cannot make anything happen in the real, physical world. The best we can do is try to act, and God, being benign, acts for us, doing (most of) the things we try to do. It would be unfortunate if Philonous was forced to conclude that we are impotent, for that is a philosophical claim bordering on the sceptical or absurd. The suggestion that humans are impotent, that we can only bring about changes in the world through God's co-operation, was familiar in Berkeley's historical context owing to the influence of Malebranche, whose doctrine of occasionalism, namely that the mental and physical realms are incapable of causal interaction and thus changes in one are brought about directly by God on the occasion of changes in the other, was criticized by Berkeley in the Second Dialogue. There it was argued (DHP2 220) that it is derogatory to God to think that he needs an occasion to put ideas into our minds. The obverse of this objection would be that it is arrogant of us to think that our volitions are occasions for God's actions, for occasionalism seems almost to be saying that our volition is God's command. Apart from being theologically unpalatable, this is inconsistent with the arguments for the existence of God.

There is a further objection which Hylas spots (DHP3 236), for if we are impotent and God in fact performs all 'our' actions for us, then he is responsible for doing all the shameful things we (try to) do. Since we tried to do them, we are still to blame, but so, it would seem, is God. This is a particularly nasty version of the problem of evil, because God is not merely omitting to stop us, not merely conniving with our wrongdoing, rather he performs the unacceptable actions himself.

Not surprisingly, Philonous' response to the problem of evil is to insist on the free agency of finite spirits (*DHP3* 237):

It is true, I have denied there are any other agents besides spirits: but this is very consistent with allowing to thinking rational beings, in the production of motions, the use of limited powers, ultimately indeed derived from God, but immediately under the direction of their own wills, which is sufficient to entitle them to all the guilt of their actions.

Philonous is here using the free-will response to the problem of evil. Whatever the merits of that response, it is clear that Philonous has recognized that it needs us not only to have free will but also freedom of action, i.e. the ability not only to will something freely, but also to do that which we freely will. The conflict between on the one hand making the involuntariness of perception a necessary condition of reality and on the other allowing our free agency is not adequately resolved by claiming that we are impotent to affect the physical world ourselves. That claim is theologically unacceptable to Berkeley, and also denies something which 'everyone knows', namely that they can do such mundane things as pick up books and open doors.

A slightly better suggestion made by Jonathan Dancy (editor's footnote to *PHK* 147) is that our actions are collaborative efforts: it is only with God's help that we can bring about changes in the real world. In contrast, our imagination does not need divine assistance, since 'ideas formed by the imagination' have 'an entire dependence on the will'. This proposal meets the reality objection by saying that though my actions are really something I do, and thus voluntary, they are also, and equally, something God does, and thus 'imprinted on the mind by a spirit distinct from us', making them real things.

The proposal still suffers from a nasty form of the problem of evil, but also affects the cogency of the argument for the existence of God. We are supposed to infer God's existence from those natural phenomena which are best explained as the product of divine will. In order to do this, we have to have a coherent conception of God's agency, of how he produces those phenomena. This can only be by extrapolation from our own case. But now we face a problem, since we have only two examples to extrapolate from: imagining and doing. But if doing is ultimately collaborative, it cannot be a model for God's solo actions, but nor can imagining, because (1) it only produces ideas in the mind of the imaginer, and (2) it does not produce real things. But if God's causing natural phenomena cannot be understood on the basis of our acting or imagining, it cannot be understood at all. This argument could equally have been used against the claim that we are totally impotent.

Another way of reading the 'entire dependence on the will' of imagined ideas is that the imagination is unrestricted but physical action is not. Specifically, physical action is restricted by the laws of nature in a way that the imagination is not. So instead of God performing our actions for us, or with us, he simply puts constraints on our action.

While this is certainly a difference between acting and imagining, it does not help with our current problem. First, the imagination is also constrained, not by the laws of nature but by the facts of prior experience. The advance of technology gives us many examples of things which were once unimaginable, such as conversations with people on the other side of the world. There are also things which will remain unimaginable, such as what it is like to die, because imagination is always the product of prior experience. Secondly, it is hard to see how the fact that there are some things that I cannot do prevents those things which I can, and do, easily do from having 'an entire dependence on the will'. In other words, when well within the constraints, my actions give me voluntary control over what I perceive, thus making it unreal by the criterion of reality Philonous gives.

A variation on the constraints proposal is that the laws of nature are the necessary conditions of physical action, in a way that imagination has no conditions. Thus, were the laws of nature different, my volition to type a specific letter might cause some completely different event, or none at all. So even when I am perceiving my own actions, it is not my will but the laws of nature which determine what I perceive. But this will collapse into the collaboration proposal, since according to Berkeley, only spirits can cause anything, so causal laws merely record patterns and intentions in the actions of some spirit, namely God. Hence, if my willing only had the effect it did because of the causal law, it can only have had the effect it did because of a contribution from another spirit.

These proposals pretty well exhaust the ways of manipulating the account of action to avoid the problem of the reality of perceived effects. Since they are all inadequate, we should look at ways of manipulating the criterion of reality so that ideas which are under my direct control can still be objects of sense perception and thus real.

The idea behind the involuntariness criterion of reality draws upon two very natural thoughts. One is that reality is beyond my control, and the other is that we rarely, if ever, make mistakes about whether we are currently perceiving or imagining something. It does not take much philosophical reflection to realize that acting on the world is precisely bringing it under my (rather limited) control, so the first thought is not strictly correct. What has gone wrong, as we shall see, is a confusion between the passive role of the subject in the process of perception and a lack of control over the objects of perception. Consider the second thought, that we do not mistake perception and imagination. For one thing, this tells us how unimportant are the criteria of vividness and clarity for distinguishing perceptions from imaginings (*DHP3* 235), since if that was what we went on, we would be easily fooled by vivid imaginings and unclear perceptions. Neither can the criterion be that we have control over what we imagine but not over what we perceive, because not only do we have quite a lot of control over what we perceive, but also we sometimes *lack* control over the imagination. For example, the horror stories of M. R. James can easily leave one's imagination full of unwanted images, and it is precisely the inability to control them which can lead to sleepless nights. Rather, the explanation of our ability to distinguish perception from imagination with ease must be that they are very different mental processes, processes in which we play different roles.

Imagine the face of someone very well known to you, a lover or a close relative perhaps. This task is easy in the sense that you should be able to achieve it. But it takes effort, one has to put quite a lot of one's intellectual resources into it, one cannot sustain it for long, and it prevents one performing other tasks. In contrast, just looking at the face of that person takes no effort, is restful and re-laxing, and can be sustained for a very long time, even while one is engaged on thinking about other things. We might tentatively con-clude that the real mark of perception, as a mental phenomenon, is its *effortlessness*. On one perfectly good sense of the active/passive distinction, this would make perceiving passive and imagining ac-tive, and it is not surprising that I can exercise some control over events and processes in which I am passive. That is really not very different from choosing which video to watch!

This solves the problem about the reality of perceived actions by allowing that (1) we are sometimes active in bringing about the things we perceive; but (2) passive in perceiving them; and (3) the question of whether ideas are under voluntary control is not critical in deciding their status as real or not. We can sometimes cause what we perceive by sense, but then the perceiving of it is effortless in a way that imagining the same thing is not. Of course, if someone was in the unfortunate situation of only ever perceiving their own actions and nothing else, in other words being in control of all that they perceive, then reality would for them be very strange. Most importantly, they would not be able to conceive of a distinction between misleading or illusory experiences and trustworthy or true ones, for, in Berkeley's system, that involves discerning the patterns imposed on our experience by the laws of nature, i.e. by the will of God. So the fact that perception is not only passive but also often involuntary is central to our understanding of the world we live in, though it is only the passivity which is a criterion of reality.

When I act I typically cause both myself and others to have ideas. The ideas I cause in others are unproblematically part of the real world, because they are involuntary for the person who perceives them. But the ideas I have which I have caused are voluntary for the person who perceives them, yet since my actions are part of the real world, it follows that involuntariness cannot be a necessary criterion of reality. So we need a criterion to separate my perceptions of my own actions from my imaginings, and the key here seems to be that in imagining there is effort involved in keeping an image before my mind, but there is no similar effort involved in sustaining a perceptual 'image'. It is not implausible to think that this is one of the phenomena Berkeley was trying to pick out with his vividness criterion.

There is one potential difficulty for this account. In most cases of perception we attend to some specific part of the array of sensible things, and this attention involves effort, so it is active, not passive. Even if there can be perception without attention, that is a side issue, since some sense perception involves attention and Berkeley needs to claim that *all* perception is passive.

Whether attention is a genuine problem for the Berkeleian position being proposed depends upon a question which appears to be empirical: does attention affect the content of perception, affect what we perceive, or only what we do with our perception? To use a modern analogy: is attention pre-production or post-production? If attention affects the content of perception, then it looks as if perceiving is not in all cases entirely passive or effortless, and Berkeley is again stuck without a criterion of reality consistent with his account of action. But if attention affects only what we do with the raw data of perception, if it only affects how we process our perceptions, then there is no problem.

200 · CHAPTER 6

6.3 Free Will and Knowledge of Other Minds

The third, rather difficult, problem for Berkeley's account of action concentrated on our perception of our own actions. It did not question the central thesis that in acting we are directly, and indirectly, affecting the ideas in the minds of others, i.e. affecting what others perceive. We can now change the perspective to that of someone who is, as it were, a *recipient* of these actions. In other words, we shall now move from the first-person to the third-person perspective on actions. We should then ask how an observer of actions might *know* that what she perceives is the product of another finite mind. To which the answer is that she discerns, in the phenomena, a pattern which reveals the other intelligent, active being as the cause of those ideas. This inference must be related to her knowledge of God's existence, since that derives from the same evidential source, which creates difficulties for our free will. Specifically, if we know about other minds, both finite and infinite, by causal inference from the patterns in our perceptions, then we face a choice. Either the patterns which reveal to us the existence of finite minds are contained within the global patterns which reveal to us the infinite mind of God, or they are separate. On the first option, our actions are in fact a product of God's intentions, so we are not free at all, and on the second, our actions are free, but create exceptions to the laws of nature, so science is less than universal.

It is worth pausing for a moment to note that the first option does not leave us without any reason to believe in other finite minds, as has been suggested by Bennett (*Locke, Berkeley, Hume*, 221). The inference from the data of our experience to a mental cause makes use of the thought that a mind has plans and intentions which it seeks to fulfil in its actions. It is perfectly possible that my perceptions of your behaviour are part of the pattern which leads me to God's existence, and yet that behaviour also displays a different, more local, pattern which is best explained as its being the intentional behaviour of another, finite, rational being. The overall picture, i.e. everyone's behaviour plus all the non-human world, might be best explained as God's actions, but that is not inconsistent with a part of that behaviour being revelatory of your intentions as well. But given that the inference to another mind is the inference to the cause of my ideas, if I am to infer that your volitions caused some of my ideas, and also be led by those ideas to God's existence, God must be the cause of your volitions. So we can allow Berkeley to combine the thought that we have knowledge of other minds with the thought that all perceptions are directly or indirectly caused by God, as long as we allow God to reveal the other minds by giving their volitions causal efficacy as part of his more general plan. Berkeley's problem with other minds is not their existence but their free will.

We can take a stance from which the dilemma I posed does not appear too problematic: why should science be universal? Why not think it a good thing that human behaviour is not encompassed by the hard laws of mechanistic physics? Surely the slightest experience will teach us that one cannot account for fickle and un-predictable humans with the tools designed to predict the regular and unchanging motions of the planets?

There is more than a grain of truth in this response, and Berke-ley would have probably endorsed it, but it achieves less than it appears to. For a start, the problem arises even if we do not want to reduce human action to physics but merely make the two com-patible. Also, we must distinguish Berkeley's perfectly reasonable instrumentalism from the less defensible view, with which Berkeley occasionally toys, that science is *entirely* at the service of practical concerns. There may be no benefits and several disadvantages to be gained from applying physics to human actions, but that does not settle the question of whether physics encompasses our actions. A good case could be made for the practical benefits of treating science and the explanation of human behaviour as operating on different domains, but the question of how they are related will not go away. Instrumentalism is a way of interpreting successful scientific theories (they are not true, just good inference rules), but it does not lay down in advance a criterion of success for science. Even if it turns out that all science is useful, the practice of science recognizes a criterion of success which is independent of usefulness. The point of instrumentalism is not to change science, but to show that we can understand science without thinking that scientific theories are aimed at some sort of unobservable, theoretical truth. Now it may just turn out that the best physical theories *are* universal. The accepted physics of Berkeley's day was Newtonian mechanics, which pictures the physical world as consisting of discrete objects changing their properties in rule-governed ways. The rules governing these changes are of two very different types. One type describes future states on the basis of past states under the assumption of no interference. The other describes the consequences of interference on the states of an object. Typically, interference in the career of any particular object comes from its crossing paths with another physical object. The interaction and its consequences are described by the laws of mechanics, and the occurrence of an interaction was equally covered by those laws. Whether there can be other sorts of interference, from outside the physical system, which is something required by many accounts of free agency, depends upon whether there are further laws governing the properties of the whole physical system, such as a law requiring the conservation of energy across the system. This requirement for extra laws leaves open the possibility of keeping the useful mechanics while leaving space for freedom of action. But physics is in fact more ambitious than this, more imperialistic: it tries to encompass any apparently external influence within its explanatory framework. One mark of this completeness is determinism, the claim that the past plus the laws of physics logically necessitate the future. But even determinism is not essential for completeness. When we look at the quantum level, physics may not be deterministic, but its indeterminacies are specific and discoverable, so an indeterminate system will not do anything surprising: it may not be determinate whether a particular particle emerging from an experimental set-up will have property P or not, but the chance of it having P is quite precise. This does not leave any room for intervention from outside the system of physics. If there are any exceptions to the universal-ity and completeness of physics, these will show up within physics itself and should not be judged in advance by philosophers, even by an instrumentalist. None have shown up so far. So we cannot simply dismiss the possibility of conflict between human agency and science.

Another deflationary response would be a form of compatibil-ism: all the actions of finite spirits do form subpatterns within the larger, global pattern of God's actions, but that does not mean that we are not free when we act as we do. Freedom consists in our ac-tions deriving from our decisions, and they can do this even if they are determined, or otherwise fixed, by the laws of nature. Whether or not compatibilism can be made to work in other metaphysical systems, there are two reasons why it seems not to be an option for Berkeley. One is that compatibilism would appear to make our knowledge of other finite minds impossible, for all the patterns in our experience would simply point to God. We must explain how, under compatibilism, we can know of minds other than God's. The other is that the compatibilist immaterialist has to choose between saying either that we are impotent, with God in fact directly bring-ing about what we take ourselves to have done, in order to fit in with his intentions for the physical world, or that God indirectly ensures that our actions fit his intentions by affecting our deci-sions. As we saw above, the suggestion of impotence is not really acceptable to Berkeley, and the other suggestion leaves him in an even worse situation over the problem of evil, because God would be responsible not only for our bad actions, but also for our bad intentions.

The tension between the ineluctability of physics and our appar-ent free will is not unique to Berkeley, and Philonous rightly insists that (DHP3 260):

Whenever therefore any difficulty occurs, try if you can find a solution for it on the hypothesis of the *materialists*. . . . And in case you cannot conceive it easier by the help of *materialism*, it is plain it can be no objection against *immaterialism*.

Unfortunately Philonous' dialectical point is not philosophically very satisfying. It is true that if the materialist cannot give us an adequate account of free will either, we cannot use the issue as a reason to prefer materialism, but we might take it as reason to withhold assent from *both* views. Rather than leave things here, I want to propose a way out of the problem for Berkeley, which combines what is correct in the two deflationary responses just mentioned.

The good points are: (1) that physical laws do not have any role to play in the explanation of behaviour; and (2) that the conditions for free action may not be such as to conflict with physics. However, rather than begin with the account of free will, I shall start with other minds. We have discussed three distinct arguments that Berkeley has for the existence of God: the inference to the best explanation, the causal argument, and the dependence argument. The first two are similar in their strategy, since they both take certain data which are agreed to point to the existence of something other than myself and my ideas and argue that they point to the existence of another mind (of a special kind, viz. infinite). A crucial step in this argument is Berkeley's theory of signs: we discover that certain experiences are correlated like sign and signified. Thus there is no natural or essential connection between, say, the sound of rain on the windows and the damp underfoot when I go out, but experience reveals a connection. Since it is not natural or essential, but yet is regular and, to all intents and purposes, unchanging, Berkeley thinks of the connections between ideas as being like the arbitrary connections between words or symbols and what they signify. Such arbitrary connections allow us to move quickly in thought from sign to signified. In the case of artificial or human languages and sign systems, signification is fixed by 'common custom', but in the case of this natural language, the language of nature, signification must be fixed by its creator, namely God.

Now the problem that Berkeley faces over other finite spirits can be rephrased: we learn about God through reading the language of nature, but if everything finite spirits do is also part of nature, learning about those things will only tell us more about God, not about the other finite spirits. If all the significance of ideas comes from the infinite spirit, then discovering what they signify will not tell us anything about finite spirits. The solution I want to offer Berkeley is that we learn about finite spirits through their language, and that human language is very different from the language of nature. There is no conflict between certain ideas having one natural signification and a completely different human signification.

There are two important points to note. The first is how, even if we accept that ideas of the natural world stand in the relation of sign to signified, it is odd, or at best metaphorical, to call this a language. The oddity comes from there being only one type of speech act possible with this language: the only thing that an idea can naturally signify is the occurrence of another idea, it can at best say 'such-and-such will happen'. In a real language one can not only assert facts, but also ask questions, express emotions, give orders, etc. Berkeley's divine language can do none of these things.

Is arithmetic a counter-example, being a language without moods? No, since arithmetic only makes sense in a wider linguistic context. If one finds a scrap of paper with '$2+2=5$' written on it, one does not know whether this is a false assertion, an unusual wish, an order (think of Orwell's *1984*) or a child's question. No further parts of arithmetic could settle this question, rather the sum must be embedded in some other linguistic conventions.

So if we are to say that we know about finite minds through their use of language, we are referring to something much more sophisticated than a mere sign–signified relation. I know of the existence of finite minds by seeing them express anger or fear, by hearing their questions and feeling their doubts. Treating nature as a system of signs does not reveal any of these things about the mind of God. Hence there is a resource we have when trying to discover about other finite minds which is completely distinct from anything we appeal to when we understand natural occurrences as emanating from the divine will.

Of course, the Bible, in parts, encourages its readers to see certain natural occurrences as expressions of divine anger or pleasure, but (1) there is no implied generalization that, say, all floods express divine anger, (2) there is always some other source of communication between God and man, such as a warning through a prophet, and (3) if these events are miracles, they are *ex hypothesi* breakdowns in the normal sign–signified relation. So my account of the differences between the language of nature and human language would not be unacceptable to Berkeley on theological grounds.

Further, and this is the second point, it is different parts or aspects of our experience which reveal to us the mind of God and the minds of others. If we try to discover about the mind of God through the significance of natural phenomena, we must do some science, and in doing science we quickly discover that the superficial regularities which we took to be sign–signifier relations are merely symptoms of much deeper and less obvious regularities. I gave the example above of hearing the rain on the window and that signifying wet grass underfoot, but this is an oversimplification. To give just one example of a hidden complexity, the correlation I notice depends upon the rate of evaporation, which is in turn correlated with temperature, pressure, and wind speed. But we shall find that even those correlations depend upon others to do with the molecular structure of liquids. So while Berkeley can say that the rules of thumb by which we organize our everyday life reveal the benevolence of the infinite spirit, it is not in those rules of thumb that we are reading the language in which that infinite spirit wrote the story of the world.

In contrast, our knowledge of finite spirits really does draw upon the materials encountered in our daily, unanalysed experience.

When we see in someone's face an expression of joy or pain or concern, there is no more basic signification on which this power of expression rests. Delving into the physiology of facial expressions may tell us a lot about how the natural world works, but it will not tell us anything more than we already knew about this person's pain and anguish.

So the aspects of our experience which we use to infer the existence of other finite minds are different from those we use to infer the existence of God. What, then, of free will? The significance of free will for Berkeley, as for many other philosophers, is that it is a necessary condition for moral responsibility. One element of this is that if we are to be responsible for an action, we must have caused it, which is why the occasionalist account of action faced a nasty form of the problem of evil. So Berkeley must hold that the volitions of finite spirits are the causes of some of my ideas. Then the question arises: if we have free will, how can God ensure that the ideas we freely cause are consistent with the patterns he puts into the natural world? There are three possible answers. God might cause our intentions, but this option again appears to threaten our free will and introduce the problem of evil. Alternatively, God might use his foreknowledge of what we freely choose to structure the natural world in such a way that our actions are consistent with it. Finally, careful attention to the question of what exactly finite spirits are the causes of may make the problem go away. It is this third option I want to consider here.

We need to keep in mind the distinction between ideas and the persistent physical objects which they compose, a distinction which has been mentioned several times already and is discussed at length in Chapter 8. We learn that someone is in pain by the look of anguish on her face. If we then turn our attention to explaining that look in terms of muscle contractions and nervous activity, we may be considering the same public, persistent object, namely her face, but we will be considering different ideas. But as I argued above, the laws of nature, the regularities which lead us to God, are defined over ideas we have when we conduct these more probing investigations. So we can say that what a single physical object, the human body, does can lead us to two different minds as causes, namely God and a finite spirit, because it is different ideas in the collection which composes that body which lead us to each of the two minds. There is a problem about our free agency only if we assume that it is the very same things which are the products of our volitions and God's. But since the products of volitions are ideas, the problem does not arise, for the very same ideas are not caused by both us and God. For example, if someone speaks to me, the ideas which compose the words I hear are caused by them, but if I begin to enquire further about how speech is produced, the ideas of their voice box and the sound waves it produces are caused by God. If we consider human behaviour as it first strikes us, the ideas we have are caused by other finite spirits. But if we think of it, i.e. the very same bodily motion, as a natural object and begin to enquire after it in that way, then the ideas we have, which are still ideas of (i.e. composing) that behaviour, are now caused by God. It is the patterns in those ideas which constitute the laws of nature.

6.4 *The Self*

Berkeley's inference to the existence of God and his account of our everyday knowledge of other finite minds both presuppose that, prior to establishing that there are others, I have a conception of my own mind as a type of thing of which there might be more than one. There are two problems with how one might have such a conception, only one of which is addressed by Philonous. Hylas realizes that we cannot have an idea of ourselves, so asks why, if we can have a notion of ourselves without an idea, we cannot have a similar notion of matter. To answer this, Philonous has to give an account of the source of our notion of ourselves which does not rely upon our having an idea of the self. Even if he can do this, another problem arises because of Berkeley's nominalism.

The proposal is that by some sort of acquaintance with our selves we form a conception of spirit which allows us to understand the possibility of other minds. For this to be the case, we have to form a conception of spirit as a *type* of thing of which there can be more than one example. Being a nominalist, Berkeley believes that everything which exists is particular, so somehow confrontation with just one particular has to enable us to think of that particular as being of a type. While Berkeley has an account of how general thought is possible about the sensible world, there are problems applying it to spirits, since we are only ever directly acquainted with one spirit, namely ourselves. He never addresses this conceptual problem of other minds.

The discussion of our ability to conceive of spirits occurs at *DHP3* 231–4 and consists of three challenges by Hylas and their responses. The second two challenges and responses were added in the 1734 edition, which indicates, first, the importance Berkeley attached to the issue, and secondly that by then he had abandoned the projected part 2 of the *Principles* which was to deal with spirits. Unfortunately, the second and third response consist largely of quite self-conscious repetition of the first. The third challenge introduces the Humean or bundle theory of the self, which Berkeley had toyed with in the *Philosophical Commentaries*. It is worth quoting Philonous at some length (*DHP3*):

I do nevertheless know, that I who am a spirit or thinking substance, exist as certainly, as I know my ideas exist. Farther, I know what I mean by the terms *I* and *myself*; and I know this immediately, or intuitively, though I do not perceive it as I perceive a triangle, a colour, or a sound. . . . and that which perceives ideas, which thinks and wills, is plainly it self no idea, nor like an idea. (231)

Whereas the being of myself, that is, my own soul, mind, or thinking principle, I evidently know by reflexion. . . . I say lastly, that I have a notion of spirit, though I have not, strictly speaking, an idea of it. I do not perceive it as an idea or by means of an idea, but know it by reflexion. (233)

How often must I repeat, that I know or am conscious of my own being; and that I my self am not my ideas, but somewhat else, a thinking active principle that perceives, knows, wills, and operates about ideas. I know that I, one and the same self, perceive both colours and sounds: that a colour cannot perceive a sound, nor a sound a colour: that I am therefore one individual principle, distinct from colour and sound; and for the same reason, from all other sensible things and inert ideas. (233–4)

There seem to be two distinct thoughts here which are not obviously compatible. One is that the self must exist and be distinct from any idea, because perceiving, thinking, willing, etc. all need a subject, all need something that wills, perceives, etc. Hence we can be certain of our own existence because we are certain that there is perception. This looks very similar to Descartes's *cogito ergo sum*, at least on some interpretations, and will face similar difficulties. The other thought is that I am somehow conscious of myself, that I have a form of direct but non-perceptual knowledge of myself which is variously described as 'immediate', 'intuitive', and 'by reflexion'.

The tension between these two thoughts comes from the first apparently classifying our self-knowledge as knowledge by inference, as depending upon a general premiss that there cannot be perception, volition, etc. without a spirit which perceives, wills, etc. The second, in contrast, makes our self-knowledge non-inferential, analogous to, but quite distinct from, perception. However, we may have been overhasty in assimilating the first thought to an inference. Consider again the very first claim:

I do nevertheless know, that I who am a spirit or thinking substance, exist as certainly, as I know my ideas exist.

This could be read as a claim about comparative degrees of certainty of two unrelated pieces of knowledge, but then it would not answer Hylas' objection. Rather, Berkeley intends his knowledge of the existence of his ideas to be seen as some sort of ground or basis for his knowledge of his own existence. But why does it have to be an inferential ground? We saw in the last chapter how Berkeley accepts the thought that every quality must exist in a substance, but rejects the materialists' notion of inherence in favour of the thesis that sensible qualities, i.e. ideas, exist in spiritual substance by way of being perceived. Now someone who holds that every quality exists in a substance could take three attitudes to our knowledge of that substance. He could say that when we perceive the quality we also perceive the substance, but that is phenomenologically false (*DHP1* 175; also *PHK* 136). Or he could say that we infer the existence of the substance. Now, we have already seen how Berkeley thinks that if we try to infer from qualities to substances we do end up with spirits, but any such process either presupposes that we have a prior conception of the substance, namely spirit, or it only allows us to conclude the existence of a substance about which we have a merely relative conception. Or, thirdly, he might think that while we are only perceptually aware of the qualities, this gives us direct, but non-perceptual, acquaintance with the substance which has those qualities. In perceiving ideas or qualities we are aware of the substance in which those ideas or qualities exist, and this awareness is not mediated by the general belief that all qualities exist in substances. All three of these could come in both materialist and immaterialist versions, depending upon one's conception of the substance–quality relation. The third suggestion gives both the materialist, if he accepts the argument of the First Dialogue, and the immaterialist a direct route from our perceptual experience to the existence of the self.

If we interpret Berkeley as saying that in perceiving sensible qualities we are directly, but non-perceptually, acquainted with the substantial subject of those qualities, namely ourselves, then that reconciles the apparent conflict between saying that our knowledge of ourselves depends upon our knowledge of our own ideas and saying that it is 'immediate' and 'intuitive'. Unfortunately, this account of our knowledge of the self suffers from a major problem, which is not Hume's problem that we do not have an idea or impression of the self, for Berkeley explicitly disavows that, but

Kant's problem that we do not have identifying knowledge of the self. Berkeley assumes that the first-person pronoun refers to a substantial item, a spirit. If so, we need to ask for the grounds on which we attribute the ideas we do to a single self. Specifically, how do we know that the ideas I call my own are not in fact had by two or more spirits, and how do we know that some of your ideas do not belong to the same subject as mine? Perhaps there is just *one* finite spirit, one substance in which all ideas, whether yours or mine, exist. Clearly, the most usual ground for determining the subject of an idea is consciousness. Berkeley needs to give an account of why all and only those ideas which are co-conscious—that is they can occur together in consciousness—belong to one subject. He must avoid Locke's definition of the identity of the subject in terms of co-consciousness, for this is incompatible with regarding the self as a substantial item distinct from the ideas which it perceives.

It is impossible to guess how Berkeley would have dealt with this problem. We know he planned a second volume of the *Principles*, which was to deal with spirits, but we do not have even a manuscript. In his first letter to Johnson he wrote:

As to the Second Part of my treatise concerning the *Principles of Human Knowledge*, the fact is that I had made considerable progress in it; but the manuscript was lost about fourteen years ago [1715], during my travels in Italy, and I never had leisure since to do so disagreeable a thing as writing twice on the same subject.

Perhaps we should take the 'considerable progress' with a touch of scepticism, for in writing the *Three Dialogues* he had written twice upon the same subject with great success and no trace of distaste. Most likely he found himself choosing between equally unacceptable alternatives. The substantial theory of the self appears to open up in the mental world those very possibilities of scepticism which he was so keen to foreclose in the physical world. But the alternative, bundle theory cannot be made to work if ideas of sense are just physical qualities which compose the world, for then he would have to say that my mind is a bundle which included such elements as the colour and shape of the coffee cup, and all the other parts of the world that I perceive.

6.5 Conclusion

This chapter has been suggestive rather than conclusive. I have isolated three major areas of difficulty for Berkeley, namely action, freedom, and the self, tried to focus on the most serious of the difficulties, and in all but the last case, made a speculative proposal as to how he might respond.

Berkeley is regularly criticized for his accounts of perception, or conception, or of physical objects or existence unperceived, but not often for his accounts of action, free will, and the self. One reason for this is that he wrote so little about them that it would seem churlish to focus on them. Given the positive and constructive nature of this book, some discussion was unavoidable. When we do look at these topics, we see that Berkeley has some good things to say, but much work to do. It is here that his metaphysics is most likely to fail.

Appendix: Did Berkeley Hold a Volitional Theory of Action?

Jennifer Hornsby (*Actions*, 52) has argued that Berkeley does not in fact hold the traditional version of the volitional theory spelt out in 6.1, on the basis of *DHP2* 217:

> PHILONOUS   Now I desire to know in the first place, whether motion being allowed to be no action, you can conceive any action besides volition.

Hornsby argues on the strength of this that Berkeley holds only volitions to be actions and bodily movements to be not actions themselves but merely their effects. Apart from the wording of *DHP1* 196, quoted above, there are two problems with this interpretation. One is that we have a very strong intuition that my moving my arm *involves* my arm moving. If my action in moving my arm is to be identified with my volition (or, for Hornsby, my trying to move it), then my action and my arm's moving are distinct existences and the former could exist without the latter. Hornsby deals with this by saying that if we describe my action as 'moving my arm' then that entails that my arm moves, but this is just a feature of how we describe the action. While this way of dealing with the intuition is adequate, it uses a conception of logical entailment, as a function of how we describe the world, which was not available to Berkeley. Hence he would have found the view that no bodily movements are actions very counter-intuitive. Secondly, the passage Hornsby cites admits of more than one interpretation. When Philonous says that motion is no action, he is considering a materialist hypothesis (*DHP2* 217):

> HYLAS ... All I contend for, is, that subordinate to the supreme agent, there is a cause of a limited and inferior nature, which concurs in the production of our ideas, not by any act of will, or spiritual efficiency, but by that kind of action which belongs to matter, *viz. motion.*

Rejecting the claim that the motions of unthinking matter cause our ideas does not commit Berkeley to the claim that bodily motions are not actions. The important point of classifying something as an action or not *in this context* is to decide whether it can be a cause. It is perfectly consistent with the claim that no motions are causes, i.e. they are not active and thus not actions in one sense, to say that bodily motions are actions, by which he means that they are the effects of volitions. Furthermore, the difficulty of conceiving any action 'besides volition' is, to my ear, ambiguous. It could be a difficulty with conceiving any action which is not itself a volition, or with conceiving any action occurring without a volition. Either would do for Philonous' dialectical purposes at that point.

CHAPTER 7

Properties and Predicates

7.1 Definitions and Background

So far we have established that the objects of perception are ideas, which are particular property instances relativized to a perceiver at a time, such as the green of the leaf for me now. Perceivers are minds or spirits, which are substantial, persisting, immaterial individuals. Minds or spirits have the ability to act, i.e. to cause ideas of sense in both themselves and others, though finite minds do not cause most of their own ideas of sense. Ideas perceptually depend upon the mind that perceives them, and ontologically depend upon the mind that causes them. Ideas themselves are causally inert.

In this chapter we shall address an issue about such ideas and their relations to other ideas. The idea which is the green of the leaf for me now is a distinct item, a distinct object of perception, from the idea which is the green of the leaf for me later, or for you now. The question to be addressed is whether these ideas have anything in common, whether they share something, namely greenness. We use the same word, 'green', to describe them all, so the question amounts to whether there is some further *thing*, the property of being green, of which they are all instances or which they all exemplify. This is the traditional problem of universals.

It is worth noting that the emphasis already placed on the relativization of ideas to perceivers at a time, and our interpretation of this, helps to avoid an unnecessary puzzle. For Berkeley is a self-confessed nominalist, i.e. someone who thinks there are no such things as properties or qualities, and yet the basic elements of his ontology are ideas, which he regularly describes as 'sensible qualities'. But we can see that there is no contradiction when we remember that what the nominalist denies is the existence of properties or qualities conceived of as universals, whereas sensible qualities, or ideas, are not universals but *particular* property instances such as the colour of this table (to me now).

Particularity, with which much of this chapter will be concerned, is rather difficult to define in terms which are any easier to understand. One way is to use the notion of singularity: grief is such that there can be lots of it, but Peter's grief for his mother is unique. Other people's grief may be similar, may in fact be indistinguishable, but they are not one and the same thing as Peter's grief. The property of grief, if there is such a thing, is non-particular, but the particular instance of grief which is Peter's grief for his mother is a particular. Equally, all physical objects (and minds) are particular: however similar Peter is to his twin or doppelgänger, they are numerically distinct—there are two of them, not one.

Before going on to discuss and evaluate Berkeley's nominalism, we need to clarify what we mean by properties and what exactly the nominalist is denying. A good starting-point is the undeniable fact that when we come to describe the world around us, we usually pick out objects and say they have certain qualities or that they are of certain kinds. Of course, thought and language can do much more than this (as Berkeley was well aware, e.g. *PHK* Intro 24), but such attributions of properties to objects can be reasonably thought of as fundamental to our judgements. Within this class of attributions, there is a distinction between attributing a quality and attributing membership of a kind, a distinction which is quite clear in our everyday speech, even though some words can perform both functions. Take, for example, 'gold', which names both a kind of substance out of which objects may be composed and a colour. In the television comedy *Blackadder II* one of the characters, Lord Percy Percy, takes up alchemy in the hope of turning base metals into gold. He fails, but claims to have succeeded in making a lump of the purest green. The joke turns upon his failing to grasp the distinction between qualities, such as the colours green and gold, and kinds, such as iron and gold.

There is also a distinction within kind terms between count nouns and non-count nouns. You can intelligibly ask 'How many horses (or trees or . . .)?' but not 'How many water (or gold or . . .)?' Though we (nearly) always attribute properties to something, count nouns, or sortals as Locke christened them, have an especially intimate connection with individual, identifiable objects in the world. Applying a sortal term to some object commits one to various claims about its identity. Thus if I say that this object is a pen, then I am ruling out the possibility that it is one and the same thing as an object which has a different location in space and time, or one which is not a writing instrument, or one which is made of jelly. In contrast, if I say the object is (made of) gold, then, though I need to identify it when I make the judgement, I have no further commitments about the identity of the object over time and through change (beyond that it exists now and is now gold). Similarly if I attribute to the object a quality such as rigidity. However, non-sortal kinds are distinguished from qualities in being acceptable answers to the question 'What is it made of?' We can in fact distinguish three questions we ask about the objects we encounter: what is it like?, what is it made of?, and what is it?, answers to which are respectively qualities, non-sortal kinds, and sortals.

The importance any given philosopher attaches to these distinctions depends upon the metaphysical place he gives to the re-identifiable individuals to which we attribute these properties. In Berkeley's case physical objects of the various kinds we delineate are all merely bundles of ideas. The only kind terms which apply to ideas rather than physical objects are the sortals 'idea' and 'sensible quality'. This is because at the fundamental level of description there are only two kinds or sorts of thing: minds and ideas. So, despite the fact that physical objects are composed of ideas, every kind term which applies to a physical object cannot be applied to ideas, and every kind term which can be applied to ideas cannot be applied to physical objects. With qualities the matter is slightly more complicated. Some qualities, such as colour and perhaps shape, are qualities of individual ideas or collections of ideas in a mind at a time. Other qualities, such as rigidity or growth, are not qualities of ideas in a mind at a time, but are qualities of objects composed of ideas in more than one mind or at more than one time. One does not perceive a rigid idea, or an idea of growth, because there is no such idea to be had: rigidity and growth are not qualities of particular ideas. Qualities of particular ideas, and perhaps also of collections of ideas in one mind at one time, are what Berkeley intends to pick out with his phrase 'sensible qualities'. Qualities not of particular ideas but of interpersonal, intertemporal collections of ideas are still qualities and not kinds, but, like the kinds, are always predicated of something more complex than an idea.

A nominalist, i.e. someone who denies that there are properties, does not thereby deny that some things are horses and others trees, that some things are made of gold and others of iron, that some things are square and others oval. One way of expressing nominalism is to say that every claim which is apparently about a property, such as 'red is a colour', can be paraphrased as one which is not about properties but objects, such as 'everything red is coloured'. There are some notorious problems in carrying out the details of this policy of paraphrase, but there is a deeper problem. If the paraphrase is to be consistent with nominalism in a way that the unparaphrased sentence appeared not to be, this must be because referring to the colour red commits us to its existence in a way that predicating red of an object does not commit us to the existence of redness. Though this is intuitively so, it is far from obvious why it should be the case. Fortunately that issue need not detain us since it is unlikely that Berkeley thought of nominalism in this language-bound way.

Traditionally nominalism is opposed to Platonism. The Platonist holds that properties are a special kind of entity which exist eternally, outside of space and time, and it is certain that Berkeley was opposed to this view. However, not everyone who denies Platonism is a nominalist. The defining claim of Platonism is that properties are completely independent of the objects which exemplify them, and one might deny this while still thinking that properties are real things. Such a view would hold that the claim 'There is something in common between all things which are *F*' commits one to the existence of properties over and above, but necessarily dependent on, the things which have them. We can call this view Aristotelianism. The Aristotelian does not hold that properties exist in some distinct reality from the physical objects which exemplify them. On the contrary, they have spatial locations and causal powers. Yet they are still a different kind of entity from physical objects: while physical objects can have different parts at different places at a single time, they can only be wholly present at one place at one time, whereas properties, according to the realist, are wholly present in each of the places where an object exemplifies them.

To simplify the terminology, and to allow the nominalist to say that things do have properties, we shall say that it is *universals* which the realist accepts and the nominalist denies. So what is common to all forms of realism about universals is the claim that there are two different types of entity in the world, universals and particulars. Different forms of realism disagree about how to characterize universals, but that does not matter to the nominalist, who simply holds that there are only particulars. Which is not to say that there are not different forms of nominalism, for some hold that particulars are physical objects, such as Socrates or that tree, whereas others hold that they are particular property instances, such as the shape of Socrates' nose or the colour of this leaf, and that objects consist of collections of such particular property instances, or tropes. Others might accept both sorts of particular.

It is easiest to see what it is that the nominalist is denying by looking at the main reason for accepting that there are universals of one sort or another. The argument goes back to Plato and runs like this. We have to accept that sometimes two things are of the same kind or share a quality. For example, I can see two trees from my window. So what makes it the case that these are both trees, especially since they may look so different? It seems to many philosophers that we cannot answer this question without saying at some point that there is something the two trees have in common. But what they have in common cannot be another particular, so it must be some other kind of entity. Everyone agrees that x and y are both trees because there is some property F such that x is F and y is F. One natural reading of this is that it is saying there is some third thing, distinct from x and y, which can be predicated of x and y. Since particulars cannot be predicated of anything, this third thing is not a particular but a universal. The challenge to the nominalist is to explain how it can be that both x and y are F without bringing in non-particular entities.

7.2 Berkeley's Commitment to Nominalism

Nominalism is a working assumption of Berkeley's philosophy. There is a strong connection between empiricism and nominalism, and it is here that Berkeley most clearly follows Locke. In fact, the nominalist principle Berkeley endorses as beyond question— 'But it is a universally received maxim, that *everything which exists is particular*' (*DHP1* 192)—is almost a direct quotation from Locke (*Essay*, III. iii. 1 and 6). But Berkeley should be more careful here, for not only is nominalism questioned by some of his philosophical adversaries, such as Descartes and Malebranche, but it is also not obviously the view of common sense, of the vulgar. We do all talk as if several distinct ideas had something in common when we say they are all green, and this talk seems unavoidable: we could make no sense of our experience without it. The nominalist must either argue that such talk is misguided or give an account of it which is consistent with his nominalism. The first alternative would fall under Berkeley's definition of scepticism (*DHP1* 173), since it involves denying the 'reality and truth' of something plainly apparent to the common man. So Berkeley, like Locke before him, takes the latter option and attempts to show that the commonalities we find between distinct ideas are in fact the work of the (finite) mind.

Berkeley's position is rather subtle here, because he wants to respect both the obvious truth that various ideas have things in common, such as being green, and the nominalist thesis that we never come across universals in our sense experience. Locke reconciled these two pressures with his theory of abstraction, which is meant to show how we can create general ideas from the materials provided by experience solely of particulars, but Berkeley emphatically rejects abstraction. As we shall see, Berkeley's resolution of the tension takes him in the direction of a much more sophisticated theory of thought.

To make it completely clear that Berkeley intends to be a full-blooded nominalist and does not endorse the Aristotelian view, consider how to interpret the claim that everything which exists is particular. This can only make sense if it is meant to indicate a contrast between universals and particulars. Supposing that the contrast is not the nominalist claim that particulars exist but universals do not, then it must be the Aristotelian claim that particulars have separate existence but universals do not. So we must ask: separate from what? Clearly the view is that universals do not exist separately from the particulars which exemplify them, so correlatively it must be being claimed that particulars *do* exist separately from the universals they exemplify. That amounts to saying that there could exist bare particulars without qualities, an idea Berkeley would undoubtedly find absurd.

Furthermore, we should ask where these particulars appear in

Berkeley's ontology. There are two options: minds and ideas. If minds are the particulars whose possible separate existence is contrasted with universals, then ideas, which certainly cannot exist separately from minds in Berkeley's metaphysics, are the universals. This view sits comfortably with the claim I made in Chapter 5 that Berkeley thinks ideas are sensible qualities and all qualities must exist in some substance, which in this case is the mind that perceives them. Unfortunately, it is in flat contradiction of the discussion at *DHP3* 245 of the question whether two people ever perceive the same idea. There Philonous asserts that we often say they do, on the grounds that their ideas are very similar, but strictly speaking they are never one and the same. But if ideas are Aristotelian universals wholly present at each instantiation, then two people may perceive one and the same idea. Nor can the bare particulars be ideas, for ideas are by definition sensible things, but at *DHP1* 175 Philonous is quite clear that nothing is perceived except qualities. Finally, at *PHK* Intro 7 Berkeley writes:

It is agreed on all hands, that the qualities or modes of things do never really exist each of them apart by it self, and separated from all others, but are mixed, as it were, and blended together, several in the same object.

It would be a mistake to interpret this as a statement of Aristotelianism. The Aristotelian claims that qualities do not exist separately from particulars, whereas what Berkeley writes here is merely that they do not exist separately from all other qualities. This is not even inconsistent with Platonism, which might allow that universals exist in groups or clusters but separate from particulars.

We now need to examine the premiss that we do not meet with universals in our sense experience. This follows immediately from the claim, argued for at *DHP1* 174–5, that the only objects of perception are particular property instances. The argument there turns upon assuming SMP (the Simplest Model of Perception). According to SMP, there can be no perceptual errors: all mistakes arise from the judgements we make on the basis of our perceptions. Suppose that the property of being green were an object of perception, then there would be a common component in the perception of a green leaf and a green bottle. Since that common component, the property of being green, occurs in both perceptual experiences, and how things seem is determined, according to SMP, by what is perceived, they would seem the same to all perceivers (or the same perceiver at different times). But it is simply false that all perceivers experience the similarity between all green things. There could be perceivers who did not think a green bottle and a green leaf had anything in common, who insisted that they looked quite different in all respects.

One response would be to say that, because such a huge variety of appearances are all equally appearances of being green, greenness is not one of the perceptible properties. But the problem recurs. However specific you make the shade occurring in two distinct perceptual experiences, it is always possible for someone to have those experiences and fail to perceive the identity. For example, there could be two marbles which, when placed next to each other, are indistinguishable, but when mixed with a hundred others, few would perceive their sameness of colour. According to SMP, the content of a perception is fully determined by the properties of the perceived object (which is why there can be no perceptual error). So if the perception of A differs from the perception of B, then A differs from B. Hence, if it is possible to perceive two shades as not the same, they are not the same. It follows that we only ever perceive particular colour instances, and likewise for the other qualities.

The claim that ideas are private and do not persist is not essential to Berkeley's nominalism. That two minds, or one mind at different times, could perceive the same particular property instance has no bearing on the question of whether two distinct objects of perception can have something in common. So we can summarize Berkeley's reasons for agreeing with the 'universally received maxim' that everything which exists is particular: only minds and perceived ideas exist; minds are particulars and all perceived ideas are particulars.

7.3 Against Abstraction

Berkeley's positive account of how there can be properties without universals is best understood in the light of his criticisms of its major rival, Locke's theory of abstraction.

7.3.1 *Locke's Theory*

Locke's theory of abstraction came quite late in the long development period of his *Essay concerning Human Understanding*. Though abstraction is first presented in the essay as if it were an activity of the mind plain for all to see (II. xi. 9), the discussion in book III chapter iii makes it clear that his attribution to us of the ability to form abstract ideas is in fact the solution to a problem arising from the conjunction of his nominalism, his empiricism, and his philosophy of language.

[1] Nominalism: everything which exists is particular.
[2] Empiricism: all ideas come from (inner or outer) sense experience.
[3] Philosophy of language: every meaningful word signifies an idea, which determines its meaning.
[4] Fact: there are meaningful general terms in our language.

The problem arises because, if everything which exists is particular, our (inner and outer) sense experience can only be of particulars, so sense experience can only furnish us with ideas of particulars. But our general words signify ideas, and given the meaning of general terms, those cannot be ideas of particulars or groups of particulars (Locke is careful to distinguish between generality and plurality at III. iii. 12: 'for Man and Men would then signify the same'), and thus, it appears, cannot derive from sense experience.

As we shall see, a perfectly reasonable response to this puzzle, and the one Berkeley adopts, is to reject one of the premises [1]–[4]. Locke, however, finds a resolution in the claim that we have an ability to abstract, i.e. take ideas of particulars and turn them into ideas suitable to be the signification of general terms. Unfortunately there is some unclarity as to exactly what an abstract idea is meant to be, and Berkeley is often accused of unfairly exploiting this in his criticisms.

Locke gives two very clear examples of the process of abstraction. The first occurs when Locke introduces abstraction as an 'Operation of Mind' (II. xi. 9):

Thus the same Colour being observed today in Chalk or Snow, which the Mind yesterday received from Milk, it considers that Appearance alone, makes it a representative of all of that kind; and having given it the name *Whiteness*, it by that sound signifies the same quality wheresoever to be imagin'd or met with; and thus Universals, whether *Ideas* or Terms, are made.

The second comes in the chapter 'Of General Terms', in which abstraction is presented as a solution to the puzzle outlined above (III. iii. 7):

There is nothing more evident, than that the *Ideas* of the Persons Children converse with, (to instance them alone,) are[,] like the persons themselves, only particular. The *Ideas* of the Nurse, and the Mother, are well framed in their Minds; and, like Pictures of them there, represent only those Individuals. The Names they first give to them, are confined to these Individuals; and the Names of *Nurse* and *Mamma*, the Child uses, determine themselves to those Persons. Afterwards, when time and a larger Acquaintance has made them observe, that there are a great many other Things in the World, that in some common agreements of Shape, and several other Qualities, resemble their Father and Mother, and those Persons they have been used to, they frame an *Idea*, which they find those many Particulars do partake in; and to that they give, with others, the name *Man*, for Example. . . . Wherein they make nothing new, but only leave out of the complex *Idea* they had of *Peter* and *James*, *Mary* and *Jane*, that which is peculiar to each, and retain only what is common to them all.

The first thing to note about these two examples is that *whiteness* is a quality, but *man* is a kind. By giving these examples, Locke makes it clear that he intends abstraction to cover both these, so he is offering a single solution to the puzzle. However, closer inspection reveals that the process of forming ideas of kinds presupposes that one has already formed ideas of qualities. The process which Locke describes the child as undergoing involves comparing her complex ideas of her mother and father, for example, and noting that they differ in some respects but that they have 'some common agreements of Shape, and several other Qualities'. She then forms an idea which applies to all and only those individuals which also have the properties held in common by all members of the original sample. All this appears to presuppose that the child already has ideas of the qualities which all humans 'partake in', which are certainly not going to be ideas of particulars. In other words, on Locke's account the generality of kind terms is parasitic on the generality of quality terms, and the first example gives the fundamental process of abstraction without which there could not be general terms at all.

Berkeley is well aware that Locke's Abstraction covers two different processes (*PHK* Intro 7–10). He also distinguishes a third process, that of separating ideas of qualities which cannot themselves be separated, e.g. separating the idea of colour from the idea of extension, though there can be nothing coloured which is not extended. Berkeley's example of kind-term abstraction is borrowed from Locke (*PHK* Intro 9), but his example of quality abstraction differs (*PHK* Intro 8):

... the mind by leaving out of the particular colours perceived by sense, that which distinguishes them one from another, and retaining that only which is common to all, makes an idea of colour in abstract which is neither red, nor blue, nor white, nor any other determinate colour.

While Locke's example of an abstract-quality idea was *whiteness*,

Berkeley's is *colour*. The significance of this is not that colour is determinable, whereas white is determinate, since despite white being more determinate than colour, it is itself a determinable of the several shades of white. So neither example is of a fully determinate property. The significant difference is that everything visible is coloured in some way or other, but not everything visible is white, and so the abstractionist claim is even less plausible in the former case.

Locke's description of the formation of abstract ideas of qualities is liable to two interpretations, which we can call subtraction and selection. On the subtraction interpretation, the process of abstraction takes one idea as input and produces another as output, the abstract idea, by subtracting those elements of the input which are not in common to all things which have the quality in question. This is clearly the model suggested by the example of the kind term 'man', but fits less well with quality abstraction, because, as Berkeley is keen to point out, it may not be possible to make the necessary separations. On the selection interpretation, the input and output ideas are the same. What the process of abstraction does is draw the thinker's attention to a specific feature of the input idea or ideas which are held in common by all things with the quality or all members of the kind.

Though much ink has been spilt on the question of how best to interpret Locke on this point, for our purposes it does not matter. So long as we remember Locke's theory of language:

[3] Every meaningful word signifies an idea, which determines its meaning,

selective attention to a part or aspect of an idea can solve the problem of generality only if that part or aspect is itself somehow general. The suggestion that we come to the idea of whiteness by separating an idea of white from its circumstances of time and place (and extension), and the suggestion that we selectively attend to the idea of white and ignore its circumstances, have in common the objective of isolating the idea of whiteness which is to serve as the meaning of the general term 'white'.

7.3.2 Criticism of Locke

Critics of Locke's theory of abstraction will inevitably concentrate on two issues: whether we do in fact have such a capacity, and whether the process of abstraction which Locke describes can really produce ideas suitable to be the signification of general terms. Berkeley makes both criticisms in the Introduction to the *Principles*. The success of the first criticism depends on whether we take introspection to be a good guide to which mental faculties we possess. Though discussion of abstraction in the *Three Dialogues* is restricted, it does appear and at the first occurrence Philonous says 'Without a doubt you can tell, whether you are able to frame this or that idea' (*DHP1* 193), before going on to claim that he cannot frame the abstract ideas of motion or extension in general. But, it is open to the defender of abstraction to argue that, despite introspective appearances, we do in fact have the capacity to form abstract ideas, since that is the only explanation of how we manage to give meaning to general terms.

For rhetorical reasons Berkeley picks up on Locke's claim that abstraction is difficult and only seems easy because of familiarity. This attempt to ridicule is not an example of Berkeley at his best, but he does make good points along the way, one of which is that very young children master general terms (*PHK* Intro 14):

> Is it not a hard thing to imagine, that a couple of children cannot prate together, of their sugar-plums and rattles and the rest of their little trinkets, till they have first tacked together numberless inconsistencies, and so framed in their minds *abstract general ideas*, and annexed them to every common name they make use of?

Setting aside, for the moment, the question of whether abstract ideas are necessarily inconsistent, Berkeley is making the very good point that however we come to give meaning to general terms, it must be possible for children to do it. The point does not directly count against abstraction, but it warns us against any over-intellectual account of the process. For example, it seems easier to understand the general term 'man' than it is to define it. Similarly, finding what is in common to all triangles is a task we might set a student, but only long after they have grasped what a triangle is. As we shall see, Berkeley's own account makes generality a practical rather than intellectual attainment.

The weight of Berkeley's argument must then be with the claim that the process of abstraction does not produce ideas suitable to be the meanings of general terms. The most common interpretation of this argument begins by attributing to Berkeley the premiss that ideas are mental images, and correlatively that an idea of something is an image of that thing. Now take the alleged abstract idea *man*. To be truly general, this idea cannot be 'either of a white, or a black, or a tawny, a straight, or a crooked, a tall, or a low, or a middle-sized man' (*PHK* Intro 10). The objection is then that no mental image can be suitably indeterminate so as to be an image of all these different sorts of man. Furthermore, Locke says at one point that our abstract idea *triangle* 'must be neither oblique nor rectangle, neither equilateral, equicrural, nor scalenon, but all and none of these at once' (*Essay*, IV. vii. 9). It would seem that no mental image could have the properties described, because they are inconsistent. Sometimes a final twist is added to the argument, in the form of the claim that were an indeterminate or inconsistent image possible, it would simply be an image of an inconsistent or indeterminate object.

As an argument against abstraction, this is weak. First, it is far from clear that Locke, or any other abstractionist, holds that ideas are all mental images. Being an empiricist, Locke must hold that all (non-abstract) ideas are possible contents of inner or outer sense experience, but this only commits him to imagism about ideas if he holds an imagistic theory of perception, and he does not. Secondly, it appears that mental images can after all be indeterminate, to some degree at least. A famous example is the mental image of a speckled hen, which does not have to be the image of a hen with a determinate number of speckles. Thirdly, it seems far from essential that abstract ideas have inconsistent properties. If abstraction is some sort of subtraction or selection, then it will not generate inconsistent ideas out of consistent ones. Finally, the example of the speckled hen shows that an image can be indeterminate without being an image of an indeterminate object. In fact, the intrinsic properties of an image alone cannot determine what it is an image of, because every image is subject to more than one interpretation.

Many critics conclude that Berkeley failed to pinpoint what is wrong with abstractionism. However, there is a different line of interpretation, owed to Jonathan Dancy (*Berkeley*, chapter 3), which draws upon two features of Berkeley's discussion, namely his shift from Locke's example of *whiteness* to *colour*, and his comment that 'whatever hand or eye I imagine, it must have some particular shape and colour' (*PHK* Intro 10). The objection to Locke is then that forming the abstract idea of, say, a hand would involve thinking of it as having some colour, for being coloured is common to all hands, but not as having any particular colour, since no particular colour is common to all hands. This is impossible: nothing can have a determinable property (colour) without having it in some determinate way. The objection can look like a simple sophism if we do not remember that an abstract idea of some kind of thing, say hands, must contain every feature which is common to all hands and no feature which is not. Having colour is common to all hands, but each of the determinate colours is not common to all hands, so must be excluded from the abstract idea. Hence the abstract idea of a hand must be the idea of something which is coloured but is *not* red or green or any other particular colour. And that is an idea which it is impossible to form.

If this is Berkeley's objection, it fails, for it only applies to abstract ideas of kinds and not to ideas of qualities, and also it is based on a logical error. There is a difference between conceiving that something is not red and not conceiving that it is red, a difference which is preserved by a theory which holds that abstraction is subtraction (or selection). What the abstractionist needs is a conception of a hand as having some particular colour but there being no particular colour which the hand is conceived as having. This is possible, unlike the conception of a hand as having some particular colour but no particular colour.

Peter Geach (*Mental Acts*, §§ 6–11) has pointed out that determinables do present a particular problem for abstractionists, since whenever one is attending to something's being coloured, one is necessarily attending to its particular colour, so selective attention (or subtraction) alone cannot determine whether one's abstract idea is of *colour* or of *red*. However, it is not plausible that this is the criticism that Berkeley had in mind.

I think that we get the best understanding of Berkeley's objection not by looking at the passages where he is trying to ridicule the abstractionist, but at those where he is trying to be constructive (*PHK* Intro 11):

But it seems that a word becomes general by being made the sign, not of an abstract general idea but, of several particular ideas, any one of which it indifferently suggests to the mind.

The core of this point is that general words do not refer each to a single idea of a peculiar type, but rather apply to more than one idea. If we remember the distinction Locke made between 'man' and 'men', between generality and plurality, we can understand Berkeley's point in terms of there being different relations between, on the one hand, singular terms and the ideas they apply to, and on the other hand, general terms and the ideas they apply to. A singular term refers to a single idea or collection of ideas, whereas a general term is related to several ideas or collections, and the relation is not that of plural reference. We can see these distinctions in practice: 'The cabinet minister declined to comment' involves singular reference, 'The cabinet ministers declined to comment' involves plural reference, and 'Jones is a cabinet minister' contains a singular term ('Jones') and a phrase which does not seem to have the function of reference at all ('cabinet minister'). Locke makes the mistake of thinking that 'cabinet minister' in 'Jones is a cabinet minister' refers to something, and then tries to find something special for it to refer to, something which is acceptable to his nominalism, namely the abstract idea of a cabinet minister derived by a mental operation from ideas of particular cabinet ministers. It would seem that Berkeley's objection contains the kernel of an important distinction between referring to something and describing it. He never uses these terms, but if we look carefully we can see that he is quite careful to distinguish between straightforward signification or denotation and signifying or denoting 'indifferently'.

However, it is open to the abstractionist to respond that he can accept the distinction between referring and describing, but still to insist on the need for an abstract idea to give the meaning of general terms. Here we shall have to help Berkeley out a little, though it is not too hard to do so. If a single, abstract idea is to give the meaning of a general term, then that idea must describe or indifferently denote all the particulars to which that general term applies. So the question we should ask is whether an idea, howsoever abstracted it may be, can perform the describing function. Locke and Berkeley agree that ideas can denote, can be of particulars such as Jones, so they must disagree on whether some ideas can denote *indifferently*. At this point Berkeley will say that were there such things as abstract ideas, they would simply refer to Platonic universals, things which cannot exist in space and time, and thereby fail to solve the problem of generality.

There seems to be a much deeper problem here which Berkeley may have sensed. For an empiricist, all ideas derive from experience and consequently only apply within experience: their source limits their field of application. The explanation for this is to do with how the ideas represent. Hume makes this clearest, but he is just articulating an assumption common to all empiricists (*Treatise*, I.

i. 1). He distinguishes the contents of experience, which he calls impressions, from the ideas involved in thought and judgement, which allows him to address the question of their relation:

> By *ideas* I mean the faint images of these [impressions] in thinking and reasoning . . .
> . . . The first circumstance, that strikes my eye, is the great resemblance betwixt our impressions and ideas in every other particular, except their degree of force and vivacity. The one seem to be in a manner the reflexion of the other . . . *all our simple ideas in their first appearance are deriv'd from impressions, which are correspondent to them, and which they exactly represent.*

Hume clearly thinks of ideas as images of impressions, but what is important is that he thinks of them as images in the sense of copies or facsimiles. Now a copy is related to the original by both a degree of resemblance and a causal connection, and while there can be many copies made of a single original, a copy can only ever be a copy of one thing. This generates a problem for abstract ideas. If an abstract idea is a copy or image of what it applies to, then it cannot apply to all things of a certain sort, since it does not derive (causally) from them all. Suppose, with Locke, that I form my idea of white by abstracting from my ideas of chalk, snow, and milk. The idea I so form may resemble the colour of this piece of paper, but (assuming nominalism) it cannot be a copy or image of that colour because it does not derive from my idea of the paper. Though this point can easily be confused with an objection based on assuming that ideas are mental images, it in fact only relies on the implicit causal constraint in the empiricist theory of ideas. The causal constraint is natural because the 'of' in 'idea of *x*' is taken to be a referential relation. Without the causal constraint, the claim that we can only have ideas of what we have experienced would be at best a contingent truth about the human mind. A copy or image necessarily derives from and refers to the original, so while it may achieve plurality (referring to several things), it cannot

234 · CHAPTER 7

achieve generality. This is a problem for abstractionism which has wider implications, because it shows up an incompatibility between nominalism and a causal or derivational account of representation, which is an instance of a more general incompatibility between nominalism and the attempt to give the meaning of a general term or concept by specifying its reference.

We can gain some indirect evidence for attributing this view to Berkeley by looking at how exactly he thinks abstraction introduces error into philosophy. For example, one might initially be struck by the way that the idea of motion in general is dismissed in the First Dialogue as impossible to frame (*DHP1* 193), but the idea of an instrument in general is allowed to be coherent in the Second Dialogue (*DHP2* 218). Berkeley is not here being inconsistent. In the First Dialogue Hylas suggests that matter has motion in general but no particular motion, whereas in the Second Dialogue he suggests that it is some particular instrument, but not knowing what sort of instrument it is, he conceives of it as an instrument in general. Now, Berkeley can allow that we do have a general idea of an instrument, and thus that we can think of something we have not experienced as being an instrument, without knowing even what sort of instrument it is. But the general idea is the idea of a particular instrument made general by its use. The philosophical error arises from first taking this general idea to be an abstract idea, and then taking ideas to be copies or images of their objects, thinking that there can be something which corresponds to that abstract idea without being some more specific particular idea.

7.3.3 *Rejecting the Assumptions*

Berkeley's biggest insight is that the theory of abstract ideas is driven by a theory of meaning, a theory which requires each word to stand for an idea (*PHK* Intro 18):

First then, 'tis thought that every name hath, or ought to have, one only precise and settled signification, which inclines men to think there are certain *abstract, determinate ideas,* which constitute the true and only signification of each general name. ... Whereas, in truth, there is no such thing as one precise and definite signification annexed to any general name, they all signifying indifferently a great number of particular ideas.

Experience furnishes me with an idea of, for example, John. So when I use the word 'John', I have this idea in mind. This raises the question of which idea I have in mind when I use the word 'man'. If it were the idea of John, then 'John' and 'man' would mean the same, and similarly for every other idea of a man or some men that I might gain from experience. Hence we need a special type of idea to give the meaning of general terms. Now, Berkeley is here rejecting this theory, at least for general names, on the ground mentioned above that their relation to particulars is not simple but 'indifferent' signification.

One element of Berkeley's rejection of the ideational theory of meaning is the simple descriptive point that we often use words meaningfully and yet have no idea before the mind (*PHK* Intro 20):

. . . it will be found that when language is once grown familiar, the hearing of the sounds or sight of the characters is oft immediately attended with those passions, which at first were wont to be produced by the intervention of ideas, that are now quite omitted. May we not, for example, be affected with the promise of a *good thing,* though we have not an idea of what it is?

The point here is that the purpose of a speech act may not be to produce an idea in the audience but, in cases such as the promise of a good thing, it is to produce a response (pleasant expectation and possibly co-operation in some project). While this response may be achieved through the 'intervention of ideas', it need not be, and the words serve their purpose when they produce the response, whether or not they also produce ideas in the mind of the audience.

A problem which Berkeley did not raise is that the ideational theory has difficulty with the publicity of meaning. It seems that I can know what your words mean without knowing what ideas they conjure in your mind. Of course, some people do attach distinctive or unusual private meanings to their words, and very occasionally this does not show up in use, but they are still breaking the rules and misusing language. Berkeley was well aware of the public nature of meaning, as this exchange from the Second Dialogue makes clear (*DHP2* 216):

> PHILONOUS   Tell me, Hylas, hath every one a liberty to change the current proper signification annexed to a common name in any language? . . .
> HYLAS   No; I should think it very absurd. Common custom is the standard of propriety in language.

It is hard, if not impossible, to explain the public nature of the rules of language if the meaning of a word is determined by the idea it produces in men's minds.

We can avoid all the problems of abstract ideas if we drop the claim that every meaningful word must stand for an idea which determines its meaning. We could equally avoid the problem by dropping nominalism or empiricism, but Berkeley does not consider these options.

Rejecting abstractionism also has consequences for the nature of thought. It is an assumption in Locke that the ideas one has before the mind determine what one is thinking about. Thus if I have an idea of Mary in mind, I am thinking about Mary. Hence abstract ideas are necessary not only for general words but also for general thoughts: if I am to think of the colour white or being human, I must do so by having an idea which determines my thought to be about whiteness or humanity. We can call this the *content assumption*: the content of a thought is completely determined by the character of the ideas one has when thinking it. If there are no abstract ideas, and if there are no inherently general ideas deriving from some other source (premises of empiricism and nominalism), then not only must we give a different explanation of the meaning of general words, but also of how we come to think general thoughts.

In rejecting abstractionism, Berkeley is also rejecting the content assumption.

Before we go on to investigate what Berkeley might offer as an alternative theory of thought, it is worth pausing to note that rejecting the content assumption involves weakening, or at least qualifying, one's commitment to empiricism. The essence of empiricism is that all ideas derive from experience. The content assumption adds that it is the ideas that we have which determine what we are thinking, and putting the two together the two entail that we are only able to think about what we have experienced. This last claim is normally taken to be as central to empiricism as the first, for much of Locke's attack on rationalism in book 1 of the *Essay* is aimed at the claim that certain very general principles, such as 'Whatever is, is' and ''Tis impossible for the same thing to be, and not to be' (or, crucially for Descartes, 'Every event has a cause'), are not grasped prior to experience. Once we drop the content assumption, that opens the possibility that, while all *ideas* derive from experience, there are certain things we are able to think, the ability to think which does not derive from experience. Of course, it does not follow from dropping the content assumption that the ability to think about whiteness or humanity is *innate*, and we shall see how such abilities are, according to Berkeley, still dependent upon experience. However, it is only because he has dropped the content assumption that Berkeley is able to respond to the problem Hylas raises about our idea of God, namely that we are not able to think of God or spirits since we have no experience of them (*DHP3* 231):

PHILONOUS   I own I have properly no idea, either of God or any other spirit . . . I do nevertheless know, that I who am a spirit or thinking substance, exist as certainly, as I know my ideas exist. Farther, I know what I mean by the terms *I* and *myself*.

With the content assumption in place, this response would be impossible.

7.4 Properties without Universals

So far all we have seen of Berkeley's position has been negative: he has rejected universals, abstract ideas, and Locke's theory of meaning. This still leaves him the difficult task of answering the property realist's challenge to explain how two things can be the same, i.e. can both be green or round or heavy, and yet be different. The realist explanation is that they have something in common, namely the properties of greenness, roundness, or heaviness. A nominalist such as Berkeley need not deny the truth of this claim, but cannot allow that it can explain how two things can both be green, say, since to say that they share the property greenness *just is* to say that they are both green. According to the nominalist, the realist mistakes a trivial reformulation for a substantive explanation. And yet there is still a fact in need of explanation.

What Berkeley says to address this need in the Introduction to the *Principles* looks circular (*PHK* Intro 12):

an idea, which considered in it self is particular, becomes general, by being made to represent or stand for all other particular ideas of the same sort.

The problem with this claim is that one thing a nominalist is trying to do is to account for what it is that makes different particular ideas 'of the same sort'. However, in a later work, the *Alciphron*, there is a striking echo of this passage with a small modification which makes it clear that Berkeley intends to give a fairly standard nominalist account of sameness of sort (Dialogue 7, § 7, 1st and 2nd editions only, p. 334):

EUPHRANOR   But may not words become general by being made to stand indiscriminately for all particular ideas which from mutual resemblance belong to the same kind, without the intervention of any abstract general idea?

There are two parts to this proposal: that sameness of property can be reduced to resemblance, and that generality in representation is a product of what we make our words and ideas do.

7.4.1 *Properties as Resemblances*

From a certain perspective, it can seem very easy to be a nominalist. A predicate or a general concept, such as oblong, 'indifferently denotes' a set of things. We can call this set its extension. Then the choice between realism and nominalism is the choice between two answers to the question 'How does the predicate get to have that extension?' The realist says that it refers to a universal, oblongness, which is shared by all the items in the extension. The nominalist says that we simply decide to assign it that extension rather than any other. By the standard of Ockham's razor, nominalism certainly looks attractive.

Unfortunately, the matter is not as simple as that, for there is an apparent dilemma for the nominalist. If it is a human act to give a predicate, such as 'oblong', a particular extension, then we must have some way of picking out that extension. It would be circular to say that it is the set of oblong things. And if we define 'oblong' in other terms, then either we face an infinite regress or the problem recurs somewhere else with some other predicate. The alternative way of picking out the extension is by enumerating all its elements. But we cannot do that, since we have not yet discovered all the oblong things, which is to say that there are elements in the extension of 'oblong' which we do not know, and thus cannot enumerate. The extension of 'oblong', like that of most of our predicates, is potentially infinite. Of course, where we can easily enumerate the extension, as with the predicate 'is a table in my room on 1 January 2000', then the nominalist is on strong grounds. It would be a very extreme realist who thought that there was a universal corresponding to that predicate.

So the challenge for the nominalist is to show how we can pick out the extension of a predicate, without circularity or regress, when we do not know all the elements of that extension. And it is quite important that the answer to this problem is not too intellectual, for, as Berkeley noted, young children have no problem grasping general terms and using them with understanding. When someone understands a term such as 'oblong', they know that it is associated with a particular extension, and when faced with a shape, they have some idea about how to answer the question 'Is this oblong?'

The solution which Berkeley appeals to is that the extensions of most of the predicates we are interested in are determined by a relation of resemblance. A given shape is oblong in virtue of its resemblance to other oblong items. What one needs in order to grasp the extension of 'oblong' is some suitable examples and an ability to spot resemblances.

We should begin by noting that, on pain of circularity, resemblance is here to be considered as subjective resemblance. Two things objectively resemble each other to the extent that they have properties in common, they subjectively resemble each other to the extent that someone judges them similar. The nominalist says that it is because this shape strikes us as similar to that oblong that it is also to be denominated an oblong.

One notorious problem with this proposal is that subjective resemblance is not transitive, but sharing a property with, or falling under the same predicate as, something is transitive. It is perfectly possible for A to resemble B (to degree n) and B to resemble C (to degree n) but A not to resemble C (to degree n). If the nominalist is claiming that resemblance to every item of type F is both necessary and sufficient for being an F, then C both is and is not the same type (F) as A. There are several ways out of this problem. One is to suggest that it is resemblance to a specific F, or group of Fs, which is necessary and sufficient for being F. This would have the consequence that there must be a common set of paradigm examples of F-ness, otherwise everyone would be using the predicate 'F' to mean something slightly different. But in most cases, different people can use predicates with exactly the same meaning despite having different opinions about which are the paradigm examples. They will all agree that each other's paradigm is an F, just not that it is a paradigmatic F. So, for example, I may think that a blackbird is a paradigm bird, whereas you, coming from New Zealand, think a kiwi is. We both agree that each other's paradigm is a bird, but if what we meant by 'bird' was determined by resemblance to the paradigm, then we might disagree about some cases, such as emus, which resembled your paradigm more than mine. The problem with the resemblance-to-a-paradigm theory is that when we do disagree about what the paradigm examples of our general concepts are, that disagreement does not necessarily amount to a disagreement about what we mean.

There are other, more elaborate, attempts to solve the problem of transitivity, but none is really satisfactory. The reason for this is that they all try to capture the determination of predicate extension in terms of some sort of *natural* subjective resemblance, but few, if any, predicates work like that. What we need is a compromise, a theory which combines the attractions of the initial position we considered, in which we simply select one of the infinitely many possible extensions to assign to the predicate, either arbitrarily or on pragmatic grounds, with the need to account for how we grasp these extensions where they are open-ended. We can achieve this by looking not for paradigms but for limiting or boundary cases. Colour terms are a good example, for sameness of colour is clearly a matter of similarity: no one can grasp colour concepts without being sensitive to the similarities between things of one colour and differences from things of other colours. Yet, the boundaries between colours are arbitrary: when someone learns to use the terms 'red', 'orange', and 'yellow', they learn to divide part of the spectrum into three categories, but we could have equally had a language which divided the same part of the spectrum into four or six or even just one category. Understanding 'red' involves on the one hand being able to recognize the similarities between red things and on the other knowing that, similarities notwithstanding, there is a distinction to be made between red and orange. The distinction between red and orange is a matter of convention within a language community, and is quite likely to differ between different communities, thus giving them a different colour vocabulary.

The problem with the paradigms theory was that we do not in fact share paradigms, that members of a language community can mean the same by their general terms and yet disagree about which are paradigmatic examples. In contrast, if someone disagreed with us about whether there was a distinction to be drawn between red and orange, even a rather indeterminate and fuzzy distinction, then she would not be using our colour vocabulary, she would mean something different by her words.

Though Berkeley never addresses the question of exactly how sameness of quality is determined by resemblance, the present proposal should be very attractive to him, since it keeps a role for resemblance while also making it clear that we choose our general terms for our own purposes, by deciding where to draw boundaries which limit the uniting effect of similarity.

7.4.2 Concepts as Abilities

Throughout the last section I have spoken about understanding a general term or grasping a general concept, taking the former to be sufficient for, if not identical to, the latter. Now it was one of the features of Locke's theory of abstraction that it explained what it was to understand a general term, namely to have an appropriate abstract idea. Having denied that there are such things as abstract ideas, Berkeley needs to offer a different explanation. In fact, he needs to offer a completely different theory of thought, because whatever he thinks is involved in grasping a general concept, it cannot consist solely of having an idea before the mind. We saw this when he rejected the content assumption.

What Berkeley says is simply that when we have a general

thought, a particular idea is being made a sign of a whole class of ideas (*PHK* Intro 12):

And as that particular line [which the geometer draws and we perceive] becomes general, by being made a sign, so the name *line* which taken absolutely is particular, by being a sign is made general. And as the former owes its generality, not to its being the sign of an abstract or general line, but of all particular right lines that may possibly exist, so the latter must be thought to derive its generality from the same cause, namely, the various particular lines which it indifferently denotes.

That even having a particular idea is not necessary, he makes clear at *PHK* Intro 20:

general names are often used in the propriety of language without the speaker's designing them for marks of ideas in his own, which he would have them raise in the mind of the hearer.

What Berkeley writes here is strikingly similar to some versions of the use theory of meaning. Take, for example, Hilary Putnam's summary in *Reason, Truth and History* (18):

Concepts are signs used in a certain way; the signs may be public or private, mental entities or physical entities, but even when the signs are 'mental' and 'private', the sign itself apart from its use is not the concept.

It is hard to say whether Berkeley really did hold something we would want to call a use theory of meaning, partly because he may not have fully realized the essential nature of generality to thought. Without some general element, some predication, I cannot think something assessable as either true or false. To illustrate this, think of the till receipts one gets from supermarkets which itemize one's shopping. A simple list of groceries like this can be accurate or inaccurate only if we know whether it is a list of what you have bought, or what you need to buy, or . . .: a concatenation of particular names says nothing on its own, without the addition of the thought that the items on the list are all of some type or other, such as 'what you have bought today'.

If generality is an essential component of all thoughts and judgements which can be true or false, then Berkeley's brief remarks take on a special significance. And what he seems to be saying is that generality involves a sign, be it a word, a symbol, or an idea, which has the property of indifferently denoting a class of particulars. Locke tried to explain how some words and ideas had generality by looking for ideas which had a special nature, being abstract, in virtue of which they denoted each of a class of particulars. Berkeley's alternative appears to be that somehow we *make* particulars into general signs. We do not do this by changing their nature, for when the geometer uses a particular triangle to stand for all triangles, he does not change anything about that particular triangle. So if making a particular into a general sign does not involve doing something *to* it, it must consist in doing something *with* it. What makes the difference between my idea of Mary being simply an idea of Mary and it being a sign for all children is what I do with it. It can be a little difficult to see how this works with ideas because all ideas are of particulars, so ideas which are being used in a way which makes them general have a dual function. Words, however, are not in themselves words for anything, either particular or general, so it is easy for us to separate the different functions, denoting a particular and denoting indifferently a class of particulars, and attach them to different words. I use the word 'Mary' so that it applies only to Mary, but I use the word 'child' so that it applies to any child, i.e. to anything similar to Mary within the conventional limits (however childlike, an 18-year-old is not a child).

What is particularly attractive about this interpretation of Berkeley's account of general thought is its consonance with his overall metaphysical position. It is sometimes thought that since the only things Berkeley countenances in his ontology are minds and ideas, he has no choice but to say that all thinking is just the having of ideas. That would force him into explaining generality in terms of special ideas. But ideas are passive whereas minds are active, so as well as the things before the mind, Berkeley can appeal to the activities of minds when he is trying to explain generality. General thought is not the passive state of having an idea, but is the active state of using an idea or word in a certain way. Which is to say that having a concept is having an ability to do something, and thinking with that concept, exercising it, is doing that thing.

7.5 Conclusion

Berkeley is a nominalist. What I have tried to make clear is that his ontology of minds and ideas does not create any special problems for him as a nominalist. Like many other nominalists, most of whom are materialists, he can appeal to resemblance to make his nominalism work. He can also appeal to conventions, both public and private, about the use of words and about what counts as being of one type rather than another. Because of his emphasis on the active nature of the mind, in his theory of thought he will naturally tend towards the proposal that concepts are abilities, that meaning is use. There may be alternatives, but the important point is that, to make his nominalism work, Berkeley needs some theory of thought or other.

There are objections to nominalism which Berkeley must deal with, but he is not any better or worse off in this respect than any other nominalist. Someone who is convinced that no form of nominalism can be made to work thereby has a route to object to Berkeley's whole metaphysical picture. But it is not an easy objection to make, for either the realist accepts that as well as universals there are particular property instances, in which case the arguments for the mind-dependence of sensible qualities still stand, or she denies there are such things, in which case sensible qualities are universals. Admittedly, if sensible qualities are universals, they are not mind-dependent, but nor are they material. So the arguments against matter can still go ahead.

CHAPTER 8

Objects and Identity

8.1 The Bundle Theory of Objects

In Chapter 5 we concluded that to be part of physical reality an idea had to be perceived by the senses. Sense perception is involuntary and thus not something God can undergo. In Chapter 6 we saw that there was a reason to change Berkeley's criterion of sense perception from involuntariness to passivity, but God is essentially active (*DHP2* 213–14), so sense perception is still exclusive to finite minds. Thus an idea is real, as opposed to merely imagined, if, and only if, it is actually, but passively, perceived by a finite spirit. As Philonous puts it at *DHP3* 260:

Every thing that is seen, felt, heard, or any way perceived by the senses, is, on the principles I embrace, a real being.

If we interpret this as not merely being a claim of sufficiency, but also necessity (Philonous' cautious phrasing is to allow for the existence of spirits, whereas we are here only concerned with physical existence), then God cannot create a real idea which is not perceived by the senses of some spirit or other. In other words, there can be no reality corresponding to what is only imagined and never perceived. This is Berkeley's most infamous thesis, which seems obviously false to most readers. In this chapter we shall explore whether it is necessarily in conflict with our everyday view of the physical world.

Now ideas may be the building-blocks of the physical world, but Berkeley, in line with common sense, also countenances talk of ordinary physical objects such as books and trees and stars. Such objects differ from ideas in being perceived by different people and at different times, i.e. they are persisting, public objects, whereas ideas are fleeting, private objects. The focus of our discussion will be how Berkeley thinks physical objects are constructed out of ideas. This will allow us to address the question many readers of Berkeley find pressing: can he account for the existence of physical objects during the intervals when no finite spirit is perceiving them? We are already in a position to reject the interpretation offered by Knox's famous limericks:

> There was a young man who said 'God
> Must think it exceedingly odd
> If he finds that this tree
> Continues to be
> When there's no one about in the Quad.'

To which God replies:

> Dear Sir:
>   Your astonishment's odd;
> I am always about in the Quad.
> And that's why the tree
> Will continue to be,
> Since observed by
>   *Yours faithfully,*
> GOD

This cannot be correct. For we have seen that Berkeley's criterion of the real requires the perception of the real world to be involuntary or passive, and none of God's perceptions is like this. In other words, while any idea God perceives thereby exists, it is not part of the physical world unless it is sensed by a finite spirit.

One account of persisting, public objects is that they are substances, i.e. they are the things which possess the properties by which we know them. Now Berkeley is not averse to the idea of substances in general, for he agrees that qualities cannot float free of something which has them, and also that spirits are substances. However, he objects to sensible objects, i.e. the things we perceive, being regarded as substances. The qualities we perceive are all 'had' or perceived by spirits, which prevents them from floating free. And we perceive nothing but qualities, so there is no ground in experience to think of sensible things as substances distinct from their qualities (*DHP1* 175):

PHILONOUS   It seems therefore, that if you take away all sensible qualities, there remains nothing sensible.

HYLAS   I grant it.

PHILONOUS   Sensible things therefore are nothing else but so many sensible qualities, or combinations of sensible qualities.

HYLAS   Nothing else.

Here he is diverging from the views of both his rationalist and his empiricist predecessors. The rationalists think that physical objects must be substances distinct from their properties in order for them to be able to persist through change of their properties. In other words, it is reason, not experience, which teaches Descartes, in the Second Meditation, that his lump of wax is something which can continue to exist despite all its sensible qualities changing and thus is something distinct from those sensible qualities. So he agrees with Philonous' first claim but not the second. The empiricist Locke also thinks that we must deny the second claim, but not on grounds of pure reason. He thinks that our experience forces us to suppose that qualities inhere in something distinct which unifies them into the groupings we experience. Consequently our ideas of physical objects include the idea of substance (*Essay*, II. xxiii. 3):

. . . we must take notice, that our complex *Ideas* of Substances, besides all these simple *Ideas* they are made up of, have always the confused *Idea* of *something* to which they belong, and in which they subsist.

So Berkeley's innovation is not in his description of what experience reveals to us, but in his claim that to think of the physical world as containing public, persisting objects, we do not need to think of those objects as substances in which their revealed qualities inhere. Rather, he is proposing that we think of physical objects as nothing more than the sum of their qualities. This is nowadays called the bundle theory of objects.

Berkeley says very little about this view of objects, so perhaps he thought it no great innovation. After all, everyone seemed to be agreed that we perceive nothing but sensible qualities, and to suppose the existence of anything else would be to suppose something unperceivable, which Berkeley thinks misguided and impossible. As he sees it, it is the doctrine of physical substance which is unusual and in conflict with common sense. So he confidently begins the *Principles* with the bundle theory and hardly mentions the matter again (*PHK* 1):

By sight I have the ideas of light and colours with their several degrees and variations. By touch I perceive, for example, hard and soft, heat and cold, motion and resistance, and of all these more and less either as to quantity or degree. Smelling furnishes me with odours; the palate with tastes, and hearing conveys sounds to the mind in all their variety of tone and composition. And as several of these are observed to accompany each other, they come to be marked by one name, and so to be reputed as one thing. Thus, for example, a certain colour, taste, smell, figure and consistence having been observed to go together, are accounted one distinct thing, signified by the name *apple*; other collections of ideas constitute a stone, a tree, a book, and the like sensible things; which, as they are pleasing or disagreeable, excite the passions of love, hatred, joy, grief, and so forth.

In the *Dialogues* the bundle theory is stated twice, once by each speaker, but only in the Third Dialogue (*DHP3* 248, 261). The statement by Philonous makes it clear that Berkeley is rejecting the claim that physical things are to be identified with substances which have the qualities we perceive. He also uses the word 'congeries' rather than 'collection'. This is to emphasize that prior to the work of the mind in drawing these ideas together and giving them one name, they do not have a natural unity (*DHP3* 249):

> I see this *cherry*, I feel it, I taste it: and I am sure *nothing* cannot be seen, or felt, or tasted: it is therefore *real*. Take away the sensations of softness, moisture, redness, tartness, and you take away the cherry. Since it is not a being distinct from sensations; a *cherry*, I say, is nothing but a congeries of sensible impressions, or ideas perceived by various senses: which ideas are united into one thing (or have one name given them) by the mind; because they are observed to attend each other. Thus when the palate is affected with such a particular taste, the sight is affected with a red colour, the touch with roundness, softness, *&c.* Hence, when I see, and feel, and taste, in sundry certain manners, I am sure the *cherry* exists, or is real; its reality being in my opinion nothing abstracted from those sensations. But if by the word *cherry* you mean an unknown nature distinct from all those sensible qualities, and by its existence something distinct from its being perceived; then indeed I own, neither you nor I, nor any one else can be sure it exists.

On the basis of these two passages, we can summarize the theory thus. Experience consists of a continuous flow of particular ideas. When we recognize these ideas as falling under types, such as being red, round, soft, or sweet, we can discern patterns in the stream of experience. In particular, we can discover that ideas of some types are often accompanied by ideas of other types. Since ideas had by different minds and at different times can be of the same type, there is no reason why accompaniment should be limited to one mind at one time. Thus, if yesterday I noticed that the red round thing I saw felt soft, and today I see something similar and you taste the sweetness, then that is evidence that this redness and roundness accompany softness and sweetness. When we find these patterns in experience, we collect together the particular ideas which accompany each other and regard them as forming a unity, a thing. And since similar collections occur at different points of our experience, we introduce names for types of thing, such as 'cherry' or 'tree' or 'book'.

It is worth emphasizing that this is a three-stage process. In the first stage we start with the perception of particular ideas, and on the basis of resemblance group them into types, such as red or round. The second stage is when we notice that certain ideas go together in groups. Thus we might notice that the qualities of brownness, hardness, flatness, etc. tend to appear together. On the basis of this, we start talking of an object which has these qualities. Which is to say that we treat the occurrence of these qualities, at different times and experienced by different minds, as all belonging to the same thing. According to Berkeley, this is a matter of collecting them together to form a 'congeries'. The alternative is to say that at this stage we introduce the concept of a substance. Either way, a structure is imposed upon, or discovered in, our experience whereby qualities which were independent at stage one are connected together into groups and fit to be denoted by a single label. In the third stage we notice that the same process of collection produces very similar bundles of qualities, that is bundles containing ideas of the same types, and we introduce a label for bundles of that type, such as 'table'. It is very rare in practice that anyone introduces a label at the second stage, which would be in effect a proper name for a particular collection of ideas, prior to introducing one at the third stage, but it could be done. Now the first stage is the process of introducing quality terms and the third stage is the process of introducing kind terms, both of which we discussed in Chapter 7. It is the second stage which is important and definitive of the bundle theory of objects. And the first objection the bundle theory faces is that the second stage cannot be coherently described, for there is no way of describing our experience without reference to physical objects. If it were true that there is no coherent description of experience more basic than that involving physical objects, then it could not be correct to see physical objects as constructed out of something more basic.

Before discussing this objection, we should clarify the irrelevance of developmental psychology to the bundle theory. The three-stage process described above is not intended to be an empirical description of the temporal stages in human development. Rather the relation between the stages is one of logical and explanatory priority. The first is possible without the second and the second without the third, but not vice versa. Also, it is the materials which are available at the first stage which explain how the second stage can occur, and those available at the second stage which explain the possibility of the third stage. It is perfectly consistent with this hierarchy that a child should achieve all three stages simultaneously, or go from having none to all three via an intermediate period of indeterminacy which cannot be described in these terms at all. Not only does this talk of stages not commit the bundle theorist to any empirical claims about child development, but also it does not commit him to the psychological possibility of stripping away the layers of conceptual complexity we have imposed on our experience. What matters is not whether we ever went through stages one and two, or whether we can go back to those stages, but whether the account of logical and explanatory priority is coherent. If it is, then the bundle theorist must address the further question of whether at stage two we introduce bundles, or congeries, composed of qualities, or whether we introduce substantial subjects in which the qualities inhere.

To return to the question of the coherence of stage two, this depends upon whether there is a way of conceiving the world at stage one which provides an adequate basis for the introduction of objects. It would be wrong simply to assume that objects are (logically) secondary in our experience, for it is perfectly possible that there is no way of conceiving of the physical world except in terms of objects. Berkeley does not seem to have thought about this problem, for he is very careless about distinguishing between talk of persistent public objects and talk of ideas. In fact, at many crucial points he takes being perceived, which is sufficient for the existence of an idea, to be sufficient for the existence of objects such as 'Wood, stones, fire, water, flesh, iron, and the like things' (*DHP3* 230). But the possibility of illusions shows that my current perceptual experience, while it is sufficient for the existence of the ideas of brownness and hardness, is not sufficient for the existence of my table. The ideas in one mind at one time cannot guarantee the existence of a public, persisting object composed of ideas in several minds at several times. So we must be more careful than Berkeley here, and ensure that the input to stage two is not described in these terms. What we need has been called, by Strawson, a feature-placing language. Examples of feature-placing sentences include (Strawson, *Individuals*, 202):

Now it is raining.
Snow is falling.
There is coal here.
There is gold here.
There is water here.

English grammar is not unique in allowing a sentence construction for asserting that some feature is present without attributing that feature to any object. Each of these sentences could be replaced by a single word: 'Rain!', 'Snow!', etc., but we should be careful to note that being equivalent to a single-word sentence is neither necessary nor sufficient for being a sentence of a feature-placing language. The single-word sentence 'Rabbit!' indicates the presence of *a rabbit,* and the concept of a rabbit is the concept of a persisting public object. Rather the feature-placing sentences which ground the introduction of rabbits as persisting public objects must be along the lines of: 'There is brownness here and there is furriness here and there is . . .', eventually enumerating all the perceptible qualities of a particular rabbit which we want to talk or think about. The qualities in this list must not be attributed to objects,

254 · CHAPTER 8

and thus cannot include sortal terms such as 'animal', but they must be located in time and space and relativized to observers. Coincidence in time and place is obviously important in bringing suitable collections to our notice, but there is no a priori reason why we should not construct an ontology which included objects with qualities that could not be simultaneously experienced.

8.2 Can we Really Do without Non-Mental Substances?

As we have noted, many philosophers prior to Berkeley would have accepted the three stages described above, but not his account of the second stage. According to Berkeley, we move from the feature-placing description of the world to the postulation of persisting, public objects by collecting the features together into amorphous bundles. The bundles are amorphous because any one is not intrinsically more appropriate than any other, rather trial and error teach us which bundles are useful to talk and think about and which are not so useful. The alternative theory is that at stage two we have to recognize (or 'suppose', according to Locke, *Essay*, II. xxiii. 1) the existence of substances, distinct from qualities and in which the qualities subsist. There are four main reasons for favouring the substance approach, and we need to see what the bundle theorist in general, or Berkeley in particular, can say about each of them.

8.2.1 *Qualities Cannot Exist on their Own*

We saw in Chapter 5 that it was a commonplace of philosophy in Berkeley's time that particular quality instances, such as the colours I see or the sounds I hear, were not capable of independent existence. There can only be redness in the world (as opposed to the Platonic universal RED) if there exists something else apart from the redness on which the redness depends. The view can be summarized as the claim that substances are the subjects of the qualities, and as such it is encouraged by language, for when we move away from feature-placing languages, we start using the construction of subject and predicate. The predicate corresponds to the quality, so one naturally expects the subject term to correspond to something different, and thus one supposes it refers to the substance which has the quality.

Berkeley's attitude towards this philosophical doctrine is complex. In the *Principles* he explicitly rejects the doctrine (*PHK* 49):

> As to what philosophers say of subject and mode, that seems very groundless and unintelligible. For instance, in this proposition, a die is hard, extended, and square, they will have it that the word *die* denotes a subject or substance, distinct from the hardness, extension and figure, which are predicated of it, and in which they exist. This I cannot comprehend: to me a die seems to be nothing distinct from those things which are termed its modes or accidents. And, to say a die is hard, extended and square, is not to attribute those qualities to a subject distinct from and supporting them, but only an explication of the meaning of the word *die*.

And yet, as we noted in Chapter 5, he does seem to endorse the more general thought that qualities cannot exist except in some relation to a substance. For example, in the Third Dialogue Philonous says (*DHP3* 234):

> I know what I mean when I affirm that there is a spiritual substance or support of ideas, that is, that a spirit knows and perceives ideas. But I do not know what is meant, when it is said, that an unperceiving substance hath inherent in it and supports either ideas or the archetypes of ideas. There is therefore upon the whole no parity of case between spirit and matter.

The point here, that the alleged relation between sensible qualities and matter is unintelligible, but the relation between sensible qualities and spirits, being perception, is perfectly intelligible, could have been made without adding in the extra thought that spirits are the 'support' of ideas. Berkeley also often writes of ideas 'subsisting' in the mind, which is a term used by philosophers to indicate a sort of dependent, or lower-status, existence. Which suggests that for Berkeley the Cartesian hierarchy of existence (God > created substance > qualities: see 5.3) is a commonplace. What he is denying is that ideas 'inhere' in spirits, and that sensible qualities are modes or accidents of the substances to which they are related by inherence, whatever that may be. This allows him to say that physical qualities depend for their existence upon mental substance, without his having to say that those qualities are to be *predicated* of the mind (*DHP3* 249–50). The thinking is neatly summarized at *DHP3* 237:

> That there is no substance wherein ideas can exist beside spirit, is to me evident. And that the objects immediately perceived are ideas, is on all hands agreed. And that sensible qualities are objects immediately perceived, no one can deny. It is therefore evident there can be no *substratum* of those qualities but spirit, in which they exist, not by way of mode or property, but as a thing perceived in that which perceives it.

This combination of an acceptance of the need for substances and a rejection of the standard relation between substances and the qualities that depend upon them is crucial to Berkeley's metaphysics. For it is only this that allows him to continue insisting that sensible qualities exist in the minds which perceive them and yet some of them have sufficient independence from us to be counted parts of the real, physical world and not just our imaginings. (See Chapter 5.)

8.2.2 *Physical Objects Instantiate or Exemplify their Qualities*

This point can be seen as a further complication for the view outlined in response to the first point, for there we said that sensible qualities did exist in, or depend on, a substance, namely the mind which perceives them, but that the qualities cannot be predicated of that substance. Now we face the fact that the qualities *can* be predicated of physical objects: the table *is* brown, the rabbit *is* furry. The theory that the table and the rabbit are substances, and that qualities are modes or attributes of substances, fully explains what we mean when we make these predications, for we are saying that the substance has the attribute. This explanation is unavailable to Berkeley, or any bundle theorist for that matter, so there is a need for an alternative explanation of what it means to predicate a quality of an object.

We get an indication of Berkeley's answer to this difficulty in the passage from the *Principles* quoted above (*PHK* 49):

And, to say a die is hard, extended and square, is not to attribute those qualities to a subject distinct from and supporting them, but only an explication of the meaning of the word *die*.

The idea here seems to be that we introduce the word 'die' not to name a substance but to indicate a bundle of qualities, so to say that a die is hard is merely to say that hardness is one of the qualities which constitute being a die. The copula denotes a relation between two things, a collection of ideas and a single idea, but the relation is not instantiation or exemplification but containment: the single idea is contained in the collection of ideas. Since instantiation and exemplification are relations which have puzzled philosophers for millennia, but containment is comparatively straightforward, this looks to Berkeley like a great advance in philosophical clarity.

There are, however, some problems with this theory. The most serious is that it does not allow us to distinguish between contingent and essential predications. Suppose we are considering a die which is hard and green. It is plausible that were it not hard, it would not be a die, for soft objects will not roll and settle in the right way to determine which face is uppermost. So being hard is plausibly part of the meaning of 'die'. But this die is also green, and it is not plausible that being green is essential to being a die, for there are plenty of non-green dice. So the greenness is not part of the meaning of the word 'die', and saying that this die is green cannot

258 · CHAPTER 8

be deemed an explication of that meaning. The solution is for Berkeley to distinguish between the false general claim 'Dice are green', which incorrectly explicates the meaning of 'die', and the true particular claim 'This die is green', which he can say correctly explicates the meaning of 'this die'. It follows that 'this die' must be analytically equivalent to a long description of the form: the die which is green, slightly scratched, about 1 cubic centimetre . . . and so on. The description must be a complete list of all the qualities the die has, divided into those which are 'essential', i.e. it has in virtue of being a die, and those which are contingent, i.e. those which may vary between dice.

Some philosophers might think that this does not really deal with the problem. In the first place, we may wish to distinguish between contingent general statements about kinds, such as 'Dodos are extinct', and non-contingent ones such as 'Dodos are birds'. Had human history been different, dodos might not have been hunted to extinction and the first sentence would be false, but had evolution not resulted in these large flightless birds but some similar-looking mammals occupying the same environmental niche, that would not make the second sentence false. Since Berkeley says that being extinct is part of the meaning of 'dodo', he cannot make this distinction, for both statements would be equally analytic: a species which was not now extinct would be just as much a different species as a species of mammals. However, Berkeley can say *something* about the difference between the two sentences, because being extinct is a property that dodos (the species) have at some times in history and not others, whereas being birds is something always true of them, and this distinction can be reflected in the definition. While this helps to a certain extent, it still leaves the problem of such sentences as 'Dodos are now (AD 2002) extinct' and 'It is possible that dodos are not now (AD 2002) extinct'. If the first is analytic, and analytic truths are necessary, then the second is false, but intuitively we think both can be (and are) true. There are two options for Berkeley here. He could bite the bullet and accept that it is not possible that dodos are not now (AD 2002) extinct, or he could deny that analytic truths are necessary. The first option looks simply implausible, so he must take the second. The sense in which 'Dodos are extinct' is analytic is that being extinct is part of the meaning of 'dodo'. But before they became extinct, it was not, and had they not become extinct, it would not have become part of the meaning. So it is contingent that being extinct is part of the meaning of dodo, and consequently, that dodos are extinct comes out as contingently true. One objection to this line of argument is that it threatens to make *everything* contingently true, since it is equally contingent that being a bird is part of the meaning of 'dodo', since we may never have discovered that dodos are birds (compare: we may never have discovered that whales are mammals). This objection only works if we assume that analyticity is our only grasp on necessity. In describing the possibility that 'extinct' had not become part of the meaning of 'dodo', we referred to the possibility that dodos did not become extinct. However, when describing the possibility of 'bird' not being part of the meaning, we did not refer to the possibility that dodos are not birds, because there is no such possibility. It seems that our grasp of what is or is not possible is at least partially independent of our grasp of which sentences are analytic. So Berkeley can say that analyticity does not entail necessity, but nor does it entail contingency. Berkeley's disdain for language and his fear that it often obscures the facts (*PHK* Intro 25) can be extended to questions of necessity and contingency.

8.2.3 *Constancy of Meaning*

A related problem is about how discoveries might change the meanings of our terms. To keep to our dodo example, when it was discovered that they had become extinct, according to Berkeley our word 'dodo' changed its meaning: it now means '*extinct*, large, flightless . . . bird'. Suppose, then, that one person says, before the extinction, 'Dodos are drab' and another says, after the extinction,

'Dodos are brightly coloured'. On all accounts the first speaks the truth and the second does not, but we want to add further that they disagree with each other, that their claims are a priori inconsistent. If the terms have changed meaning, however, the claims are only inconsistent if the terms are coextensional, and that is not an a priori matter.

Before dealing with this, it is worth pointing out that on Berkeley's account error *is* possible, for it is not the collection of ideas in one person's mind which constitutes being a dodo, and thus gives the meaning of the word, but the collection put together by co-operating humans. In other words, if someone asserts that 'Dodos are brightly coloured' he is claiming that being brightly coloured is one of the qualities in the dodo collection, but since he does not alone determine the membership of that collection, he may be mistaken. There still remains the point that if the first speaker and the second speaker do mean something different by 'dodo', then they have not contradicted each other. The important claim in this argument is that the meaning has in fact changed. It is not clear that Berkeley must accept this. The two speakers differ in what they believe 'dodo' to mean, since if the second speaker had taken drabness to be part of the meaning of dodo, he would not have claimed that they are brightly coloured. And also, if error is to be possible, Berkeley cannot allow the meaning of a term to be identified with what the speaker takes it to mean. The second speaker's mistake, according to Berkeley, is over the meaning of the term. If we add the thought that a property such as being extinct is always going to be a time-relative member of the collection—that is, the collection will include the property of being extinct-in-AD 2002—then we do not need to say that the first speaker's ignorance of the impending extinction of the dodo determines that the collection of ideas he named 'dodo' did not include being extinct. In other words, what looks like a change in meaning is really an increase in understanding. Both before and after the extinction, speakers refer to the same collection of ideas by 'dodo'; the difference lies in what they know about that collection.

8.2.4 Persistence through Change

One of the most influential and traditional reasons for thinking that the move from feature-placing descriptions to talk of individual objects required the introduction of substances was the problem of saying what continued to exist when the qualities something possessed changed over time. Right now I am sitting down, but a few minutes ago I was standing up. For this to be a change, as opposed to merely a difference (as in 'A is sitting but B is standing'), it must be one and the same person who is both standing and sitting, but at different times. And this seems to force us to recognize the existence of something distinct from the changeable qualities, namely something which undergoes the change. One way of doing this would be to say that each thing which undergoes change has some unchanging quality which remains constant throughout all the variations of its other qualities. The problem is finding such a quality. There are some cases where this seems fairly straightforward, such as animals, for they must be alive both before and after any change in order for it to be the animal which is changing. If the change involves death, then the animal no longer exists, just a corpse. But this does not work in full generality, for there is also the change of dying. Of course, death is not a change which an animal undergoes, but it is a change for all that, a change which something, probably the animal's body, undergoes. So even if some kinds of thing have essential properties which cannot change without that thing ceasing to exist, there can still be changes in respect of that property which need to be accounted for somehow or other. It would seem that there is no choice but to introduce something distinct from the qualities of objects which can remain constant through changes in those qualities.

The bundle theorist's response to this has an important, but often unexpressed, premiss, namely that coming into or going out of existence is not a change in the problematic sense. If something exists at one time and not at another, that is a difference between how things are at the two times, but it does not look like a change in anything (except, trivially, in 'how things are'). It would be absurd to think we must explain the coming into existence of one thing in terms of a change in the qualities of some distinct thing. There are some such cases, e.g. when changing the shape of a piece of clay brings a bowl into existence, but not all coming to be can be like that unless we commit ourselves to the existence of a determinate, fixed quantity of some eternally existing material out of which the whole universe is made. But if creation and destruction are not changes in the problematic sense, the bundle theorist can say that an object changes, say from sitting to standing, when it is composed at one time of one type of idea/quality (=sitting) and at another time another idea/quality (=standing). Consider this analogy: when a new child is born or a grandparent dies, a family changes. We often talk of a family growing, which is a verb of change, which amounts to saying that gaining and losing members constitutes a change in the family. There are two ways of thinking of families as objects, which can be seen in contrasting answers to the question whether the whole of a family can be present at a single time. We might say, at a wedding for example, that the whole family is present, by which we mean all the living members of the family are present. But we might equally say that the whole family is not present, since the dead (and unborn) members are absent. We are only ever likely to say the latter when thinking of recently departed members, but it is a coherent option. Each answer corresponds to a conception of families as objects, either as something which is wholly present at different times, though its constitution differs over time, or as something which is spread out through time, with only part of it ever existing at once. The first type of persistence through time has been called endurance and the second perdurance (Lewis, *On the Plurality of Worlds*, 202–

4). It is thinking of persistence as endurance which requires us to find an enduring object distinct from the changing qualities. If we are seriously to propose that families endure through time, in this technical sense, then they cannot simply be collections of their members, because collections perdure, not endure. If we think of families as collections of their members, bound together by ties of blood and marriage, then the family can undergo change by having different members alive at different times.

A physical object such as a tree or a chair changes its properties over time. If the physical object is nothing but a bundle of qualities, then it does not endure through change but perdure, and perdurance means having only some of its elements existing at any one time. Change for a perduring object, then, consists in different elements existing at different times. As the qualities which compose it come into being and go out of being, the object changes its qualities. This neat proposal works for Berkeley because the qualities we are talking about are ideas, and, like family members, ideas are particular, dated things which go in and out of existence.

8.3 Collections of Ideas

There are two questions we now need to address. One is what determines whether a given idea is a member of a particular collection of ideas. The other is whether the answer to the first question allows Berkeley to give collections of ideas the same criteria of sameness and difference as the physical objects they are meant to be identical with. Our common-sense beliefs about physical objects include the belief that they can be perceived either by an individual on her own, or by several people at once, or by different people over time, it being one and the same thing which is perceived in all those cases. They can persist through time both changed and unchanged, but they do not survive all changes. There cannot be two objects of the same type in the same place at the same time. If two objects are in fact not distinct but identical, then they must be in the same places at all times. And they can continue to exist even though no one is perceiving them.

The inevitable objection to Berkeley is that the only way to give an answer to the first question which meets the requirements of the second is to say that what determines whether a quality is a member of a given bundle is which object has the quality. A bundle of qualities has the same criteria of identity as an object only because the identity of the bundle is determined by the object which has the qualities. Consequently, the object must be distinct from the bundle, so there are substances as well as qualities. We can only meet this objection by spelling out the details of Berkeley's thesis that objects are nothing but collections of ideas.

8.3.1 *Human Choices*

Berkeley's answer to the first question is elegantly simple: it is our decision which determines which idea belongs to which collection. Collections of ideas, as opposed to the ideas which are collected therein, do not have real existence, for they depend upon our will. For Berkeley the real world consists of ideas, which are particular quality instances. For their own, parochial, purposes humans impose a structure upon that world (*DHP3* 247–8):

Let us suppose several men together, all endued with the same faculties, and consequently affected in like sort by their senses, and who had yet never known the use of language; they would, without question, agree in their perceptions. Though perhaps, when they came to the use of speech, some regarding the uniformness of what was perceived, might call it the *same* thing: others, especially regarding the diversity of persons who perceived, might choose the denomination of *different* things. But who sees not that all the dispute is about a word?

First we group ideas together in terms of similarity, which introduces properties or universals. Then we group the ideas together into collections on the basis of our experience of which ideas go together, where 'going together' is intended to be a projectible characteristic on which we can base predictions. These predictions fall into two categories, those which depend upon experience of particular collections, as in the prediction that this tulip will have a yellow flower, and those which depend upon experience of several similar collections, as in the prediction that this bulb will grow into a tulip, whereas this bulb will grow into a daffodil. The second sort of prediction turns upon particular collections being instances of kinds, all of which have common properties.

We can illustrate this with the famous example of the oar in water (*DHP3* 238). The oar partially submerged in water looks crooked. The question 'Is it really crooked?', as we saw above, means 'Is crookedness part of the meaning of "that oar"?' Now we have two sorts of experience to draw upon. First, we could say that other oars do not bend or break when put in water, so being an oar, we can expect this thing not to do so. In other words, being straight (to the touch) when appearing crooked in water is part of the meaning of 'oar'. If the thing we are confronted with does not have those properties, if it is crooked when in water, it is, by definition, not an oar. That leads us to the second area of experience, for we now need to ascertain whether this thing has the right properties to be an oar, and one of those is not being crooked when in water. Here we can appeal to its feeling straight to the touch when submerged, its looking straight when taken out of the water, our failure to touch its blade by putting our hands where the blade appears to be, and so on. On the basis of this evidence, we would seem to get along best in the world, to make the most useful predictions, if we regarded the crookedness as an illusion, which is to say that the visual idea of crookedness is not part of the collection which constitutes this oar: it is discarded for being misleading.

So our choices about which ideas go in which bundle are not completely unconstrained, for they are based on experience and aim to achieve useful predictions, but the criteria on which they are to be evaluated are entirely pragmatic. All we can ask about them is: do they work? If we had different practical purposes in life, our predictive goals would be different. We can see this at a local scale with our colour words, for the decisions an interior decorator might make about whether some fabric was green or not might differ from the decision most of us would make, simply because the interior decorator is concerned only with how that fabric will look when used, for example, to upholster a chair. The interior decorator is concerned with a restricted set of appearances, and thus makes different choices. Now Berkeley thinks that our basic or core concerns in life are pretty universal, and also that God has created the world so that they can be met (*DHP3* 258):

PHILONOUS we ... place the reality of things in ideas, fleeting indeed, and changeable; however not changed at random, but according to the fixed order of Nature. For herein consists the constancy and truth of things, which secures all the concerns of life.

Whether we share his belief or not, the most it can tell him is that we can succeed, *by the pragmatic standards*, in deciding which ideas to collect together. It does not tell us that the pragmatically successful collections of ideas correspond to a feature of the world independent of us, for (*DHP3* 246):

Words [are] framed by the vulgar, merely for conveniency and dispatch in the common actions of life, without any regard to speculation.

8.3.2 *Identity*

Berkeley lived in a time when many philosophers were confused about identity, resulting in many strange and implausible definitions and distinctions, and he was rightfully disdainful of their disputes (*DHP3* 247):

But if the term *same* be used in the acceptation of philosophers, who pretend to an abstracted notion of identity, then, according to their sundry definitions of this notion (for it is not yet agreed wherein that philosophic identity consists), it may or may not be possible for divers persons to perceive the same thing. But whether philosophers shall think fit to call a thing the *same* or no, is, I conceive, of small importance.

What led to the confusion was a failure properly to grasp the distinction between two uses of the phrase 'the same'. Sometimes we use the phrase to indicate sameness of type or qualitative identity, as when we say that the words 'pin' and 'nip' contain *the same* letters in a different order. And at other times we use it to indicate sameness of token, or numerical identity, as in the children's game where one has three cardboard cut-out letters and must rearrange *the same* letters to make two different words. Confusion sets in because in the first sense not only are the same letters in different places at one time, but also they might differ (very slightly) in their qualities at a time, whereas in the second sense, if letters are to be the same, they must be in the same place at the same time and share all their qualities at a time. This led some philosophers to think that the latter was strict identity and the former was not really identity at all but only a vulgar confusion. Furthermore, qualitative identity seems to depend upon what type of thing we are considering: so, for example, whether 'cheese' is the same as 'CHEESE' depends upon whether we are asking about (qualitative) sameness of word or shape. Consequently some philosophers insisted that strict identity, being absolute, must be independent of how we describe the objects.

Berkeley saw that the resultant position was mistaken, for the answers to counting questions depend upon the answers to numerical-identity questions, but they also depend upon how one describes the objects one is counting (*PHK* 12):

That number is entirely the creature of the mind, even though the other qualities be allowed to exist without, will be evident to whoever considers, that the same thing bears a different denomination of number, as the mind views it with different respects. Thus, the same extension is one, or three, or thirty six, according as the mind considers it with reference to a yard, a foot, or an inch. Number is so visibly relative, and dependent on men's understanding, that it is strange to think how any one should give it an absolute existence without the mind. We say one book, one page, one line; all these are equally units, though some contain several of the others. And in each instance it is plain, the unit relates to some particular combination of ideas arbitrarily put together by the mind.

Berkeley is absolutely right that numerical identity, just as much as qualitative identity, depends upon how we describe the objects. There is simply no saying whether this is the same as that (where the objects are picked out in different ways) without first deciding what sort of thing we are dealing with. Suppose someone shows us a cup, then smashes it into small pieces and picks up the pieces. If he asks whether what he has in his hand now is the same as what he had in his hand a few moments ago, despite having watched the whole process, we do not know how to answer. It is not the same cup, because he no longer has a cup in his hands at all, but it is the same matter (give or take a few chips). Without a description to relativize the identity question, we cannot answer it. This is not a shortcoming on our part, for there is no determinate answer. The strict, absolute notion of identity is incoherent.

Berkeley sometimes writes in a way which implies that we can use the strict, absolute notion of identity for ideas, and Hume certainly thinks we can. This must be because ideas, unlike physical objects, are what they seem and seem what they are. Consequently, when you ask the question 'Is this the same as that?' of two ideas, either one has picked them out the same way, in which case the answer is trivially 'Yes' , or one has not, in which case it is equally trivially 'No'. This is sometimes described as the transparency of identity for ideas. However, despite appearances, it does not resurrect strict identity, because to know that the negative answer is correct, one must know that the two things picked out are both ideas: in other words, the answer was only trivial because of the hidden assumption that the question 'Are they both ideas?' has already been answered. Of course, that question is so easy to answer that it is easily overlooked, but it must still be answered, making the identity again relative to a description.

Berkeley also sees that if questions of numerical identity are relative to a description, it must be because the description *builds in* criteria of identity. When we call something a book or a cup, we are giving instructions about how to determine questions of identity. Not all descriptions have this feature, for when I say something is red, that gives you no information about how to tell whether some candidate for being the same thing is in fact identical with it or not. In 7.1 we called the first type of descriptive word 'sortals', for they tell us what sort of thing we are dealing with. Now, if sortals include criteria of identity as part of their meaning, it seems to Berkeley that a disagreement about identity between two people who 'agree in their perceptions' must boil down to a disagreement about language (*DHP3* 248):

> Or suppose a house, whose walls or outward shell remaining unaltered, the chambers are all pulled down, and new ones built in their place; and that you should call this the *same*, and I should say it was not the *same* house: would we not for all this perfectly agree in our thoughts of the house, considered in itself? and would not all the difference consist in a sound? . . . Why so silent, Hylas? Are you not yet satisfied, men may dispute about identity and diversity, without any real difference in their thoughts and opinions, abstracted from names?

We can best understand Berkeley's view by the use of an extended metaphor. The world we perceive, the real world, consists of a two-dimensional array of ideas, the two dimensions being the perceiver and the time of perception (each perceiver has a subjective timescale, but communication allows us to relate them to each other). Language, and the attendant process of conceptualization, involves drawing lines on the array which make enclosed spaces, and giving all the ideas in such an enclosure a single name. There are clearly many different ways of doing this, especially since a large part of the array, the future, remains unknown to us. The practicalities of language and communication itself impose one set of constraints on how we do this, for we want words which are few enough and easy enough to learn. The purpose of the whole operation is to enable us to live our day-to-day lives. If I eat bread today and it nourishes me, I need to know which of the things I confront tomorrow in the larder will also nourish me. So we introduce a word 'loaf' with criteria of identity over time, and it turns out to be useful, for if the loaf was good to eat today, it will probably be good to eat tomorrow but not next week. Other words, with different criteria of identity, which I might have introduced, would not have been so useful. For example, a word 'schmoaf', which applies to all and only those things which are in the same place in the larder as the bread is today, would probably lead to food poisoning. These different words would not have made the world any different, for all words do is draw lines around the ideas which constitute the world, but they might have made it less easy to live in that world.

8.3.3 Natural Kinds

There might be thought to be a tension in Berkeley's thinking here. For on the one hand he tells us that 'words are of *arbitrary* imposition' (*DHP3* 247), that men 'might *choose* the denomination of different things' (*DHP3* 248), and 'several distinct ideas [are] united into one thing by the mind' (*DHP3* 246); on the other hand, that 'men combine together several ideas . . . observed . . . to have some connexion in Nature' and 'the more a man knows of the connexion of ideas, the more he is said to know of the nature of things' (*DHP3* 245). The talk of arbitrariness and choice, and even the term 'congeries', suggest that it is only facts about us which impose any constraint upon our language. If we consider the ideas as they are in themselves, there is no reason to group them one way rather than another. In contrast, talk of connections in nature and the nature of things suggests that there are facts about the ideas themselves which do, or ought to, constrain our language. The implication here is that while we are free to draw shapes on the array of ideas as we please, some of those shapes will be correct and others will not. This is the image of nature itself having a structure, which Plato summed up when he talked of language aiming to carve nature 'where the joint is' (*Phaedrus*, 265 E).

This issue is very similar to that of whether the resemblance between ideas on which we base our general words is subjective or objective. In fact it is just an instance of that problem. And in discussing that problem we noted that in Berkeley's theistic metaphysics the world is made for us, or better, with us in mind. At first this seems to collapse the distinction between subjective and objective, because God knows which similarities we will experience and creates the world to enable us to exploit those similarities. However, on closer inspection it is clear that God faced a choice. He could have created objectively similar ideas, and given us the faculties to discern those similarities, or he could have created us with certain subjective responses, and created the world to make those responses helpful. Given that Berkeley thinks that the way for there to be objective similarities would be for distinct particulars to instantiate a single universal, and that there are no universals, he is committed to God having taken the second option. Similarly, if we have a Berkeleian metaphysics without God, the non-existence of universals will still entail the impossibility of objective similarities.

The situation with respect to natural kinds is slightly different, for here we are not concerned with similarities between ideas, but connections between ideas. The connections Berkeley has in mind are either co-occurrences (the table looks brown and feels hard) or sequences (the pen moves across the paper and a black line appears). Now for Berkeley, since God causes all ideas we perceive by sense, these connections and sequences we observe are determined by God's intentions. Consequently, there is more than a pragmatic difference between a concept that gets it right and one that does not, for only the former correctly picks up the connections and sequences that God intended. In other words, the array of ideas on which we draw our concepts is actually structured by God's intentions—there is a third dimension of variation which makes some ideas cluster together naturally. Because whether two ideas co-occur, or whether a sequence of ideas occurs, is an objective fact independent of any judgement or decision we make, it is something God can use to create natural kinds in the world. This realism about natural kinds allows that there are several alternative languages or conceptual schemes, and that we choose our language largely constrained by practical considerations, and yet there is a clear sense in which one of these languages is better than the others, for it is the one the categories of which correspond to the kinds of thing God intended us to find in the world. It carves nature at its joints.

However, we should be uneasy at this combination of nominalism about qualities with realism about kinds. Take, for example, the co-occurrence of hardness and brownness exhibited by my table. The realist about kinds says that the co-occurrence of these two qualities is not a matter for my choice. I could choose to ignore it, but if I did, my conceptual scheme would not match up to the patterns to be found in nature. But this overlooks an ambiguity in the term 'quality'. For Berkeley, the qualities which God causes to co-occur, or to occur in sequence, are particular ideas relativized to a person at a time. So God intends the brownness-to-me-now to co-occur with the hardness-to-me-now. But the co-occurrence which would make it natural to divide the world up into tables and non-tables would be brownness (in general) and hardness (in general). In order for God to cause this, he would have to cause ideas of one type (brown) to occur alongside ideas of another type (hard). Now, of course God can do this, because he knows whether two ideas are of the same type or not, but this is because he knows about us, about how we categorize ideas. Whether two sensible ideas are both brown, say, depends upon whether humans find them suitably similar. God cannot make it an objective fact, i.e. one independent of human nature, that brown ideas occur with hard ideas, because it is not objective whether ideas are brown or hard. This does not leave God powerless, for he knows what we will find similar, how we will choose to group ideas, and consequently he can fix the ideas we have so that we do construct an easy and convenient conceptual scheme, but it is a conceptual scheme we impose on an unarticulated nature for all that.

It is worth pausing for a moment to consider what the atheist Berkeleian of 4.5 would be able to say here. For such a philosopher it is simply a brute fact, not susceptible to explanation, that we have the ideas we do when we do. He would agree with Berkeley that there are no natural kinds, that in regarding something as a tree we are not trying to mirror some independent distinction, but merely to assist ourselves in the business of day-to-day survival. Where he would differ from Berkeley is over the expectation that there is a conceptual scheme which will enable us to make predictions and furnish all the necessities of life. For the atheist it is entirely possible that every concept we introduce should ultimately prove to be unsuccessful, to hinder rather than help us. Berkeley allows that we can never be certain that any given concept will stand the test of time, that it will not be shown to be misguided by future experience, but the existence of God gives him the reassurance that there are some concepts to be found which will work, for the world is benign. The atheist, in contrast, not only lacks assurance that any given concept will work, but also that the whole project of trying to conceptualize the world of experience makes sense. It remains an open possibility that the world is unconceptualizable. Both the theist and the atheist can agree that in *perception* we have perfect knowledge of the world, for the world is composed of ideas, and ideas are dependent upon being perceived by us, so there is nothing in an idea that we do not know about when we perceive it (*DHP1* 206):

PHILONOUS ... Do you not perfectly know your own ideas?

HYLAS I know them perfectly; since what I do not perceive or know, can be no part of my idea.

But when we move away from considering perception to conception and judgement, a difference emerges. Here the goal is not knowledge but practical success in the business of life. According to the theist, the world of ideas, through God's foreknowledge and benign intentions, is sufficiently well correlated to the way our minds work to ensure that we can construct a conceptual scheme which will enable us to go about the everyday business of life. The atheist, however, has no such guarantee: it remains open that there is no conceptual scheme which lives up to the vagaries of the world.

8.3.4 *Direct Perception*

According to common sense, we can directly perceive physical objects—that is, ordinary things such as tables and trees are among the things that we see, hear, feel, touch, and taste. But if physical objects are just collections of ideas spread out across perceivers and over time, how can this be? We can only perceive what is present at the time of perception, and collections of ideas, being perduring objects, are not wholly present at the time of perception. Furthermore, some of the ideas which go to make up an object are other people's ideas, and since ideas are private, I am unable to perceive them. And yet Berkeley endorses the commonsensical view that we do directly perceive physical objects, both implicitly by talking of physical objects as things perceived, and also explicitly, for example (*DHP3* 230):

Wood, stones, fire, water, flesh, iron, and the like things, which I name and discourse of, are things that I know. And I should not have known them, but that I perceived them by my senses; and things perceived by the senses are immediately perceived . . .

He also thinks that the ordinary, non-philosophical conception of an object is a collection of sensible qualities (*PHK* 37; *DHP3* 237, 261). So if Berkeley cannot both claim that physical objects are collections and that we perceive them by sense, our common-sense conception would also be inconsistent.

Berkeley defines sense perception in terms of immediate perception. So the question becomes whether a physical object can be immediately perceived. The distinction between mediate and immediate perception is introduced in the important passage about perception at the beginning of the Dialogues (*DHP1* 174):

PHILONOUS   Pardon me, Hylas, if I am desirous clearly to apprehend your notions, since this may much shorten our inquiry. Suffer me then to ask you this farther question. Are those things only perceived by the senses which are perceived immediately? Or may those things properly be said to be *sensible*, which are perceived mediately, or not without the intervention of others?

Now, Philonous' objective here is to establish a definition of sense perception which will allow him to rule that certain ideas we might be alleged to have on the basis of sense experience are not themselves perceived by sense and thus need not be regarded as parts of the sensible world. To do this he makes a distinction between two ways of perceiving and claims that it is necessary for an idea to be perceived by sense that it be perceived immediately. The mediate/immediate distinction seems to be:

An idea X is mediately perceived if (1) it is perceived, and (2) its being perceived depends upon the subject also perceiving some distinct idea Y.

Suppose that whenever I have the (olfactory) idea of over-cooked cabbage, I also have the (visual) idea of my school dining hall. Whether or not the first idea is an idea of sense, the second is not because I would not be having it were I not to have had the idea of cabbage; it depends upon the first and is thus mediately perceived. Typically we would call the second idea an idea of memory, but it suffices for Berkeley's purpose to agree that it is not an idea of sense, because it fails a necessary condition for being a sense perception (*DHP1* 175):

PHILONOUS This point then is agreed between us, that *sensible things are those only which are immediately perceived by sense.*

Clearly we shall need to make some modifications to this definition to allow for difficult cases such as ideas perceived in groups, but the basic point is clear: an immediate perception is independent of all other perceptions. It is not important for present purposes exactly what Berkeley thinks the dependence relation is, except that it must be something under voluntary control and in which we are active, for only thus can he restrict the contents of reality to what is immediately perceived. He talks of mediately perceived ideas being 'suggested' (*DHP1* 204), and this is clearly meant to include memory, subjective associations, and some inferences.

This distinction of Berkeley's between mediate and immediate perception is significantly different from the normal distinction between direct and indirect perception. Suppose that I indirectly perceive someone on closed-circuit television. This is only possible because I directly perceive something else, namely the television screen, hence perceiving the person appears to be a case of mediate perception. However, Berkeley would deny this because he would deny that I perceive the person at all. If the only ideas before my mind are ideas of an image on a TV screen, then an image on a TV screen is all I perceive, for perception is nothing more and nothing less than having ideas before the mind, and the content of perception, what one perceives, is fully determined by which ideas one has before the mind. Sense perception, immediate perception, and mediate perception are all *species* of perception in this sense, for they all consist in having ideas before the mind. I cannot perceive something other than the TV screen without having further ideas (*DHP1* 203). If we add to the story that seeing the CCTV image reminds me of seeing the man yesterday, then I do perceive him, for ideas of him are before my mind. This (memory) perception of him is suggested by, and thus depends upon, my current sense perception, which makes it a mediate perception and not a sense

perception. Berkeley will insist that all alleged cases of indirect perception are either mediate perceptions involving suggestion or not
perceptions at all. Either way, there is no indirect sense perception.

As we have already noted, common sense holds that physical
objects can be the direct objects of sense experience. It would
seem that, if Berkeley is not to go against common sense on this
point, he must say that physical objects, i.e. collections of ideas, can
be immediately perceived. However, after discussing an example
similar to that of the closed-circuit TV, namely a portrait of Caesar,
Philonous appears to claim that a physical object such as a coach is
not immediately perceived, despite the fact that we often speak as
if it is (*DHP1* 204):

> Though I grant we may in one acceptation be said to perceive sensible
> things mediately by sense: that is, when from a frequently perceived
> connexion, the immediate perception of ideas by one sense suggests to
> the mind others perhaps belonging to another sense, which are wont
> to be connected with them. For instance, when I hear a coach drive
> along the streets, immediately I perceive only the sound; but from the
> experience I have had that such a sound is connected with a coach,
> I am said to hear the coach. It is nevertheless evident, that in truth
> and strictness, nothing can be *heard* but *sound*: and the coach is not then
> properly perceived by sense, but suggested from experience. So likewise
> when we are said to see a red-hot bar of iron; the solidity and heat of the
> iron are not the objects of sight, but suggested to the imagination by the
> colour and figure, which are properly perceived by that sense. In short,
> those things alone are actually and strictly perceived by any sense, which
> would have been perceived, in case that same sense had then been first
> conferred on us. As for other things, it is plain they are only suggested
> to the mind by experience grounded on former perceptions.

Berkeley's line of thinking here is that anything the perception
of which depends upon some previous experience is mediately
perceived and thus not perceived by sense. Thus whatever is perceived by sense would also be perceivable by someone without
any previous experience. Someone with no knowledge or experi-

ence of coaches would therefore immediately perceive the same as Philonous, when the coach passed by outside on the street. And that person could not be said to be perceiving a coach at all, so it follows that Philonous did not *immediately perceive* the coach either.

This argument contains a mistake which, when removed, leaves Berkeley in a perfectly good position to say that we do perceive physical objects by sense. The mistake lies in the claim that the person with no previous experience could not be said to be perceiving a coach at all. What is true is that the sounds that person hears do not suggest to her mind any of the other characteristics of a coach, whereas they do to Philonous. But this only entails the needed premiss if perceiving the coach necessarily involves having those other ideas suggested to the mind. That Berkeley believes this is implied by the comment 'from the experience I have had that such a sound is connected with a coach, I am said to hear the coach'. However, suppose that some time after being in the room with Philonous, the inexperienced person sees a coach and comments that she has never heard one of those. It would be perfectly proper for Philonous to say 'Yes you have, that time you were in the study with me.' In other words, to say at the time that the person can hear a coach might be misleading, for it carries the implication that she knows it is a coach that she can hear. But when we get to a situation in which that implication has been cancelled, it is perfectly reasonable to say that she did hear the coach. Berkeley's 'strict sense' is not really a proper sense of the term 'hear' at all. One source of Berkeley's mistake must be the thought that someone who hears a coach must have more to their experience than someone who merely hears sounds. But the general principle, that if one person perceives something by sense and another does not, then there must be some sensible quality (idea) the first is aware of which the second is not, is not true. Consider a beach on a desert island. The lid of a chest is just visible above the sand. In scenario one the lid is attached to nothing, in scenario two it is attached to a treasure chest. Now we can fairly say that someone in scenario two can see the treasure chest, since nearly always we see things by seeing only a part of them. But in scenario one there is no treasure chest to be seen, only part of a chest, so someone in that situation can only see part of a chest. Saying this does not commit us to saying that there is something extra in the content of the experience of someone in scenario two. They both see a lid, and neither sees any more of a chest than that, yet one and not the other sees a treasure chest.

The last argument appeals to the common-sense thought that sometimes you can see something by seeing only a part of it. In fact we almost never perceive the whole of something at once. This principle is not in conflict with anything Berkeley needs to say, and thus he could use it in his attempt to reconcile his views with common sense. If we can say that the inexperienced person who hears the sound of a coach hears a part of the coach, then we can say that she hears the coach, just like Philonous, though she does not know it. To know she hears the coach, she would need to have the other ideas suggested to mind as well. Berkeley can allow that we immediately perceive the collections of ideas which are physical objects in virtue of immediately perceiving their parts.

Unfortunately for Berkeley, he is unlikely to persuade the spokesman of common sense that the sound of a coach is a part of the whole coach in the same sense that the lid of a chest is a part of the whole chest. Ideas are parts of collections, but not all of them are spatial parts (e.g. colours), and common sense seems only to allow that one can perceive an object by perceiving a spatial part.

Since Berkeley thinks that our ordinary conception of an object is as nothing more than a collection of sensible qualities, he does have the option of saying that if common sense claims we can perceive physical objects, it is correct when we perceive an idea or group of ideas which form a spatial part of that object, but otherwise misguided by its own lights. Unfortunately, since a spatial part of a physical object is itself a public, persistent object, there is a question whether we ever do perceive by sense even the parts of objects. This cannot be answered by appeal to their parts, on pain of an infinite regress, so Berkeley would have to admit (as he appears to in the coach passage) that neither his theory nor common sense can allow that physical objects are among the objects of perception. However, since common sense clearly does allow that, the reasonable response would be to take Berkeley's difficulties here as evidence that our ordinary conception of an object is as something more than a collection of sensible qualities. And if this were the case, Philonous would have lost the dispute with Hylas, since he would be denying the reality of sensible things.

So Berkeley really does need to have an account of how, by perceiving just a few members of a collection, we can be said to perceive the collection, and this account must be consistent with what we ordinarily say about sense perception. Ideally, we would extract from our common-sense intuitions a principle similar enough to the claim that one can see an object by seeing only a part of it, but which applies to hearing a coach by hearing the sound of it and all the other cases. So consider the circumstances in which you might say that you heard a violin in another room. You might have heard it being played, or being tuned, for example. But had you heard the violin being dropped on the floor, or being smashed with an axe, you would not normally say that you had heard the violin. We can construct similar examples for any object which has a typical sound, be it a cat or a motor car. The point seems to be that we say we hear an object of a certain kind when the sound we hear is a typical sound for an object of such a kind to make. The point also applies to sight, though normally we are seeing spatial parts of an object. So you might be said to see a coach when you see a typical coach appearance, but not when what you see is not a typical appearance of a coach (or any of its parts). To give an exaggerated illustration, suppose that Cinderella's coach returns to its pumpkin shape to make parking easier. If one saw the pumpkin appearance, one would not normally have been said to have seen a coach, since that is not a typical appearance of a coach. This suggests the following principle:

> One perceives an X by sense when what one immediately perceives is a typical sensible quality of that X.

('X' is a placeholder for a kind concept applying to physical objects.) Now the question of whether hearing the sound of a coach constitutes hearing the coach depends upon which sound one is talking about. If it is a typical sound, such as the metal-banded coach wheels rattling along a cobbled street, then one can hear the coach, even if one does not know it. If it is not a typical sound (e.g. the sound of the coach being blown over in the wind), then even if the sound suggests the coach to you, you do not have a sense experience of the coach.

The last point to clear up is which sensible qualities count as the typical ones. One way of doing this would be to say that the typical qualities are those which follow from the essence of the kind. Given Berkeley's conceptualism, which sensible qualities followed from the essence of the kind would not be an objective, judgement-independent fact, but rather a feature of the concept we humans have introduced on the basis of experience. So any appeal to the essential nature of the kind would ultimately be an appeal to someone's experiences and how those had affected their judgements. In effect, something follows from the essential nature of a kind if perceiving it causes someone who has fully grasped the concept to think there is an object of that kind. Thus:

> A sensible quality of an X is typical if, and only if, experiencing that sensible quality would suggest, in the mind of a perceiver with the concept of X-hood, in normal conditions, the idea of an X (i.e. other sensible qualities of an X).

If we accept this proposal, then we see how Berkeley's infamous passage about the coach correctly ties the notion of perceiving physical objects to what is suggested, i.e. in mediate perception, but

282 · CHAPTER 8

draws the false consequence that we do not have sense experience of physical objects. The mistake was to think that the perception of the physical object is constituted by the mediate perception. Rather, which mediate perceptions occur in some suitable observer in normal conditions determines whether an immediate perception of an idea constitutes the (immediate, direct) perception of a physical object.

8.4 Existence Unperceived

8.4.1 *The Shape of the Problem*

Readers of Berkeley's philosophy are often frustrated by how little he says about the question of what happens to the physical world when no one is perceiving it. There seem to be three possible answers: it ceases to exist; God always perceives it; and it has a merely hypothetical existence deriving from the possibility of perception. (These correspond to the Simple View, the Disjunctive View, and the Reductionist View of 5.6.) Since the first option is alleged to go against common sense, it is normally assumed that Berkeley must hold either the second or the third. I argued against the second at the beginning of this chapter, so it would seem that we are left with no choice but the third. However, before developing this further, it is worth pausing for a moment to consider the first alternative. If Berkeley is right that, for the physical world anyway, to be is to be perceived, then it is an obvious consequence that nothing can exist unperceived. Berkeley does not think that this claim is, as it stands, sceptical or in conflict with common sense. There are two possible explanations of this, namely (1) that Berkeley did not think common sense was committed to the physical world continuing to exist when unperceived by us, or (2) that he thought he could endorse the common-sense belief while maintaining that for sensible things, to be is to be perceived.

When Hylas tries to bring out the conflict with common sense which many readers find in Berkeley's philosophy, Berkeley side-steps the issue by having Philonous give a glib and unsatisfying answer (*DHP3* 234):

HYLAS . . . Ask the first man you meet, and he shall tell you, *to be perceived* is one thing, and *to exist* is another.

PHILONOUS   I am content, Hylas, to appeal to the common sense of the world for the truth of my notion. Ask the gardener, why he thinks yonder cherry-tree exists in the garden, and he shall tell you, because he sees and feels it; in a word, because he perceives it by his senses. Ask him, why he thinks an orange-tree not to be there, and he shall tell you, because he does not perceive it.

Since what is perceived must exist, Hylas is really making the point that ordinarily we think that what exists can exist unperceived. Philonous appears to address both the question of necessity as well as sufficiency, but there is a subtle equivocation. The question 'Why do you think that tree exists?' could be asking for a sufficient condition for the tree's existence, or it could be asking for a particular person's evidence that the tree exists. Given that being perceived is sufficient for existence, and it also provides evidence, the imagined answer is a reply to both questions. But when the gardener is asked why he thinks the orange-tree does not exist, his answer only addresses the question about evidence. For it is perfectly possible for an orange-tree to exist and not be perceived by the gardener. It is not even part of Berkeley's position, and certainly not part of common sense, that the perceptions of some particular individual are necessary for the existence of an object such as a tree. Philonous has simply failed to say anything relevant to the objection.

It looks as if Berkeley is avoiding the issue of whether common sense is committed to physical objects existing unperceived, and to many critics this is a sign that he did not have a good enough answer. However, it is striking that when he is eventually drawn into saying something on the matter, it is not because of an alleged conflict with common sense but with Scripture. The account of the creation in the Bible says that the physical world was created before mankind, and before any sentient creatures at all. Though the problem is raised and answered in terms of the Mosaic account of creation (that is, as told by Moses in the Book of Genesis), geological and fossil evidence also gives a reason to believe that the physical world existed before there were any finite creatures to perceive it.

So one explanation of why it took the biblical objection to rouse Berkeley into giving an account of existence unperceived is simply that he did not think that common sense was unequivocally committed to it. The trouble with interpreting Berkeley thus is that it seems so obviously wrong. There are three claims that common sense is undoubtedly committed to, and they do all appear inconsistent with Berkeley's views:

[1] We refer to and describe objects which have never been, and so far as we know, never will be, perceived, and we take it that some, but not others, of these descriptions are true.

[2] We do not think that the visible objects cease to exist when everyone in the room closes their eyes, or are created anew when we enter the room each morning.

[3] We think that objects go through the same processes of change when unobserved as they do when observed.

Berkeley never discusses the first. This is probably because truths about unobserved objects have no practical implications for us unless they entail something about future experiences. Suppose there is an emerald which no one has ever seen and no one will ever see. The question of whether it is green or not can have no point or purpose; in at least one sense of the word, it is meaningless. But if I am mining emeralds, the colour of unobserved ones is of import, because it will affect how much I can sell them for and thus how much effort it is worth my putting into mining them.

The third point is never addressed directly, but many things

Berkeley says bear upon it. Berkeley thinks that common sense is committed to the sensible world consisting in nothing other than the objects of perception. And the objects of perception, be they termed ideas or sensible qualities, are obviously inert. They have no causal powers (e.g. *DHP3* 236), and thus any process of change the sensible world goes through is externally caused by some mind. The current state of the sensible world only depends upon previous states *via the intervention of some agent*. So all Berkeley needs to account for the third point is suitable intentions on the part of God. A glass of water left in the sunshine will evaporate whether continuously observed or not. Which amounts to no more than that whoever is causing us to have the idea of a full glass and later the idea of an empty glass does so whether or not we have had the intervening ideas of the glass becoming progressively more empty. And Berkeley does not really need to invoke God for this, for if the patterns in our experience are simply brute but contingent, there is no reason why they should not be such that we do not need the intervening experiences to have the experiences of the beginning and the end of the evaporation process. If the materialist insists that this fact cannot be brute but needs further explanation, then he has reopened the question of explanation we discussed at length in Chapter 4.

Berkeley does discuss the second claim of common sense explicitly in the *Principles* (*PHK* 45–8), but the discussion is very unsatisfactory. In § 45 he reasserts the connection between perception and existence, but as we have seen above, that does not address the question. In § 46 he notes how everyone who thinks the objects of perception are ideas is equally committed to the objects of perception being annihilated when we close our eyes, and that many 'Schoolmen', which here includes Descartes and Malebranche, hold that everything is continually recreated, for it could not otherwise continue in existence from time to time. In § 47 he gives a fascinating argument to the effect that materialists who believe in the infinite divisibility of matter must think that the distinctions between particular objects rest on idea and thus cannot exist unperceived. And finally in § 48 he gives a direct answer, namely that if one person ceases to perceive something, others may still do so, which would be sufficient to keep it in existence. Unfortunately, this is no good, since it is easy for us to get into a situation in which we are the only finite creature aware of, say, a table, and then to close our eyes. Common sense says the table continues to exist, so either this answer of Berkeley's is inadequate, or he is tacitly invoking the thought that God is an omnipresent observer. But we have seen that God's perception is not sufficient for something to exist as part of the physical world. It seems that Berkeley does have more of a problem than he acknowledges, so we must turn to his discussion of the creation to look for a solution.

8.4.2 *Lady Percival's Objection*

The discussion of the Mosaic account of the creation in the Third Dialogue has no echo in the *Principles*. Since the *Dialogues* carefully maintain a dramatic fiction, acknowledgement was not possible, but we know from letters that it was the wife of Berkeley's friend Sir John Percival who first raised the objection that the physical world existed before there were any finite minds to perceive it. Whether one takes this to be established by the Bible, or by geology and the fossil record, or by cosmology, it is hard to deny.

The discussion between Hylas and Philonous (*DHP3* 250–4) has Hylas struggling to turn an intuitive hunch of incompatibility into a solid objection. The effect of this is to distract our attention a little from the main point, and cover up the fact that Hylas does not test the new theory very searchingly. In response to the point that everything that is in God's mind exists eternally, so creation must consist in something other than the creation of ideas, Philonous claims that to come into existence as a physical thing is to become perceptible (*DHP3* 251–2):

When things are said to begin or end their existence, we do not mean this with regard to God, but His creatures. . . . when things before imperceptible to creatures, are by decree of God, made perceptible to them; then are they said to begin a relative existence, with respect to created minds. Upon reading therefore the Mosaic account of the Creation, I understand that the several parts of the world became gradually perceivable to finite spirits, endowed with proper faculties; so that whoever such were present, they were in truth perceived by them.

Now it is unclear whether this should be read as a form of phenomenalism. There is a natural reading of 'perceptible' on which something is only perceptible if there is someone nearby to perceive it, and the final claim about 'whoever such were present' refers only to those actually present, not those who might have been present. Hylas tries to press the point by making a distinction between 'relative or hypothetical existence' and 'actuality of absolute existence', and arguing that Philonous cannot allow the physical world the latter sort of existence until animate creatures exist. This is an unfortunate way of putting the point, because the conflation of relative and hypothetical allows Philonous to answer one charge and ignore the other. He challenges Hylas to make sense of non-relative existence, which just amounts to mind-independent existence. On pain of going through the whole argument again, Hylas gives up the point and begins looking for another one. But this is a mistake, for even if we deny the possibility of absolute, mind-independent existence, there is still a distinction to be made between that which has existence because God has decreed it possible for someone to perceive it, and that which has existence because it is actually perceived.

The creation challenge seems to force Berkeley into saying that it merely being possible for someone to perceive something, even though no one exists to perceive it in fact, is sufficient for that thing to exist. If the physical world existed before sentient beings were there to perceive it, then it existed in virtue of the possibility of perception, and we can equally say that my table exists when I close my eyes in virtue of the possibility that I still had my eyes open and would be perceiving it. Philonous summarizes the view thus (*DHP3* 253):

> May we not understand [the creation] to have been entirely in respect of finite spirits; so that things, with regard to us, may properly be said to begin their existence, or be created, when God decreed they should become perceptible to intelligent creatures, in that order and manner which he then established, and we now call the laws of Nature. You may call this a *relative*, or *hypothetical existence* if you please.

Here we must read 'perceptible to intelligent creatures' as 'would be perceived by intelligent creatures, were there any', and '*relative*, or *hypothetical existence*' as '*relative*, and *hypothetical existence*'. Only thus can Berkeley allow for the world to exist before we did.

8.4.3 *Against Phenomenalism*

The trouble with this interpretation of Berkeley, as we saw in 5.6, is that he offers an argument against the position. At *DHP3* 234 Hylas tries to defend the thought that being perceived is not necessary for physical existence by suggesting that being perceivable is sufficient. Philonous replies curtly:

> And what is perceivable but an idea? And can an idea exist without being actually perceived? These are points long since agreed between us.

Berkeley is right that there is something incoherent about the suggestion that there are some ideas which are not actually perceived, only possibly perceived. If an idea just is how things appear to a specific person at a specific time, there is no way for an idea to exist without being perceived. But this objection can be met by saying that the unperceived ideas are not actual ideas possibly perceived but merely possible ideas. There is an answer to the question: 'What would so-and-so have perceived had such-and-such happened?', and the answer to that question is a possible but non-actual idea.

It is no simple mistake that led Berkeley to interpret Hylas' attempts at phenomenalism in such an incoherent fashion, for the alternative would have seemed to Berkeley to offer no solution to the problem at all, not even an incoherent one. Berkeley thinks ontologically, he is concerned with determining what sort of thing exists. Both Berkeley and the phenomenalist agree that ideas actually perceived by someone exist. The phenomenalist wants to add something further to that ontology. As far as Berkeley can see, this addition will be either ideas actually existing but merely possibly perceived, which are impossible, or merely possible ideas. But how does it help one's ontology of the actual world to say that as well as the ideas we perceive there are also some non-actual ideas?

The way to reconcile Berkeley's apparent commitment to phenomenalism with this devastating objection is to distinguish ordinary objects from the ideas which compose them. We can then see that there are two different sides to phenomenalism, which we might call the ontological and the metaphysical. The ontological aspect is the claim that physical objects consist of actual and possible ideas or experiences. This is the view that the objection is aimed at. The metaphysical aspect is the claim that asserting some statements about physical objects, such as that they exist or have certain qualities while unperceived, commits one to nothing more than possible but non-actual experiences. For example, if I claim that the unseen grass is green I am committed to nothing stronger than the conditional that if someone were to look, the grass would seem green to them. To answer the creation objection, and to deal with what common sense has to say about unperceived objects, Berkeley only needs the metaphysical aspect of phenomenalism. So the substantive question he faces is whether it is possible to have the metaphysical without the ontological. In particular, if Berkeley thinks that objects are made up of ideas, can he avoid the conclusion that unperceived objects are made up (in part) of possible ideas?

If we go back to the discussion of the creation, we see that Philonous says (*DHP3* 253):

May we not understand [the creation] to have been entirely in respect of finite spirits; so that things, with regard to us, may properly be said to begin their existence, or be created, when God decreed they should become perceptible to intelligent creatures, in that order and manner which he then established, and we now call the laws of Nature?

It is clear that Berkeley sees the problem of the creation, which is an instance of the problem of existence unperceived, as there being certain truths, such as 'This planet existed before there was any sentient life on it', which need to be accounted for. And it is God's decrees which account for these truths. For it to be true that this planet existed before there was any sentient life on it, there is no need for anything to exist other than God's decree.

This leaves Berkeley in the position of saying that the earth (or any other physical object) is a collection of actual ideas had by finite spirits, and that there is a time at which the earth has been created but no members of the collection exist. At least from Berkeley's perspective, this view is radically different from phenomenalism, for it keeps the central thought that the physical world is composed of ideas actually perceived by finite minds *and nothing else*. However, it can allow that there are circumstances in which 'Such-and-such object exists' is true even though none of the ideas of which it is composed exists in those circumstances.

Now it may seem absurd to say that a collection can exist when none of its members exists, but we can construct similar situations for other collection-like entities such as clubs. Suppose a university benefactor decided to award an annual prize for the best philosophy essay. She might also decide that there should be a club whose members were all and only winners of the prize. There is nothing absurd in saying that this club exists before the prize has been first awarded, and there might equally be future times when there are no living members (owing to war, natural disaster, or philistinism), but the club would still exist. A club is just a collection of people, unified by membership rules, but it would seem that the club can, under certain conditions, exist when it has no members. Similarly, we might say that having decided to collect stamps, someone might set out to buy her first stamp, and on the way she would be a stamp collector who had no stamps in her collection.

What will strike most philosophers about such cases is that it is a matter of stipulation whether we allow clubs or stamp collections to exist without any members. There may be some practical reasons for preferring one stipulation to another, but there is no deeper fact of the matter. However, this is no objection to Berkeley's combination of the metaphysical aspect of phenomenalism with ontological idealism, since he thinks that what we say about physical objects is also just a matter of convention governed by some practical objectives but unconstrained by any deeper facts. And that is how he can have his cake and eat it on the question of existence unperceived.

CHAPTER 9

Conclusion

We saw in Chapter 3 that the single most important premiss in the whole of Berkeley's philosophy is the Simplest Model of Perception (p. 54):

> '*S* perceives *O* (by sense)' describes a two-place relation between a mind and a sensible thing/quality. The relation of *perceiving* or *being aware of* is a pure relation, much like a spatial relation (hence 'before the mind') in that it is not constituted, either wholly or partly, by any concurrent event in or state of one of the relata. . . . The only possible differences between two perceivings are in the identities of the subject or the object (the five senses are distinguished by their objects). . . .

Since the most natural and most common response to Berkeley is that he went wrong somewhere in his account of perception, most readers of this book will, I expect, be inclined to immunize themselves from immaterialism by rejecting SMP. But we must not forget the potential side effects of this immunization programme. SMP is so attractive to Berkeley because it captures the very intuitive sense in which we think that sense perception is simple openness to the world. When I look at my hand, there does not seem to me to be any point in that experience where it would make sense to say there is a potential *mismatch* between something I experience and how my hand really is. There is no part of my experience which could be a perceiving of my hand, or a representation of my hand, for the hand itself completely exhausts the experience. This is perhaps clearest if we take an example of an illusion, say the Müller-Lyer illusion (Diagram 1). The two horizontal lines are, as a matter of verifiable fact, the same length, but the bottom one looks longer. Now if one concentrates on those two lines and asks oneself 'What is there here, in my experience, which does not match up with the real lines?', one can find no answer. The only option seems to be to contrast the lines I see, which are different lengths, with the lines I measure, which are the same length. But if only the latter are the

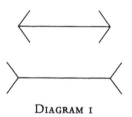

DIAGRAM 1

real lines, then we have lost the direct realist element of perception. It is totally unlike imagining something, say a waterfall, for then there unquestionably is something, the imagined waterfall, which may or may not correspond to any waterfall in the world. If a representation is to be correct or incorrect, it must in the first place be a representation. But in the case of perception, there is nothing which we experience which may or may not correspond with the world, for our experience presents itself as experience of the world itself. Perceptual experience does not seem to represent the world to us, it just presents it. If one insists on the possibility of misperception, then there seem to be only two choices. Either the external world is not the object of perception, so the hand I see is not my real hand but merely a collection of sense-data; or sense perception is not *of* the world, does not have the world as its object, but is a state of mind, an experience, which is *about* the world, in much the same way as daydreaming or thinking is about the world (see 3.3.2). The compromise position is to say that SMP is right for veridical experiences, and one of the other alternatives holds for illusions. This is known as the disjunctive account of perception, because it offers two alternative accounts of what is going on when we have sense experiences, only one of which applies at each time. However, the disjunctive account is unattractive for two reasons. First, it is very mysterious how the switch between the disjuncts occurs. Suppose I am sitting reading a book under normal conditions. Then I am perceptually open to the world. While I am sitting there, you slowly change the character of my spectacle lenses until they distort the page in front of me. Then I am no longer open to the world but having an illusory experience. How did your fiddling with the lenses have such a dramatic effect on me? How did it change me from being directly in touch with my environment to being out of touch? Surely all you did was change something in the world? Secondly, there is a problem with the notion of veridicality. Is there a guarantee that some of our perceptual experiences are veridical, i.e. are of a mind-independent reality? If, as seems plausible, there is no guarantee, then whether any are veridical will have to be assessed against some external standard, and if that standard is the scientific description of the world, it may well turn out that none is veridical and all the attractions of SMP have been lost.

Since SMP has considerable attractions, and the jury is still undecided on the viability of any alternatives, we should take Berkeley's argument for the mind-dependence of sensible qualities to be in pretty good standing. The next significant move he needs to make is instrumentalism about the unobservable parts of scientific theories. Without this instrumentalism, science would vindicate talk of matter and Berkeley would be thrown into one form of scepticism, namely denying the truth and reality of what the ordinary man takes to be the real world, namely what he perceives. While there are many objections to instrumentalism, it is still a viable philosophical position for anyone who can make a sharp distinction between what is observed and what is a theory based on those observations. With the assistance of SMP, Berkeley is able to make this distinction, but only at the cost of committing himself to conceptualism about properties and objects. With SMP and instrumentalism, Berkeley has some very strong arguments against materialism.

Berkeley was explicit and determined in his anti-sceptical objectives, so merely arguing against materialism is not sufficient: he must also provide an adequate and coherent alternative. This aspect of Berkeley's philosophy is much more difficult, and unfortunately he spent much less time on it. We know from his letters that Berkeley was very concerned about the reception of his works, and the obstacle they consistently faced was incredulity at the denial of matter. It is not surprising, then, that he should concentrate his efforts on that front and neglect the more subtle objections; but if we are to appreciate his contribution to philosophy, we must push him on those points and use our imaginations where necessary to work through the details of immaterialism.

The first important question to address is the criterion of reality for ideas. Not all the ideas we have are real things, for some are products of the imagination. There are three possible ways to make such a distinction: by some property of the ideas (e.g. vividness), by some relation between ideas (e.g. coherence), or by some relation between the ideas and something else (e.g. correspondence). There are notorious problems with using just the first and second criteria, but the third seems unavailable to an immaterialist. However, Berkeley is clever enough to use a different sort of external relation here, not correspondence but causation. The difference between imagination and sense perception is that we cause our imaginings but not our sensings. This is not normally thought to be sufficient to give a criterion of reality, because perceptual illusions are externally caused perceptions. Berkeley overcomes this problem by interpreting illusory experiences not as ones which are not experiences of the real world, but as ones which are liable to mislead us about future experiences. The visual experience of the Müller-Lyer illusion is not mistaken in itself, because the bottom line really is visually longer. What marks it out as an illusion is that, were I to predict on the basis of that visual experience of the lines that a ruler would measure them to be different lengths, I would be misled. This approach has the benefit of providing a nice explanation of why perceptual illusions persist even when we know they are illusions: the world looks how it is, even in an illusion.

Behind the superficial coherence of Berkeley's criterion of reality lies a deeper problem. He seems to be committed to saying that a sense perception is both dependent upon the perceiver's mind, being a sensation or idea, and independent of it, being real. In order to solve this problem, Berkeley has to distinguish two different types of dependence relation between an idea and a mind. The first relation, perception, is the dependence of a quality upon a substance, and cannot hold between a mind and something material. The second relation, ontological dependence, is the dependence of something that exists upon its creator for its existence. It is ideas we have which do not depend upon us for their existence which constitute perceptions of the real world.

Berkeley has achieved coherence here, but at the cost of a considerably more complex theory. And when we address the question of what it is for a spirit to act, the theory becomes even more complex: my actions ontologically depend upon me and yet they are things which happen in the real world. While I offered Berkeley a sketch of a solution to this problem, namely a means of distinguishing the voluntary/involuntary distinction from the active/passive distinction, much more work would need to be done before anything satisfactory could be said on that issue. Furthermore, it seemed to depend upon an empirical question about the nature of attention.

With respect to properties, we saw that Berkeley is no worse off than any other nominalist. Objects were more difficult. The first dif-

298 · CHAPTER 9

298 · CHAPTER 9

ficulty is that objects, unlike ideas, persist through time and change their properties. Collections of ideas can also persist through time, but they differ from our ordinary conception of objects in that they have temporal parts and they do not change their properties but their membership. It is possible for Berkeley to save most of our ordinary beliefs about physical objects within this framework, but it is not easy and far from uncontroversial. Finally, he needs to introduce a version of phenomenalism to cope with existence unperceived, a version which has the consequence that a collection can exist and have properties at times when none of its members exists. I tried to give some examples to make this more plausible, but many may feel that this involved a level of anti-realism about physical objects which is sufficient to brand Berkeley a sceptic, i.e. one 'who denies the reality and truth of things' (*DHP1* 173).

This is the biggest problem for Berkeley. He is determined to save the common-sense view that the very objects of perception are real, but the cost is an ontologically anti-realist interpretation of ordinary talk. It is true that I see my hand, and also that I see several ideas, and it is true that both my hand and the ideas exist. However, there is a marked difference, for the existence of my hand depends upon contingent facts about how humans choose to conceptualize the world they perceive. Had we had different minds, I would still perceive the ideas, they would still exist, but my hand would not. Now there are some very delicate issues to be addressed here to do with exactly what sort of anti-realism Berkeley's conceptualism commits one to. In particular, Berkeley might well be in a position to argue that, given the concept of *hand* that we do have, the counterfactual claim I made two sentences ago is in fact false: had we had different minds, my hand would still exist (though I would not be thinking about it) because what we actually mean by *hand* allows for that possibility. However, the point remains that the question of whether my hand would exist is answered very differently from the question of whether these ideas would exist. Whether the ideas exist in any hypothetical situation is independent of what sort of conceptual system we have, in either the real or the counterfactual situations. There are no two ways about it: Berkeley is *less realist* about hands, trees, tables, and all physical objects than he is about ideas, and this may well be enough to denominate him a sceptic by his own standards.

In his subtle and quick-witted defence of immaterialism, Berkeley wins many impressive victories, but he still loses the campaign which he set out upon with such confidence. It is the very manoeuvres he must use to win the battles which ultimately cost him the war. The main thing which is wrong with immaterialism is not SMP, is not the denial of matter, both of which are defensible positions, and nor is it some kind of internal incoherence. No, the main thing that is wrong with it is that immaterialism is less staunchly realistic about the empirical world of tables and trees than Berkeley would have liked.

Bibliography

Arnauld, A., *On True and False Ideas*, ed. S. Gaukroger (Manchester: Manchester University Press, 1990).

Atherton, M., 'Berkeley without God', in Muehlmann (ed.), *Berkeley's Metaphysics*.

Bennett, J., *Locke, Berkeley, Hume* (Oxford: Clarendon Press, 1971).

Berkeley, George, *Philosophical Works*, ed. M. Ayers (London: J. M. Dent, 1975).

—— *Three Dialogues between Hylas and Philonous*, ed. J. Dancy (Oxford: Oxford University Press, 1998).

—— *A Treatise concerning the Principles of Human Knowledge*, ed. J. Dancy (Oxford: Oxford University Press, 1998).

—— *The Works of George Berkeley Bishop of Cloyne*, ed. A. A. Luce and T. E. Jessop (London: Thomas Nelson, 1948–57).

—— *The Works of George Berkeley, D.D., Late Bishop of Cloyne in Ireland. To Which is Added, an Account of his Life, and Several of his Letters to Thomas Prior, Dean Gervais, and Mr. Pope, &c.*, ed. J. Stock (Dublin: John Exshaw, 1784).

Boswell, J., *The Life of Samuel Johnson*, ed. J. Canning (London: Methuen, 1991).

Burnyeat, M., 'Conflicting Appearances', *Proceedings of the British Academy*, 65 (1979), 69–111.

Dancy, J., *Berkeley: An Introduction* (Oxford: Blackwell, 1987).

Descartes, R., *Meditations on First Philosophy*, in *The Philosophical Writings of Descartes*, ii, trans. J. Cottingham, R. Stoothof, and D. Murdoch (Cambridge: Cambridge University Press, 1984).

—— *Principles of Philosophy*, in *The Philosophical Writings of Descartes*, i, trans. J. Cottingham, R. Stoothof, and D. Murdoch (Cambridge: Cambridge University Press, 1985).

Dummett, M., 'Common Sense and Physics', in G. F. Macdonald (ed.), *Perception and Identity* (London: Macmillan, 1979).

Flage, D., 'Berkeley, Individuation, and Physical Objects', in K. Barber (ed.), *Individuation and Identity in Early Modern Philosophy* (Albany: SUNY Press, 1994).

Foster, J., and Robinson, H. (eds.), *Essays on Berkeley* (Oxford: Clarendon Press, 1985).

Gallois, A., 'Berkeley's Master Argument', *Philosophical Review*, 83 (1974), 55–69.

Garber, D., 'Locke, Berkeley, and Corpuscular Scepticism', in Turbayne (ed.), *Berkeley*.

Geach, P., *Mental Acts: Their Content and their Objects*, 2nd edn. (London: Routledge and Kegan Paul, 1971).

Grayling, A., *Berkeley: The Central Arguments* (London: Duckworth, 1986).

Hornsby, J., *Actions* (London: Routledge and Kegan Paul, 1980).

Hume, D., *A Treatise of Human Nature*, ed. L. A. Selby-Bigge, rev. P. H. Nidditch (Oxford: Clarendon Press, 1978).

Jessop, T. E., *George Berkeley* (London: British Council, 1959).

Kant, I., *Critique of Pure Reason*, trans. N. Kemp Smith (London: Macmillan, 1929).

Lewis, D., *On the Plurality of Worlds* (Oxford: Blackwell, 1986).

Lipton, P., *Inference to the Best Explanation* (London: Routledge, 1991).

Locke, J., *Essay concerning Human Understanding*, ed. P. H. Nidditch (Oxford: Clarendon Press, 1975).

Luce, A. A., *Life of George Berkeley* (London: Thomas Nelson, 1949).

Mackie, J. L., *Problems from Locke* (Oxford: Oxford University Press, 1976).

Malebranche, N., *Dialogues on Metaphysics and Religion*, ed. N. Jolley, trans. D. Scott (Cambridge: Cambridge University Press, 1997).

Mill, J. S., 'Berkeley's Life and Writings', in *Collected Works of John Stuart Mill*, xi. *Essays on Philosophy and the Classics*, ed. J. M. Robson (London: Routledge, 1996).

Muehlmann, R. (ed.), *Berkeley's Metaphysics: Structural, Interpretative and*

Critical Essays (University Park: Pennsylvania State University Press, 1995).

Pappas, G., *Berkeley's Thought* (Ithaca, NY: Cornell University Press, 2000).

Pitcher, G., *Berkeley* (London: Routledge, 1977).

Plato, *Phaedrus*, in *The Dialogues of Plato*, trans. B. Jowett (Oxford: Clarendon Press, 1871).

Putnam, H., *Reason, Truth and History* (Cambridge: Cambridge University Press, 1981).

Quine, W. V. O., 'Natural Kinds', in his *Ontological Relativity and Other Essays* (New York: Columbia University Press, 1969).

—— 'Ontology and Ideology', *Philosophical Studies*, 2 (1951), 11–15.

Russell, B., *History of Western Philosophy*, 2nd edn. (London: Allen and Unwin, 1961).

—— 'Knowledge by Acquaintance and Knowledge by Description', *Proceedings of the Aristotelian Society*, 11 (1910–11), 108–28.

—— *The Problems of Philosophy* (Oxford: Oxford University Press, 1967).

Stock, J., *An Account of the Life of George Berkeley, D.D., Late Bishop of Cloyne in Ireland. With Notes, Containing Strictures upon the Works* (London: printed for J. Murray, 1776); repr. in Stock's 1784 edn. of Berkeley's works (above, s.n. Berkeley).

Strawson, P. F., *Individuals: An Essay in Descriptive Metaphysics* (London: Methuen, 1959).

Swift, J., *Journal to Stella*, ed. H. Williams (Oxford: Blackwell, 1974).

Taylor, C. C. W., 'Action and Inaction in Berkeley', in Foster and Robinson (eds.), *Essays on Berkeley*.

Tipton, I. C., and Furlong, E. J., 'Mrs George Berkeley and her Washing Machine', *Hermathena*, 101 (1965), 38–47.

Turbayne, C. (ed.), *Berkeley: Critical and Interpretative Essays* (Minnesota: Minnesota University Press, 1982).

Urmson, J. O., *Berkeley* (Oxford: Oxford University Press, 1982).

Warnock, G., *Berkeley* (Oxford: Blackwell, 1953).

Williams, B., 'Imagination and the Self', in his *Problems of the Self* (Cambridge: Cambridge University Press, 1973).

Wilson, M., *Ideas and Mechanism* (Princeton: Princeton University Press, 1999).

Winkler, K., *Berkeley: An Interpretation* (Oxford: Clarendon Press, 1989).

Wittgenstein, L., *Philosophical Investigations* (Oxford: Blackwell, 1958).

—— *Tractatus Logico-Philosophicus*, trans. D. Pears and B. McGuiness (London: Routledge, 1961).

Yeats, W. B., *The Collected Poems* (London: Macmillan, 1950).

Index